M000249214

Dear Reader,

Welcome to the Galileo Press *Discover SAP* series. T... ... . has been developed as part of our official SAP PRESS imprint to help you discover what SAP is all about and to show you how you can use the wide array of applications and tools to make your organization more efficient and cost effective.

Each book in the series is written in a friendly, easy-to-follow style that guides you through the intricacies of the software and its core components. If you are completely new to SAP, you can begin with "Discover SAP," the first book in the series, where you'll find a detailed overview of the core components of SAP, what they are, how they can benefit your company, and the technology requirements and costs of implementation. Once you have a foundational knowledge of SAP, you can explore the other books in the series covering Financials, CRM, SCM, and more. In these books you'll delve into the fundamental business concepts and principles behind the tool, discover why it's important for your business, and evaluate the technology and implementation costs for each.

Whether you are a decision maker who needs to determine if SAP is the right enterprise solution for your company, you are just starting to work in a firm that uses SAP, or you're already familiar with SAP but need to learn about a specific component, you are sure to find what you need in the *Discover SAP* series. Then when you're ready to implement SAP, you'll find what you need in the SAP PRESS series at *www.sap-press.com*.

Thank you for your interest in the series. We look forward to hearing how the series helps you get started with SAP.

Jenifer Niles
Vice President

Galileo Press, Inc.
100 Grossman Drive
Suite 205
Braintree, MA 02184

 **PRESS**

SAP PRESS is a joint initiative of SAP and Galileo Press. The know-how offered by SAP specialists combined with the expertise of the Galileo Press publishing house offers the reader expert books in the field. SAP PRESS features first-hand information and expert advice, and provides useful skills for professional decision-making.

SAP PRESS offers a variety of books on technical and business related topics for the SAP user. For further information, please visit our website: *www.sap-press.com*.

Martin Murray
SAP MM: Functionality and Technical Configuration
2008, 561 pp., $69.95
978-1-59229-134-2

D. Rajen Iyer
Effective SAP SD
2007, 365 pp., $69.95
978-1-59229-101-4

Sachin Sethi
Enhancing Supplier Relationship Management Using SAP SRM
2007, 695 pp., $69.95
978-1-59229-068-0

Martin Murray
SAP Warehouse Management:
Functionality and Technical Configuration
2007, 515 pp., $79.95
978-1-59229-133-5

Martin Murray

Discover Logistics with SAP® ERP

Galileo Press

Bonn • Boston

ISBN 978-1-59229-230-1

1st Edition 2009

Editor Meg Dunkerley
Copyeditor Julie McNamee
Production Editor Kelly O'Callaghan
Cover Designer Jill Winitzer
Photo Credit Photos.com
Layout Design Vera Brauner
Typesetter Publishers' Design and Production Services, Inc.
Printed and bound in Canada

Galileo Press is named after the Italian physicist, mathematician and philosopher Galileo Galilei (1564–1642). He is known as one of the founders of modern science and an advocate of our contemporary, heliocentric worldview. His words *Eppur si muove* (And yet it moves) have become legendary. The Galileo Press logo depicts Jupiter orbited by the four Galilean moons, which were discovered by Galileo in 1610.

Contents at a Glance

Peter Kenny
Tel: 07825 110149

Contents

PART I   Procurement and Logistics Execution

3   Inventory Management 67

4   Warehouse Management 89

5   Inbound and Outbound Logistics 109

PART II   Product Development and Manufacturing

6   Product Planning 129

PART III   Sales and Service

PART IV   Implementation and New Technologies

Acknowledgments

The author would like to thank Meg Dunkerley of SAP PRESS for her faith in the author and her patient, tireless efforts in ensuring this book was completed. Thanks also to Julie McNamee for her editing of the final draft.

Preface

In writing this book, I addressed the needs of logistics and supply chain professional that require an easy to understand overview of the logistics functionality available in SAP ERP.

I've explained the logistics functionality in SAP ERP in understandable language that isn't technical jargon or sales terminology. You won't find menu paths or SAP transaction codes in this book. This book simply describes the benefits of using SAP ERP using examples and case studies to help you understand what the logistics functionality in SAP ERP can do for the success of your company.

Who This Book Is For

If you're a supply chain or logistics manager or analyst whose company is implementing or thinking of implementing the SAP ERP business suite, then this book will help you become familiar with the logistics functionality in SAP ERP. The book describes the different logistical areas of SAP ERP. It examines these areas in full, highlighting the aspects that are important in achieving benefits for your company.

This book is also helpful for IT professionals who have focused on the logistics or supply chain but may have never worked with SAP ERP before. This book gives you the basic knowledge from which you can hit the ground running and be a productive team member of any implementation team.

Lastly, if you are a supply chain or logistics consultant considering a position with a company that has implemented SAP ERP, this book will help you see where the different logistics functions fit into the overall SAP ERP business suite.

Navigational Tools for This Book

Throughout the book, we've provided several elements that will help you access useful information:

> Tips call out useful information about related ideas and provide practical suggestions for how to use a particular function.

> Notes provide other resources to explore, or special tools or services from SAP that will help you with the topic under discussion.

> Examples provide real-world scenarios and illustrations of how the tools are used.

This is a marginal note

> Marginal text provides a useful way to scan the book to locate topics of interest for you. Each margin note appears to the side of a paragraph or section with related information.

Organization of This Book

When you examine the functionality of the SAP ERP business suite, you'll find three distinct elements:

> SAP ERP Financials

> SAP ERP Human Capital Management (HCM)

> SAP ERP Operations

Although SAP ERP Financials and SAP ERP HCM are important to your company's success, they don't contain any of the logistics functions we'll discuss in this book.

The SAP ERP Operations functionality contains the elements that logistics users are familiar with. The SAP ERP Operations functionality is characterized by these three areas:

> Procurement and logistics execution

> Product development and manufacturing

> Sales and service

This book takes these areas and delves into the distinct functionality. So let's take a look at how the book is organized.

Section 1 – Procurement and Logistics Execution

This section of the book initially introduces you to the SAP ERP environment. It then goes on to examine the procurement, inventory management, and warehouse management functionality. Finally this section ends with an examination of the inbound and outbound logistics function.

Chapter 1 – Introduction to SAP Logistics
This is an introduction for the reader to gain understanding of the SAP software environment and get a review of how the logistics function is an integral part of the SAP ERP business suite. This chapter gives a comprehensive overview of the SAP functionality that is relevant to logistics.

Chapter 2 – Procurement
This chapter gives readers an overview of the organizational structure that is used by SAP ERP for the purchasing function. It then introduces the reader to the purchasing functions in SAP ERP, such as purchase requisition, request for quotations (RFQs), purchase orders (POs), and accounts payable.

Chapter 3 – Inventory Management
This chapter describes the SAP functions used in inventory management. The logical structure of the plant is introduced as well as the goods movements within the plant, and physical inventory of material.

Chapter 4 – Warehouse Management
In this chapter, the structure of the warehouse is fully examined as well as how it integrates with the SAP Inventory Management (SAP IM) functionality. This chapter also details the movements of material within the warehouse.

Chapter 5 – Inbound and Outbound Logistics
This chapter explains the logistical movements of material in and out of the plant by detailing the goods receipt and goods issue functions.

Section 2 – Product Development and Manufacturing

The second section of SAP ERP Operations looks at the manufacturing functionality. The section begins with a discussion of the planning functions in SAP ERP followed by an examination of the manufacturing operations. The two remaining chapters in this section discuss the two important functions that support successful manufacturing: plant maintenance (PM) and quality management (QM).

Chapter 6 – Product Planning

This chapter introduces the product planning functions in SAP. The chapter will detail the functionality of SAP Sales and Operations Planning (SAP SOP), demand management, and materials resource planning (MRP).

Chapter 7 – Manufacturing Operations

This chapter reviews the structure of the manufacturing function, including master data such as equipment, bills of material (BOMs), and routings. The chapter continues with an examination of the functionality of production orders and product costing.

Chapter 8 – Plant Maintenance

Plant maintenance is important to a successful manufacturing process, and this chapter begins with an examination of the organizational structure of the plant maintenance (PM) function. The chapter also describes the preventative maintenance and maintenance processing functions.

Chapter 9 – Quality Management

Like PM, quality management (QM) is an important part of successful manufacturing. This chapter details the QM functions concentrating on quality planning, notifications, and inspections.

Section 3 – Sales and Service

The third section of this book looks at the sales and service functionality. This section covers sales order management, customer service (CS), and SAP Transportation Management (SAP TM).

Chapter 10 – Sales Order Management

This chapter introduces the SAP sales functionality. The chapter initially examines the organizational structure of the sales function and then details the sales ordering, shipping, and billing processes.

Chapter 11 – Customer Service

Following on from the examination of the sales function, this chapter reviews the customer service (CS) functions in SAP. The topics include the master data, service agreements, warranties, and processing of service orders.

Chapter 12 – Transportation Management

This chapter examines the transportation functions found in SAP. The chapter examines the planning of transporting materials, determining freight costs, and the using functionality for transporting materials.

Section 4 – Implementation and New Technologies

This section looks at successfully implementing SAP ERP using tried and tested implementation methodologies. It also examines new SAP technology that can be used by your companies, including SAP NetWeaver and other business suites, such as SAP Supply Chain Management (SAP SCM).

Chapter 13 – Implementation

This chapter covers the best approach to implementing logistics—not the how, but the how to plan for and approach. It also reviews how much the total cost of ownership (TCO) might be, and when and how much of a return on investment (ROI) to expect.

Chapter 14 – New Technologies and Conclusion

This chapter reviews the new technologies developed by SAP that will be important to logistics, including SOA and SAP NetWeaver. This chapter also touches on other SAP software, such as SAP Supply Chain Management (SAP SCM). This chapter closes with a review of the concepts that were discussed throughout the book

This book gives you the information you need to understand SAP logistics. You can use the knowledge you gain from reading this book to develop your skills to help your company successfully benefit from using SAP ERP.

PART I
Procurement and Logistics Execution

1

Introduction to Logistics with SAP

The current versions of SAP® software are the result of the nearly 40 years of development that has been driven by the needs of customers. In this chapter, we'll examine the origins of SAP, the elements of logistics within SAP, and how the logistics functionality can help you manage your company's key logistics activities.

Origins of SAP

SAP was founded in 1972 by five ex-IBM employees in Mannheim, Germany. Today, SAP is a market and technology leader in client/server enterprise application software. SAP provides comprehensive solutions for companies of all sizes and all industry sectors. SAP is the leading vendor of standard business-application software and the third largest software supplier in the world. SAP delivers scalable solutions that enable users to further advance industry best practices. SAP is constantly developing new products to help users respond to dynamic market conditions and help them maintain their competitive advantage.

SAP Enterprise Resource Planning

In 1979, SAP released its mainframe product called R/2. This was the first product designed as an enterprise-wide solution for business. The R/2 product was a hugely successful enterprise resource planning (ERP) software suite, and SAP soon dominated the German market. In the 1980s SAP developed a broader market in the rest of Europe. And, in 1992, SAP developed the client/server application called R/3. This allowed SAP to bring the software to the U.S. market, and within a few years, SAP became the gold standard for ERP software.

When businesses chose SAP as their enterprise application software, they identified the integration of the modules as a key advantage. So, while many other software companies used a best-of-breed approach and developed highly complex interfaces to integrate the separate software packages, SAP built modules into one complete software package, allowing customers to extend functionality as needed. This approach of supporting and maintaining just one system rather than several systems with different hardware platforms has yielded a significant cost saving for companies.

SAP currently has more than 36,000 customers in more than 120 countries worldwide with more than 12 million users. SAP also employs close to 40,000 people in more than 50 countries.

Americas' SAP Users' Group (ASUG)

SAP develops its software in collaboration with its customers, developers, and business experts. The current software was developed to incorporate the best industry practices. The collaboration of user groups, such as the Americas' SAP Users' Group (ASUG), with SAP ensures that the latest product reflects real-world computing needs.

ASUG has more than 45,000 members and dozens of special interest groups (SIG), which reflect specific industries, business processes, or particular technologies. Many SIGs are of particular interest to logistics users; such as Inventory Management, Procurement, Manufacturing, Supply Chain Planning, Distribution, and Transportation. One of the key aims of ASUG is to influence future SAP product releases and direction.

Currently two SAP enterprise application products are of particular interest to logistics users. The first has been the core product of SAP for a number of years, the SAP ERP software. The current release is SAP ERP 6.0 (SAP ECC is the engine behind SAP ERP, where ECC refers to ERP Central Component). SAP defines four distinct elements to the SAP ERP software: SAP ERP Human Capital Management (SAP ERP HCM), SAP ERP Financials, SAP ERP Corporate Service, and SAP ERP Operations. The SAP ERP Operations functionality contains the logistics functionality.

SAP ERP core offerings

The second software suite that SAP offers for logistics users is the SAP Supply Chain Management (SAP SCM). This business suite is separate from the SAP ERP software and is for companies that are ready to build adaptive supply chain networks. The SAP SCM software suite is one of four software suites that are part of the SAP business suite. The other software suites that your company can integrate with SAP ERP and SAP SCM are SAP Customer Relationship Management (SAP CRM), SAP Supplier Relationship Management (SAP SRM), and SAP Product Lifecycle Management (SAP PLM). Figure 1.1 shows the business suites offered by SAP.

SAP Supply Chain Management (SCM)

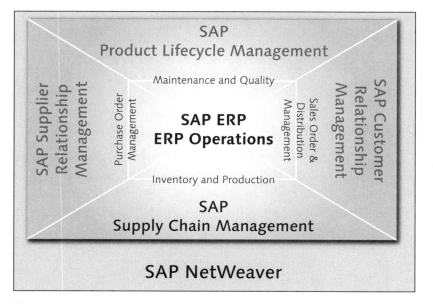

Figure 1.1 SAP Business Suite

The SAP SCM software suite includes strategic, tactical, and operational planning; supply chain execution; supply chain design; and analytics. The current release of this software is SAP SCM 5.1, which can be run as a standalone system or can be integrated with SAP ERP using the SAP Supply Network Collaboration.

SAP as market leader

In September 2007, the research company, Gartner Research, identified SAP as the market share leader for ERP and SCM software. The Gartner report on ERP software identified SAP as the market leader, as measured by total software revenues for 2006, with a total market share of 27% worldwide. The closest competitor in the ERP market had only 13.8% of worldwide ERP market share.

In the SCM software market, SAP had a market share of 19.7%, measured by total SCM software revenues for 2006. The second-ranked competitor had only 14.9%.

Now that we've examined the origins of SAP and the current logistics software, let's move on to the specific logistics functions within SAP.

SAP and Logistics

Clearly, SAP is a market leader in logistics and plans to continue to improve its offerings to customers, so let's take a closer look at what you can do with SAP logistics, in particular how the SAP software incorporates the logistics operations.

Definition of Logistics

What is logistics?

The definition of logistics comes in many varieties, but one good definition comes from the non-profit organization Supply Chain and Logistics Association Canada (SCL), which defines logistics as "the process of planning, implementing, and controlling the efficient, cost effective flow and storage of raw materials, in-process inventory, finished goods, and related information from point of origin to point of consumption for the purpose of meeting customer requirements."

Note

The word "logistics" originates from the Greek word *logos*. In ancient Greece, some military officers with the title *Logistikas* were responsible for financial and supply distribution matters. It is believed that the word "logistics" came into being as a military term describing the need to supply arms and ammunition from a base location to a forward position.

Although logistics may have originated from a military term, the business world started to use the techniques associated with the movement and supply of material at the beginning of the twentieth century. The first time logistics was associated with business was in 1919 when the Chartered Institute of Logistics & Transport was founded, which was then given a Royal Charter from King George V in 1926.

"Logistics" was first associated with the military

The logistics function at any company requires that products and services are delivered to the customers efficiently and cost effectively. The SAP ERP software provides your company with the functionality to ensure that you'll have the correct materials at the correct location at the correct time, with the correct quantity and at the most competitive cost.

The competitive advantage is achieved when your company can manage the process the most efficiently. This involves managing your vendor and customer relationships while controlling your inventory, forecasting customer demand, and receiving timely information about all aspects of the supply-chain transactions. Figure 1.2 shows the interactions along the supply chain.

Your competitive advantage

The SAP SCM software further enhances the improvements made in streamlining the logistics function by using SAP ERP to provide added visibility and system monitoring for changing conditions. This allows the traditional linear and sequential processes to produce a supply chain that can adapt, which has been called an adaptive supply chain network. This new type of supply chain possesses the flexibility to continually respond to the environment without affecting operational and financial efficiencies. An adaptive supply chain seamlessly connects supply, planning, manufacturing, and distribution operations to critical enterprise applications, and provides visibility across the supply network.

Creating an adaptive supply chain

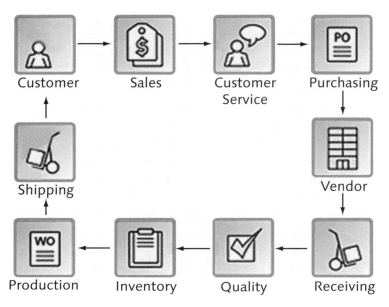

Figure 1.2 Elements of the Supply Chain

RFID technology in SAP SCM

The SAP SCM software complements SAP ERP by leveraging the transactional data to allow reactive decisions. The SAP SCM software has real-time monitoring of critical business events and allows for early identification of issues and resolution before any impact occurs. The SAP SCM software also includes new technologies such as the Radio Frequency Identification tags (RFID) and SAP Extended Warehouse Management (SAP EWM), which is especially suitable for warehouses with high volumes and complex processes. It evolved from companies in the automotive spare parts industry that needed more flexibility than was offered in standard SAP WM.

SAP ERP Operations

Within the SAP ERP software, the SAP ERP Operations functionality contains the elements that logistics users are familiar with.

The SAP ERP Operations functionality is characterized by three areas:

> Procurement and logistics execution
> Product development and manufacturing
> Sales and service

We'll examine these three areas in detail throughout the book, but for now let's take a look at how it breaks down.

The logistics function in SAP has many components, including the following:

> **Materials management (MM)**
> The MM component is the foundation for the logistics functions of a company. The component includes purchasing functionality, inventory movements, accounts payable, and the material master file, which contains the information on all materials and services used at your company.

> **Sales and distribution (SD)**
> The SD component incorporates the processes from customer order to the delivery of the product to the customer. The component includes the sales functions, pricing, picking, packing, and shipping.

> **Quality management (QM)**
> The QM component is used to ensure and improve on the quality of your company's products. The functions of this component include the planning and execution of quality inspections of purchased and finished products.

> **Plant maintenance (PM)**
> The PM component is used to maintain the equipment that is used in the production of your company's finished products. The component focuses on the planning and execution of preventive maintenance on equipment and tools used in the production process.

> **Production planning (PP)**
> The PP component manages your company's production process. The functions of this component include capacity planning of your company's production, master production scheduling (MPS), material requirements planning (MRP), and the shop floor functions of producing your company's finished products.

> **Customer service (CS)**
> The CS component manages your company's repairs and warranties services. Items can be sent back for repair, or your staff may visit

customer facilities. If your company makes finished products that are sold with warranties, the SAP CS component helps you service and repair those items with maximum efficiency.

> **Warehouse management (WM)**
> The WM component helps your company accurately manage inventory and maximize storage capacity. This component can reduce the time it takes to place and remove items from the warehouse by suggesting the most efficient location to store a material and the most efficient way to place and remove that material from the warehouse.

Additional SAP components

And, of course, there is additional functionality that integrates with the logistics area, such as transportation management, batch management, handling unit management, Logistics Information System (LIS), variant configuration, engineering change management, project systems (PS), and SAP Environment, Health & Safety (SAP EH&S). All of these can be important in the logistics area, depending on what your company requires.

Logistics Functionality

The previous section highlighted the core functionality in the SAP software that falls in the logistics area. This section goes into more depth of each of those areas and the SAP components you'll find associated with logistics.

Procurement and Logistics Execution

The procurement and logistics execution operations in the SAP software help your company to reduce costs in purchasing, inventory management, and warehouse management.

Purchasing

Purchasing in SAP

The purchasing function within SAP provides a complete procure-to-pay process, which includes requisitioning, purchase order management, and invoice verification.

SAP ERP can help your company maintain catalog content of purchased items from your vendors and enable employee self-service purchasing of material and services.

The SAP ERP software allows your company to work with your vendors with regards to invoice processing and payment, using functionality such as evaluated receipt settlement (ERS).

Inventory Management

The SAP Inventory Management (SAP IM) functions of the SAP ERP software help your company reduce costs within the plant. The functionality enables you to record and track the quantity and value of all materials in the plant. Physical inventory of the materials in the plant can be taken to ensure that your company has a high level of stock accuracy.

Inventory management functionality

With the SAP IM functionality, you can plan, enter, and document all the internal material movements within the plant.

Warehouse Management

The SAP Warehouse Management (SAP WM) functionality helps your company manage the workload within the warehouse through workload planning, wave picking, and order consolidation. The SAP ERP software incorporates the latest warehouse technology such as radio frequency (RF) and barcode scanning, which are found in successful warehouse operations. The SAP WM functionality includes the ability to create handling units for materials moved and stored on pallets or within packages.

Warehouse management, radio frequency, barcoding

Inbound and Outbound Logistics

The inbound and outbound movements in SAP ERP help your company successfully manage goods receipt and goods issuing processes.

The functionality incorporates monitoring the receipts of materials at the plant, providing advanced shipping notifications, posting goods issues, and documenting deliveries.

Goods issue, goods receipt

Product Development and Manufacturing

The SAP ERP software helps your company improve production processes. The functionality also improves efficiencies in planning and scheduling. As a result, you can lower costs, deliver higher-quality products, and boost margins.

Product Planning

The SAP functionality provides support for a number of planning procedures, including SAP Sales and Operations Planning (SAP SOP), master production scheduling (MPS), and material requirements planning (MRP).

SAP Sales and Operational Planning

SAP SOP defines what your company will produce in the year ahead, how it will be produced, and what resources will be needed. SAP SOP should include a forecast, budget, and resource requirements.

Master production scheduling (MPS)

MPS translates your company's business plan developed by the SAP SOP function into a production plan. MPS is a statement of what the company expects to produce and purchase. MPS is used for materials that have the greatest influence on your company profits or that affect the production process by taking critical resources. These materials should be given extra attention and selected for a separate MPS run prior to the MRP process.

Material requirements planning (MRP)

MRP manages the planning for your company's manufacturing process, and ensures that the materials are available for the production process and for delivery to your customers. MRP helps your company maintain the lowest possible level of inventory, as well as plan your company's manufacturing activities, delivery schedules, and purchasing activities.

Manufacturing Operations

The SAP software helps your company capture the actual production information from the orders that are in process on the shop floor.

Production techniques support

The functionality can be used for the variety of production techniques that your company may use, such as Kanban, repetitive manufacturing, and production order processing. The software can be used with a variety of planning strategies, including make to order, and make to stock.

SAP ERP can also help you accelerate time to market by centralizing the product development and innovation process, improve productivity through efficient collaborative processes, and ensure compliance with new regulations and industry standards.

Plant Maintenance (PM)

All successful manufacturing companies require a successful PM function to ensure the production process is working at maximum capacity. SAP ERP helps your company design preventative maintenance processes to keep plant use as high as possible. In addition, SAP software provides processes for spare parts and serialized components, as well as procedures for equipment breakdowns.

Plant maintenance functionality

Quality Management (QM)

SAP ERP delivers a wide range of integrated QM functionality for cost-effectively ensuring the quality of your company's products and processes. SAP ERP can support your company's Six Sigma projects by analyzing current and archived quality data. The QM function has an audit function that supports a wide range of industry standards such as ISO 9000, QS-9000, Good Manufacturing Practice (GMP), ISO 14011, and ISO 19011.

Quality management supports industry standards

The QM functionality helps your company reduce quality management costs by automating monitoring quality activities, which reduces errors in transferring data and increases accuracy. The timely availability of test results to the rest of the logistics function by integration with other SAP ERP functions can reduce time that material is held for quality control and therefore reduce warehouse costs and delivery times to the customer.

Sales and Service

The benefits of the SAP ERP software for your company can be achieved with improvements in sales order management, which produces higher levels of customer satisfaction. By simplifying and automating your company's order-to-cash process, the benefits include a reduction in operational costs as well as improved customer satisfaction when you provide accurate delivery information to your customers.

Sales Order Management

The SAP ERP software helps your company improve its management of the sales order management process, including handling sales inquiries, quotations, and order processing. Improvements can also be made in developing contracts and in the billing cycle management.

Internet sales increase revenues

In conjunction with the SAP ERP software, your company can use Internet sales software to take advantage of new markets and thus increase revenues. The SAP ERP software provides your Internet customers with real-time product availability and pricing information, and accurately calculates delivery information, which is based on production capacity, real-time stock levels, and transport schedules.

SAP ERP software also helps your company introduce sales incentive programs for your customers, including sales commissions and bonuses.

Customer Service

Providing customer service

If your company has products that offer warranties and require servicing from your company, the SAP ERP software provides functionality to manage those situations. In addition, SAP addresses service contracts, service orders, and warranty management.

The customer service functionality manages all aspects of service-order processing within the service organization, from responding to the customer's initial inquiry to confirmation and billing.

Transportation Management

Transport management functionality

As fuel costs continue to rise, it's important for your company to efficiently manage its transportation function. The SAP ERP software incorporates functionality to manage all aspects of the delivery process, tracking activities, and analyzing the profitability of delivery routes.

This section examined the logistics functionality that is available to your company in SAP ERP. The benefits of the SAP ERP software can improve your customers' satisfaction by providing accurate delivery dates and improved quality of your products. SAP can increase profitability and revenues by developing a cost-efficient production process, reduce purchasing costs by using best practices, increase revenue by expanding sales channels such as online sales, and improve analysis of logistics functions that will identify areas that can be improved.

The SAP functionality can help your company reduce operating costs by automating manual processes in the plant, reduce costs in the warehouse by creating efficient use of resources and streamlining activities, and reduce transport costs by using the transport management function of the software.

Conclusion

In this chapter, we've discussed the origins of SAP, including an overview of the present SAP product offerings, the SAP software and the logistics function, and the logistics functionality and the benefits offered by the SAP ERP software.

Now that you've completed this chapter, there are a few points that you should remember:

> SAP is the leading ERP software with more than 36,000 customers in more than 120 countries and over 12 million users.

> SAP ERP allows your company to manage vendor and customer relationships, control inventory, forecast demand, and have timely information on all aspects of the supply chain.

> SAP ERP operations functionality is characterized by three areas; procurement and logistics execution, product development and manufacturing, and sales and service.

> SAP components in the logistics area include materials management (MM), sales and distribution (SD), production planning (PP), quality management (QM), plant maintenance (PM), and customer service (CS).

The next section of this book reviews the procurement and logistics execution functionality within the SAP ERP system. The first chapter of that section covers the procurement functions, including an overview of the organizational structure used by SAP for the purchasing function. This is followed by an examination of the purchasing functions in SAP, such as purchase requisitions, Request for Quotations (RFQ), purchase orders (PO), and accounts payable.

2

Procurement

Every company has to purchase items, from the raw materials that go into making a component in a finished product to the external services needed to help in the manufacture of an item, the equipment that is required to manufacture items, and even buildings to house the manufacturing process. The science of purchasing has become part of today's efficient business operation. But before any purchasing happens, the purchasing department has to research and negotiate the best prices through policies and technology to ensure that your company is getting the right materials at the best cost.

In this chapter, we'll examine the organizational structure within SAP, along with the organization of the purchasing department, the components of the procurement process, and how accounts payable operates within the system.

SAP Organization Structure

Let's briefly review some of the technical aspects of SAP software and then examine the organizational structure that is defined in SAP.

Creating the Client Landscape

SAP instance
When your company purchases SAP software, you need to create your SAP landscape by installing and configuring the software according to your specific needs. In SAP terminology, this is called an *instance*. Your company can have more than one SAP instance, but they'll exist on different SAP systems. Within one SAP instance, a number of clients will be created. A *client* is an organizational and legal entity in the SAP system.

What is master data?
Master data is the detailed information stored in the SAP system that describes the materials, vendors, and customers you use. Master data is protected within the client, so it can't be seen from outside. The data in a client is only visible within that client and can't be displayed or changed from another client. For example, if your company has subsidiaries that also use SAP applications, they can use your physical SAP software and servers, but they use a different client. The subsidiaries would not have access to your data, nor would your company have access to theirs.

Multiple clients
SAP systems have multiple clients that each have a different objective and represent a unique environment. Clients also have their own sets of tables and user data.

After the SAP software has been installed, the technical team needs to create a number of clients that reflect the customer needs. The general client structure for an SAP implementation includes a development client, training client, quality client, and production client.

Development client
The *development client* is where all development work, such as the setup of the plants, storage locations, and configuration work, should take place. There may be more than one development client created. For example, there may be a *sandbox client*, for general users to practice and test configuration. There may also be a *clean* or *golden* development client where the specific configuration is made and from which it's then transported to the quality client for review before moving to the production client.

Training client
The *training client* usually reflects the current production system and is used primarily for training project staff and end users. When configuration is transported to the production client, it's transported to the training client at the same time. Although the training client is useful for training, it isn't necessity for a successful implementation.

Other clients may be needed for SAP NetWeaver Business Intelligence (SAP NetWeaver BI) and other SAP software, such as SAP Supply Chain Management (SAP SCM) or SAP Customer Relationship Management (SAP CRM).

To successfully manage this client environment, you need strict procedures and security so that the integrity of the clients is maintained.

Company Code

The *company code* is defined in SAP as the smallest organizational unit for which a complete self-contained set of accounts can be drawn up. It's important to be able provide data for generating balance sheets and profit-loss statements. The company code represents legally independent companies. Using more than one company code allows a customer to manage financial data for different independent companies at the same time. When a customer is deciding on its organizational structure, one or more company codes can be used.

Defining a company code

 Example

If an American company has components of its organization in Canada and in Mexico, it may be appropriate to use three company codes instead of one.

Figure 2.1 shows the data that is entered for a company code.

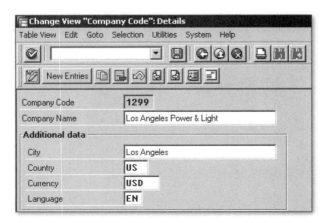

Figure 2.1 Company Code Data Screen

Plant

Plants   When you think of a plant, your mind probably goes to a manufacturing site where equipment, warehousing, and offices are located. In SAP terms, the definition of a plant can vary. From a logistics view, a *plant* can be defined as a location that holds valuated stock or as an organizational unit that is central to production planning. A plant can also be defined as a location that contains customer service or maintenance facilities. The definition of a plant will vary depending on the need of the customer. Figure 2.2 shows the data that is entered for a plant.

Figure 2.2 Plant Data Screen

The organizational structure within SAP applications allows the plant to be assigned to a company code. So a company code can have one or many plants associated with it. If you look at how your own company is structured, you can easily see which locations can be defined as plants.

 Tip

Carefully consider the plant structure before configuring the SAP system. Although it's easy to add plants in SAP software, you don't want to spend unnecessary time changing the structure.

In Figure 2.3, the plant 9002 is associated with company code 1299.

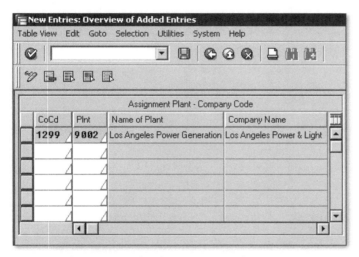

Figure 2.3 Plant Associated with a Company Code

Storage Location

A *storage location* is a section or area within a plant. It's usually defined as a specific area where stock is physically kept within a plant. There will always be at least one storage location defined for one plant, but there can be more than one, depending on the setup. Figure 2.4 shows a number of storage locations defined for a single plant in SAP.

Storage locations

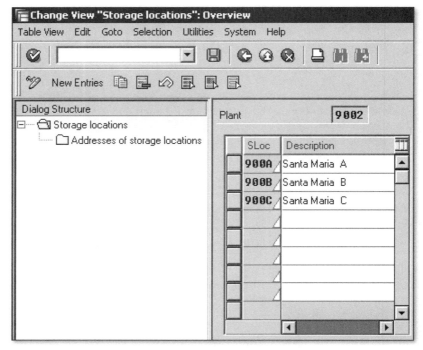

Figure 2.4 Storage Locations Associated with a Plant

There are no set rules or physical requirements for what a storage lo-cation should look like. SAP customers have a variety of very specific inventory-monitoring requirements. A physical storage location is an area that contains inventory separated from other inventory. Depend-ing on the physical size of the materials involved, this may be as small as a 2-inch square bin or as large as an entire building. Storage loca-tions can define areas of racking, shelves, plastic bins, refrigerators, tool cages, safes, and so on.

 Tip

> Create only the number of storage locations that are needed to operate an efficient inventory process. Unnecessary storage locations create un-necessary movements and reduce efficiency.

Warehouse

A warehouse is part of the SAP Warehouse Management (SAP WM) functionality, which allows the customer to further specify locations within a storage location. If you need to know more than just the contents of a storage location, the WM functions can be configured. Figure 2.5 shows a number of warehouses configured in SAP.

SAP Warehouse Management

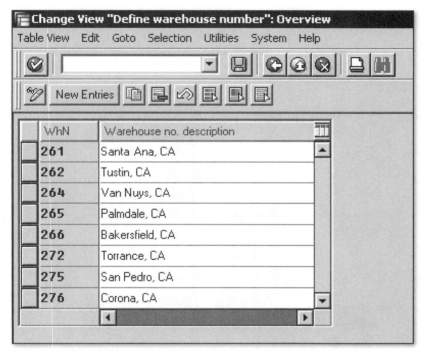

Figure 2.5 Warehouse Entries in SAP

The warehouse is a defined physical area assigned to a storage location. Using a warehouse gives a company the ability to track items down to a very low-level location, which is the storage bin. This can be important if there are thousands of items in a single storage location that are required to be moved, either in or out, with minimum time. The warehouse can be divided into storage types, sections, and bins.

Warehouses assigned to storage locations

The warehouse is assigned to a storage location or number of storage locations in the SAP system. Figure 2.6 shows the assignment of warehouses to storage locations and plants.

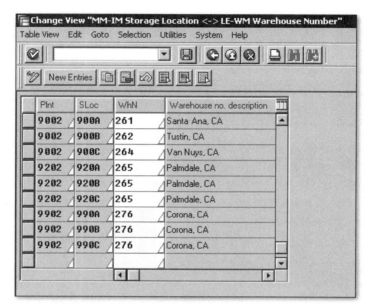

Figure 2.6 Warehouse Associated with Storage Locations

Storage Type

Areas within a warehouse

A *storage type* is an area of the warehouse that users can base searches on. Common storage types in a warehouse can be areas such as cold room, bulk storage, and high racking area. Search strategies can be configured at the storage type level that allow different types of stock placement and stock removal to be defined. Figure 2.7 shows storage types created for a warehouse.

Storage Section

A *storage section* is an area of the storage type used to divide the storage type further; for example, if the bulk storage area had two levels, each level could be defined as a storage section. Figure 2.8 shows storage sections for the storage types of Warehouse 276.

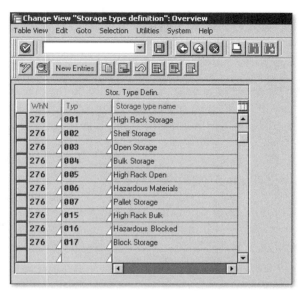

Figure 2.7 Storage Types Defined for Warehouse 276

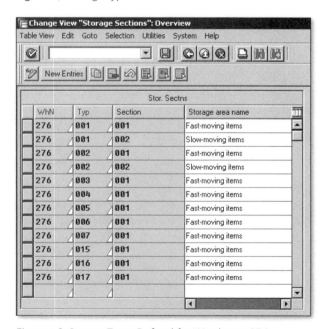

Figure 2.8 Storage Types Defined for Warehouse 276

Storage Bin

Smallest location in
the warehouse

A number of storage bins can be defined for each storage section. A *storage bin* is the lowest level of storage in the plant.

Now that you understand the organizational structure found in an SAP system, the next section will review the purchasing organization and how it integrates with the structure defined in this section.

Purchasing Organization Structure

Any purchasing function can range from simple to very complex. The largest SAP customers may spend hundreds of millions of dollars in purchasing each year and have a sophisticated purchasing department that works at many different levels, from strategic global procurement to low-level vendor relationships. SAP software can be defined to allow all purchasing departments to be accurately reflected.

Modernizing the
purchasing function

Smaller SAP customers are working to eradicate requisition cards and create a modern purchasing department. Every purchasing department is unique, but the organizational structure defined within the SAP system allows your company to adopt best practices to maximize the benefits SAP applications provide.

Purchasing Organization

A *purchasing organization* refers to a group of purchasing activities associated with all or a specific part of the enterprise.

Purchasing function
structure

For example, if a company has three plants; New York, Chicago, and Houston, there can either be a single purchasing organization that negotiates contracts for all three plants or a purchasing organization at each plant that locally negotiates with vendors.

The number of purchasing organizations depends on a several factors. For example, if the three plants all use the same materials from the same vendors, then a single purchasing organization may be more suitable; however, if the plants use different materials from local vendors, then a purchasing organization for each plant may be more appropriate. The decision to adopt the use of more than one purchasing organization may be more complex and requires a study of what materials and services are purchased across the enterprise, how those materials are purchased, and by whom.

 Tip

> The flexibility in the SAP system means that whatever purchasing structure your company has, it can be replicated in the system.

Figure 2.9 shows a number of purchasing organizations that have been configured.

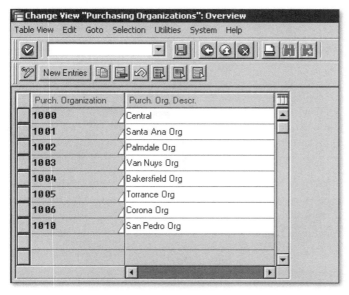

Figure 2.9 Purchasing Organizations in SAP

SAP systems provide a number of ways to configure the purchasing organization.

Purchasing Across the Whole Organization

For large companies, *procurement*, which some companies call purchasing, may take place at the highest level within an organization. If a customer has a central purchasing department that coordinates

Single purchasing organization

purchasing for all companies within the enterprise, then the purchasing organization can be configured in that manner. The purchasing organization is defined in the SAP software and then assigned to all companies. Companies such as General Motors and Coca-Cola negotiate and procure materials and services on a global basis for the companies within their organizations.

Purchasing at a Company Level

Different companies, different purchasing

Some large companies don't have a single business-wide purchasing function and may have centralized purchasing for each company. This may be appropriate for companies with entities in various countries, in which case, an enterprise purchasing department may not be possible. In this scenario, the purchasing organization is created and assigned for each company code. However, a purchasing organization may cover several companies.

 Example

A company that has a purchasing organization for Mexico may be assigned as the purchasing organization for the companies based in Belize, Honduras, and Guatemala.

Figure 2.10 shows purchasing organizations in the SAP system that have been assigned to a company code.

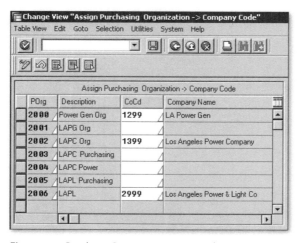

Figure 2.10 Purchase Organization Assigned to Company Code

50

Purchasing at the Plant Level

In an enterprise that has companies with large autonomous plants; the purchasing decisions may be made at a local level. A company may decide that assigning one purchasing organization to one company isn't appropriate, and it would be a better business decision to assign a purchasing organization at the plant. This scenario is advantageous when the vendors are at a local level and few vendors supply materials or services to more than one plant.

Local purchasing function

 Example

> In the oil industry, oil refineries are so large and geographically dispersed that companies may not be able to use a company-wide purchasing department because the vendors are local to the refineries and therefore require the purchasing organization to be at the plant level.

Figure 2.11 shows purchasing organizations that have been assigned to a plant.

POrg	Description	Plant	Name 1
1000	Central	9002	Los Angeles Power Generation
1000	Central	9003	Los Angeles Power Administrative
1000	Central	9004	Los Angeles Power Spares
1000	Central	9005	Los Angeles Power & Light Administrative
1001	Santa Ana Org	9515	Santa Ana
1001	Santa Ana Org	9518	Santa Ana Administrative
1002	Palmdale Org	9525	Palmdale
1002	Palmdale Org	9909	Palmdale Administrative

Figure 2.11 Purchasing Organization Assigned to a Plant

Purchasing Group

Your company can define its purchasing department below the level of purchasing organization. The *purchasing group* can be defined as a

Organization of purchasing staff

person or group of people dealing with a certain material or group of materials purchased through the purchasing organization. In larger organizations, there are often groups of employees in the purchasing department who work with certain vendors or certain types of vendors.

Ex Example

Large companies can assign each vendor a dedicated person within the purchasing organization to be the point of contact. If the company uses a vendor as a single source for a large number of materials or services— for example, for scientific testing products, a company may use VWR, Fischer Scientific, or Cambridge Scientific Products—then the purchasing department may have a group of employees who are dedicated to that one vendor.

Purchasing group for multiple vendors

In smaller companies, one single purchasing department employee may deal with a variety of vendors that fall under a specific area; for example, in a chemical company, one purchasing department employee may be responsible for all vendors that supply organic compounds. Figure 2.12 shows a number of purchasing groups that have been configured in SAP.

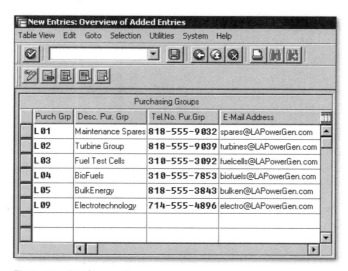

Figure 2.12 Purchasing Groups

Now that we've discussed the SAP purchasing organization, let's go on to examine the procurement processes that are used.

Purchasing Process

The SAP purchasing processes allow the purchasing department to use the best practices that are found in world-class purchasing organizations.

Purchasing Best Practices

In the procurement of materials and services, the purchasing department does more than just process orders. The modern purchasing department manages a process that ensures the items the company purchases are of the highest quality, at the lowest cost, delivered in a timely manner. The following subsections describe the best practices used in world-class purchasing department.

Best practices improve efficiency, reduce costs

Information Gathering

When a new product has been developed, design engineers often require materials or services to be procured that may be new to the company. The purchasing department is responsible for searching for suppliers who can satisfy the requirements. Purchasing departments start with their current vendors who offer the best discounts to ensure that the new material or service is procured at the best possible price.

Request for Quotation

If the material can't be procured from contracted vendors, or the price and quality aren't acceptable, the purchasing department advertises or sends potential vendors a request for quotation (RFQ), request for proposals (RFP), request for information (RFI), or request for tender (RFT). The purchasing department evaluates any reply based on a set of defined criteria to obtain the best product at the best price.

RFQs create vendor competition

Tip

If your company is going to use RFQs, you should implement a set of guidelines that will assist in the process. You probably don't want to send out an RFQ for every material or service that is purchased, so identifying the relevant items is important.

Background Review

Vendor evaluation

If a company has used a vendor before, the company will have information about that vendor within the system. SAP software has a vendor evaluation function that uses objective and subjective analysis to help in the evaluation of vendors. If the vendor hasn't been used before, the purchasing department requires references for the material or service quality. The purchasing department also investigates installation, maintenance, and warranty information. If the material is to be used in the production process, the quality department may examine samples and undertake trials of the material.

Negotiation

Produce significant price reductions

The purchasing department is also responsible for entering into negotiations with potential vendors. The agreement isn't just about price and discounts but also availability lead times and quality. The negotiation of the terms of an agreement can be prolonged, but the purchasing department must be fully aware of upcoming sales orders and production lead times.

Contract Monitoring

Monitor your contracts

After the contract is signed, the purchasing department monitors the performance of the vendor based on the terms of the contract. The purchasing department evaluates on-time delivery, checking that the correct quantity arrived, ensuring that the quality of the material was per the contract, and verifying that the invoicing was sent correctly with the correct price, delivery charge, and appropriate discounts.

Contract Renewal

After a specific time, determined by the contract, the purchasing department enters into contract renewal negotiations with the vendor. The vendor's performance with the material and other materials it supplies will be considered and evaluated.

 Example

> If the vendor has a perfect record with one material but fails evaluation constantly with other materials it supplies, contract renewal with the vendor may not be considered.

Monitoring the vendor's performance allows the purchasing department to enter into negotiations with leverage that can produce a better price for the material in subsequent contracts. If the purchasing department or the production department doesn't want to renew the contract for the material or service, the purchasing department is required to start a new RFQ process to find a new vendor for the material.

Purchase Requisition

The *purchase requisition* is the procedure by which users can request the purchase of materials or services that require processing by the purchasing department. Companies can allow certain authorized users to enter purchase requisitions directly into the SAP system, but in situations involving a particular dollar value or type of goods and services, the company may request another method of informing the purchasing department of the purchasing requisition, such as fax or email. Figure 2.13 shows a purchase requisition that has been entered into SAP. The purchase requisition includes the quantity, cost center, and purchasing group responsible for the purchase. The purchasing group monitors new requisitions and processes those for which they are responsible.

Purchase requisitions shouldn't specify vendors

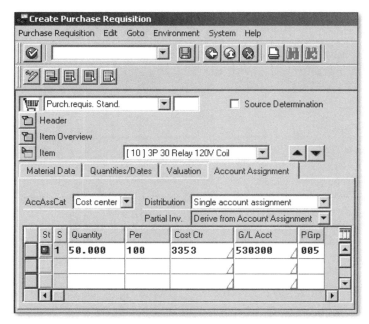

Figure 2.13 Purchase Requisition

Placing requisitions via intranet

A growing number of companies have implemented a web-based frontend to purchase requisitioning over their company intranets, and authorized users can go to a URL and enter the material or services they need instead of having direct access to the SAP system. Some companies have purchased Internet requisition software, whereas others have built their own applications in-house. The benefit of this type of application is that it can allow any employee to create a requisition without having to sign on to the SAP system or be an SAP user. This can be beneficial because it requires less administration work for your SAP security staff.

Figure 2.14 shows an example of an Internet-based purchase requisition application. The user can add a vendor, items, and quantities, and, if the application accesses a vendor catalog, a price can be shown.

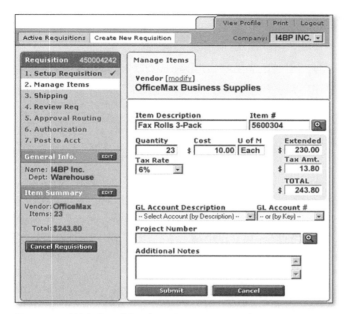

Figure 2.14 Web-Based Purchase Requisition Application

After the purchase requisition has been created, it can be converted to a purchase order (PO) or can be used as the basis for an RFQ if the material or service isn't currently purchased by the company.

Request for Quotation (RFQ)

When the purchasing department receives and reviews purchase requisitions, there may be a material or service that requires the purchasing department to offer an RFQ.

RFQs give new vendors opportunities

Many scenarios require the purchasing department to produce an RFQ:

> Material or service has not previously been purchased by the company.

> Previously used material or service has no valid vendor.

> Material or service requires a new vendor because the previous vendor's contract was not renewed.

> Material or service requires a new vendor to be found due to new government regulations or laws.

> Material or service requires a new vendor to be found due to logistical issues.

The purchasing department either publishes an RFQ from which vendors then send a quotation, or the purchasing department specifically sends the RFQ to a number of vendors that have been preselected. These vendors currently have a contract with the company, have been identified by the person who entered the requisition, or have been identified by the purchasing department after investigation.

Detailed RFQs produce accurate vendor quotes The RFQ can contain as little or as much information as the purchasing department deems necessary for a competitive bid situation. If the material or service is low cost and has little strategic impact, then the RFQ will be relatively simple. However, if the item or service is of high value, it may not be a question of just cost but other factors that determine which vendor offers the most competitive bid. In complex RFQs, the purchasing department may require vendors to supply information on quantity discounts and rebates, detailed quality specifications, delivery and lead time requirements, period of warranty, detailed drawings, and so on. Figure 2.15 shows an RFQ that has been entered into the SAP software. The RFQ shows the required material, quantity, delivery date, and the deadline date for a response.

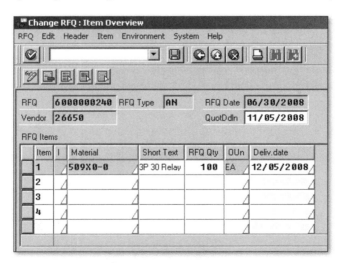

Figure 2.15 Request for Quotation

The RFQ can be transmitted to the vendor by email or EDI (Electronic Data Interchange), or it can be printed from the SAP system and then faxed or sent. Each vendor sends back to the purchasing department a quotation based on the contents of the RFQ.

Transmitting an RFQ

Quotation

The vendor sends a quotation to the purchasing department via email, EDI, fax, or mail. Each vendor's quotation is evaluated by the purchasing department to ensure that it abides by the stipulations of the RFQ that was sent out. If the vendor failed to reply in the format required, this may disqualify the vendor's bid. The purchasing department may enter into negotiations with one or more vendors before making a decision on a primary and secondary vendor. After a final decision is made, the details of the contract are entered into the SAP application, so that the information is available when a PO is created.

Vendor response to RFQs

Purchase Order

A *purchase order* (PO) is a commercial document issued by a purchasing department to the vendor. The PO specifies the material or service required, the quantities, and the negotiated price that the vendor and purchasing department have agreed upon.

PO equals vendor contract

You can create a PO from a purchase requisition that has been entered into the SAP system. It can be created as a direct result of a quotation from a vendor replying to an RFQ. In addition, you can enter a PO directly into SAP without a requisition. Your company policies on procurement determine the purchasing processes allowed.

 Tip

Allowing staff to enter POs without any requisition is a valid purchasing process, but it bypasses the requisition process and negates any possible savings and efficiencies.

The PO can only be given to one vendor via email, fax, mail, or EDI. Figure 2.16 shows a PO that has been entered into SAP.

Submitting a PO

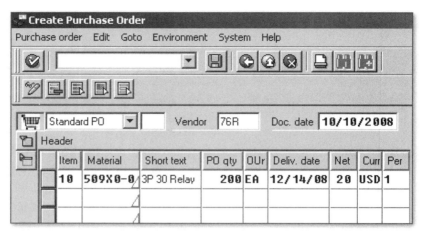

Figure 2.16 Purchase Order Entered into SAP

Vendors can receive an acknowledgement of the PO via EDI.

Different types of POs

Changes to the PO, such as additional items or quantities, can be made and communicated to the vendor via either fax or EDI transaction number 860. A number of different POs can be created for a variety of situations that occur within your company.

Outline Purchasing Agreement

Blanket PO

An *outline purchasing agreement* is often referred to as a blanket PO and is used between a company and a vendor where a set of terms and conditions are agreed upon that covers a number of materials or services that will be purchased over a period of time.

 Example

A purchasing department sets up an outline purchase agreement with an office supply company, and the office staff requisitions a variety of office supplies from the vendor's catalog. The purchasing department then purchases these items against the existing outline purchasing agreement.

Scheduling Agreement

Purchased items required at regular intervals

A *scheduling agreement* is similar to an outline purchase agreement because it's created between a company and a vendor for items over a given period based on agreed terms and conditions. However, a scheduling agreement is used where the vendor is to supply the items on a given schedule required by the company.

 Example

A company that manufactures vacuum cleaners has determined its sales forecast for the year and has put a production plan into place that manufactures 5,000 vacuums a week. This requires 20,000 feet of electrical cord for each weekly run. The company creates a scheduling agreement with the vendor of the electrical cord that will deliver 40,000 feet of electrical cord every 2 weeks.

Quantity Contract

In some instances, the purchasing department and the vendor negotiate an agreement whereby the terms and agreement of the deal are valid for a quantity of material or services over a given period of time. This is called a *quantity contract* and is used when a company has a specific requirement that has been identified.

Contract for a specific quantity of material from a vendor

 Tip

A quantity contract can be used with new vendors when you guarantee a minimum purchase. When the quantity in the contract has been exceeded, the purchasing staff can assess whether the contract should be renewed.

 Example

It the vacuum cleaner manufacturer has a special promotion that includes a handheld cleaner with every full-size vacuum purchased, the purchasing department can create a quantity contract with a vendor to provide a service to create special packaging for the promotion. The company has identified a specific quantity of vacuums that it wants to include in the promotion, and the contract with the vendor is based on that given quantity.

Value Contract

Similar to the quantity contract, a *value contract* is an agreement with a vendor in which the terms and agreement of the deal are valid for a given period of time, but are based on value rather than quantity of materials or services.

 Example

> If the vacuum manufacturer wants to analyze how consumers viewed its special promotion, the company can hire a market research company to perform in-store surveys. The sales department has a budget of $20,000 for this analysis, and the purchasing department negotiates a value contract with the market research company to allow the sales staff to requisition services against that contract.

After the vendor has been notified of the company's requirements through the submission of a PO, the materials or services are sent or provided. The vendor then invoices the company to get payment.

The next section examines the accounts payable processes in the SAP system, which is where these vendor invoices are dealt with.

Accounts Payable

Paying vendors *Accounts payable* can be defined as the money that your company owes to vendors for materials or services purchased on credit. The items appear on your company's balance sheet as a current liability. When accounts payable are paid off, it represents a negative cash flow for the company.

Let's examine the accounts payables processes found in SAP.

Invoice Verification

Verifying invoices *Invoice verification* is part of the accounts payment process where vendors are paid for materials or services that they have provided. The verification of the invoice is important to both the vendor and the purchaser because it ensures that the quantities and the pricing are correct and that neither party has made an error. The standard method of invoice verification is the three-way match.

Three-Way Match

Invoice verification using a three-way match takes the PO supplied to the vendor, the goods receipt or delivery note supplied by the vendor, and the invoice sent to the customer from the vendor. In a successful three-way match, the quantity and price of the three documents match, and the payment to the vendor is sent via check or bank transfer at a date defined by an agreement between the company and vendor. Figure 2.17 shows the entry of an invoice into SAP.

Invoice matching to PO and receipt

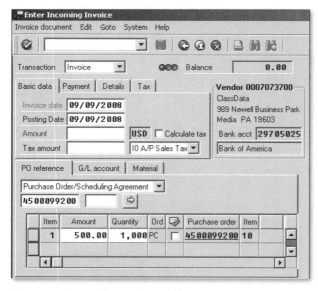

Figure 2.17 Invoice Entered into SAP

Evaluated Receipt Settlement

Instead of the traditional three-way match, some companies are working with their vendors to allow payment without an invoice, so they are performing a two-way match. This method was developed by General Motors in 1994 and is called evaluated receipt settlement (ERS). This process allows the purchasing department to electronically match the goods receipt with the PO, and if there is no variance, a payment is sent.

Two-way match

Tip

> ERS should only be considered with trusted vendors. By foregoing an invoice, your company is committed to paying on receipt. However, this is beneficial because it means that your company can take advantage of any discounts.

Evaluated receipt settlement (ERS)

The process works when a high level of communication and trust exists between vendor and purchaser. The evaluated receipt process usually includes the following elements:

> As part of an ERS agreement, the vendor is usually required to keep the purchaser informed of current prices at a more frequent period than normally expected. This reduces any price variances issues that normally arise.

> The purchasing department uses the most recent pricing information sent by the vendor when an order is placed. The PO is sent to the vendor who usually acknowledges the PO by sending an Advance Shipping Notification (ASN) to the purchasing company. The ASN can be sent electronically via EDI 856, through a fax or email.

> The vendor ships the materials to the customer with an itemized bill of lading or packing slip that references the PO.

> The purchasing department matches the goods receipt, which can be the vendor's bill of lading or packing slip to the ASN, PO, or contract, to validate accuracy.

> Instead of receiving and paying against a vendor's invoice, the purchasing department calculates payment based on price information. The type, quantity, and condition of the goods received are entered into the SAP software, which calculates the payment amount with respect to accrual or payment of tax. The goods receipt date is used as the basis for taking discounts and determining the due date of the payment. The payment to the vendor is made either by electronic funds transfer (EFT) or check.

The benefits of the ERS process are experienced by the purchasing company and the vendor. The process reduces costs, reduces errors, and eliminates activities that don't add value as described in the following list:

> **Reduced costs**

Less resources, equipment, and floor space are required thus reducing costs. An automated process eliminates lost discounts and eliminates the cost of printing invoices.

ERS benefits

> **Reduced errors**

Invoices don't need to be entered, so there are fewer keying errors. Other processes such as checking PO numbers, quantity and pricing discounts become automated and further reduce errors.

> **Eliminating activities that don't add value**

The process eliminates manual activities such as invoice entry, invoice filing, and voucher payment preparation, as well as the cost of mailing invoices.

> **More timely payments**

By eliminating the vendor invoice, the process allows the vendor to receive payment sooner.

> **Maximized discounts**

ERS results in fewer errors to resolve, thus allowing purchasing departments to take full advantage of payment discounts.

 Case Study

In 2001, a major U.S. retailer was using the traditional invoice verification process to match POs created in a standalone purchasing system, with the goods receipt and invoices entered into its aging ERP system. The errors matching the three documents caused the company to fail to pay invoices on time and often incorrectly. This produced a growing number of legal cases in which vendors filed suit against the retailer to reclaim the money owed. That year, the retailer implemented SAP ERP, and as part of the implementation, introduced ERS with a number of vendors, some of which had been involved in legal action against the retailer. By 2004, the company reported that in the two years of operating the ERS process under SAP, it had saved more than $2 million in legal costs and reduced material spending by $200,000 due to implementing best practices, including taking advantages of discounts offered by vendors for prompt payment.

Your company may already use ERS with selected vendors and already receive some of the benefits outlined in this section. The accounts payable process is important because it provides payment for the vendor for the materials and services they have provided.

Summary

This chapter has given you an overview of the organizational structure that is used by SAP software for the purchasing function, as well as introduced you to the purchasing functions in SAP, such as purchase requisition, request for quotations (RFQs), purchase orders (POs), and accounts payable.

The SAP purchasing function is important in the logistics process because it ensures that the correct material is at the manufacturing site at the lowest cost at the required time. Purchasing professionals can reduce your raw material spend by using the functionality in the SAP system. SAP purchasing functionality, such as RFQs, vendor evaluation, and contract monitoring, gives your purchasing staff the tools to negotiate with vendors and save your company money.

In this chapter, there are some key points that you should remember:

> Whether your company purchases at the enterprise, company, or plant level, SAP has the flexibility for any scenario.

> SAP contains purchasing best practices such as RFQs, vendor evaluation, and contract monitoring.

> With SAP systems, company can use RFQs and requisitions, or if your purchasing needs are simple, just POs can be used.

> Quantity and value contracts, scheduling agreements, and purchase agreements are available to your purchasing staff.

> ERS, two-way match, can be used with trusted vendors to eliminate the need to use vendor invoices.

The next chapter describes the SAP functions used in inventory management. You'll be introduced to the logical structure of the plant as well as the goods movements within the plant, and physical inventory of material.

3

Inventory Management

Inventory management is the process in which a company balances its inventory needs and requirements with the need to minimize costs resulting from obtaining and holding inventory.

You can think of inventory as the stored materials that exceed what is needed for the company to run. Companies try to reduce their inventory because the cost of holding what isn't being used is often significant. The costs of material, warehousing facilities, staff, and management of that inventory affects the profitability of the company. However, keep in mind that a company may need to hold inventory for a number of valid business reasons. It's a delicate balance.

Customers expect a company to have materials available when they require them for purchase. If a material takes two days to be manufactured, and the customer requires the item in one day, then the company must have an inventory on hand to fulfill the customer's order. In fact, the longer the manufacturing lead time for a finished product, the more inventories a company will be required to hold.

Customer expectations

Example

> A company manufactures commercial lawnmowers, and each finished product takes three days to complete. To be competitive, the company guarantees same day shipping on all orders. To ensure the company has enough stock, it keeps an on-hand balance of its top-selling models. The amount of stock on hand is calculated based on the average daily number of sales orders the company has received over the past two years.

One of the main reasons that companies often hold inventory of raw materials is because of discounts offered by vendors.

Vendor discounts   If the discounts offered by the vendor are greater than the cost of holding the inventory, then that material will be purchased and held until required. You can think of it as companies shopping at BJ's, Sam's Club, or Costco's, rather than a Seven-Eleven.

We'll examine the SAP Inventory Management (SAP IM) processes beginning with the structure of the plant where the inventory is stored, the movements of inventory within the plant, and the processes involved in counting inventory.

Plant Structure

Plant structure is important to review, and you need to know how the plant is used with SAP IM processes.

Plant

In Chapter 2, we defined the *plant* as a location that holds valuated stock or as an organizational unit that is central to production planning. The definition of a plant varies depending on what your company requires, but it should be an organizational unit that exists within your company where processes take place. Sometimes these processes involve stored material, sometimes maintenance, or sometimes production. Your company will define the organizational units based on how your company's processes operate.

When the SAP system is first being implemented at your company, many decisions have to be made regarding the company structure, especially finance decisions, as well as organizational decisions regarding the business. This is the first stage in the process of defining a plant in the SAP system, as seen in Figure 3.1.

Figure 3.1 Plant Information in SAP

Your company's logistics organization will be called upon to determine the structure of the business, the nature and number of plants to be defined, and then at a more detailed level, how each plant will be defined.

Someone must make the decision concerning whether a plant is to use just SAP Inventory Management (SAP IM) or whether the functionality available in SAP Warehouse Management (SAP WM) is required. We'll examine warehouse management in greater detail in Chapter 4, but let's look at SAP IM versus SAP WM.

If your company uses and stores a small number of materials, the SAP WM functionality may be excessive and not allow your company to be efficient. However, if your plant has a large number of locations where material is stored, or placement and removal of materials needs to be efficiently managed, then use of the SAP WM functionality may be worth considering.

 Tip

Before deciding on implementing SAP WM or just continuing to use SAP IM, review all aspects of the change, including any additional resources, additional processing time, employee training, and so on. Make an informed decision.

Storage Location

As described in the previous chapter, a storage location is a section or area within your company's plant where inventory is held. The inventory can be materials that are used in your company's production, finished goods, or maintenance items. The storage location is the lowest inventory level in the SAP IM component. Your company's logistics management must evaluate whether the storage location is the most suitable inventory structure for the plant.

SAP IM or SAP WM Although there are no rules on when the SAP WM component is to be used, the logistics management should check with SAP consultants to determine whether the SAP WM component should be implemented. Figure 3.2 shows storage locations that have been created for a plant.

The storage location can be a physical location or a logical location. In a plant, a storage location can be physically defined as a physical room, a row of shelves, a refrigerated cabinet, a trailer, or a space in the plant that is determined by lines on the shop floor. Every company has its own way of determining physical storage locations, which can be as small as a 50-centimeter square tote or as large as a building.

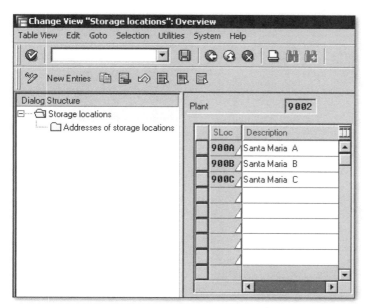

Figure 3.2 Storage Locations Defined for a Plant

The storage location defined in the SAP system doesn't need to represent a physical location in your plant. Your company may not be able to physically define individual storage locations because material is just stored in one location. However, you may want to logically define areas within the SAP system to distinguish where materials are stored in the system. There are several reasons why your company might want to create logical storage locations. For example, if each storage location has an individual physical address, your company might need to create separate storage locations so that incoming material has documentation that identifies a certain address.

Logical storage locations

Another reason your company might want to create a logical storage location is to distinguish between materials associated with production planning and material that is not. With material requirements planning (MRP), the process can include or exclude material in certain storage locations. Companies may decide not to include certain storage locations in their MRP process because they require the material not to be part of the MRP calculations. One common reason is that a

Required logical storage locations?

company has material in a storage location that is specifically held for priority customers or for priority production orders. Therefore, if material isn't physically separated, the system can logically distinguish between those materials required for MRP and those materials that are not required.

Now that you understand the plant structure and the use of storage locations, let's move on to the movements of material within the plant, called goods movements.

Goods Movements

Physical and logical goods movements

The *goods movement* processes within the SAP system refer to movements of stock inside the plant that can create a change in stock levels within the storage locations inside the plant. The movement of stock can be either inbound from one of your vendors, outbound to your customers, a stock transfer between plants, or an internal transfer posting within a plant.

When items are inside the plant, they need to be placed in an area that is appropriate for their physical characteristics.

 Example

> Materials requiring refrigeration need to be in a storage location designated for cold storage.

Items can also be moved between storage locations, for example, when a material is required to be moved to a staging area before it's used in production. This section examines the goods movements that occur in the SAP system.

Goods Receipt

From vendors or other company locations

A goods receipt occurs when there is a receipt of material from a vendor or from your company's in-house production process. Many other types of goods receipt are also found in the SAP system, including initial stock creation, which is used when SAP software is first implemented. A goods receipt of material from whatever source creates an increase in stock levels. Figure 3.3 shows a typical goods receipt for two materials. Goods receipts are discussed more fully in Chapter 5.

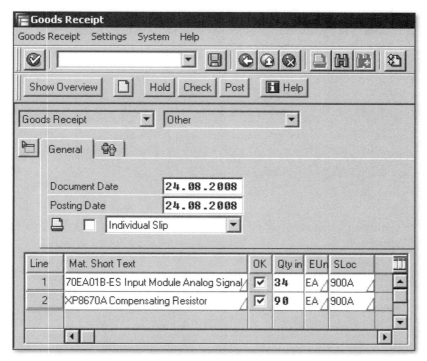

Figure 3.3 SAP Goods Receipt

Goods Issue

A *goods issue* is a reduction of stock triggered when there is a shipment to your customer or a withdrawal of stock for use in a production order. Other goods issues can be for a sample or to scrap if the material is damaged. A goods issue is the final process of an outbound delivery. Figure 3.4 shows a typical goods issue of two materials from storage location 900A that will be moved from inventory and consumed.

Goods issue is a consumption of stock

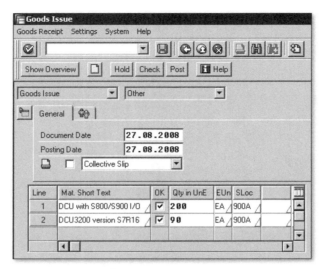

Figure 3.4 SAP Goods Issue

The outbound movements of material are discussed more fully in Chapter 5.

Returns

The returns process occurs whenever your company purchases material. Items often need to be returned to the vendor because an item is damaged, fails quality testing, is the wrong material, or is over-delivered. Part of the agreement with your vendors will be a clause that specifies the returns policy that must be adhered to.

Reasons material is returned | Some vendors won't allow a return until a Return Material Authorization (RMA) has been issued. The vendor specifies by what method the material is to be returned. They determine whether the item is to be repaired, replaced, or whether a monetary refund or credit is offered.

 Tip

Make sure your warehouse staff know the returns policy for each vendor. Making a mistake on the method of return or in the period allowed to send back a return to a vendor can be very costly.

Figure 3.5 shows a typical return that is processed in the SAP system.

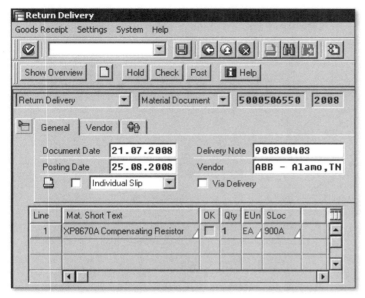

Figure 3.5 Return of Material to a Vendor

Reservations

A *reservation* is a request to hold material in the plant or storage location for movement to a process before that process begins.

Reservations identify task-specific material

 Example

A company has received a sales order from a new customer. The item that was ordered has to be manufactured, and a production order has been created. To ensure that the raw material is available for the production orders, a reservation was created.

Reservations aren't always manually created. You can create automatic reservations by a project or a production order.

Reservations identify material as being allocated for an order or project, but the material is still shown as available stock because it may be needed in an emergency for a customer or for another production

Reserved material for emergencies

order. The material may be reserved but can be reallocated if necessary.

Figure 3.6 shows a reservation that has been made in the SAP system.

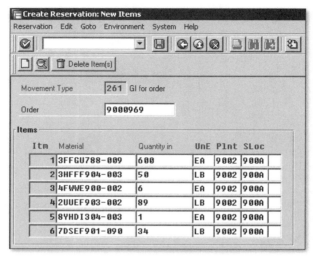

Figure 3.6 Reservation Created for a Production Order

Stock Transfers and Transfer Postings

Although your company is probably trying to reduce the number of moves that material makes in the plant, some movements are inevitably required.

Unnecessary material movements wastes resources Material is most frequently moved from the receiving area to the warehouse, the warehouse to the production staging area, the production area to the warehouse, and the warehouse to the shipping area. SAP software provides a number of transactions that facilitates the movement of material between storage locations in your company's plant.

In addition to the movements inside the plant, your company will likely need to move material to another company location. SAP functionality facilitates the movement of material between plants as well.

The terms *stock transfer* and *transfer posting* are both used in SAP applications to describe the movement of materials. However, a stock transfer refers to the physical movements of materials, and a transfer posting is used to describe a logical movement of material.

Stock transfers and transfer posting

 Example

> A delivery from a vendor was received at the loading dock, and the material, ABC, was placed in the usual storage. Another delivery of material ABC arrived from the vendor before the previous delivery had been used, due to a delay in the production order. The warehouse staff decided to move the older material closer to where it will be used on the shop floor so that the latest delivery could be stored. To do this, the warehouse staff created a stock transfer from storage location to storage location.
>
> However, when the older material was moved, the warehouse staff noticed damage to the packaging. The warehouse manager requested that a quality inspection be performed. To ensure that the material wasn't used, a transfer posting was performed moving the material from an unrestricted status to a quality inspection status.

Stock Transfer Between Storage Locations

The transfer of material between storage locations in your company's plant occurs every day because of normal plant operations.

 Tip

> Although it's extremely easy in the SAP system to move material from storage location to storage location, it uses your resources to physically move items. The costs of stock transfers can mount up if they are performed too frequently. Minimizing moves in the warehouse is important in an efficient warehouse.

Material is moved to the shipping area to fulfill customer orders, and to the staging area for production orders, because of storage limitations, for quality testing, and so on. The process of moving material between storage locations in your company's plant is made simple by SAP ERP functionality.

Reasons for moves between storage locations

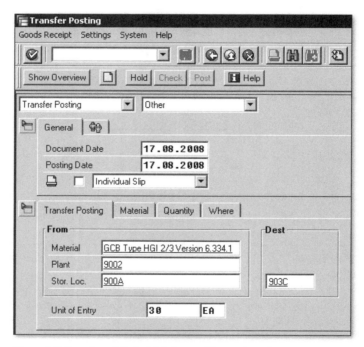

Ex **Example**

At the production plant of a chemical manufacturer, raw material is received at the loading dock and is moved to a holding area where a quality inspection is performed. After the material has passed the inspection, the raw material is moved to the bulk storage via stock transfer from storage to storage location.

Figure 3.7 shows a stock transfer of material between two storage locations in the SAP system. A quantity of 30 of the material in plant 9002 is being transferred between storage locations 900A and 903C.

Figure 3.7 Transfer of Material Between Storage Locations

Stock Transfer Between Plants

The transfer of material between plants occurs when material is moved to replenish stock levels at another plant within your company, to deliver material from a production site to a distribution center, or to move obsolete or slow-moving stock.

Tip

Before moving obsolete and slow-moving stock, compare the costs of disposing of the material locally over paying for shipping material to another plant.

If your company has a production site and a number of regional distribution centers, plant-to-plant stock transfers can be used to move the material.

Plant-to-plant stock transfers

 Example

A German car manufacturer has three manufacturing plants that produce spare parts for the European market. It has distribution centers in seven countries, which are supplied by the manufacturing plants. To move material from the production sites to the distribution centers, the company uses plant-to-plant stock transfers.

Figure 3.8 shows a stock transfer of material between two storage locations in SAP.

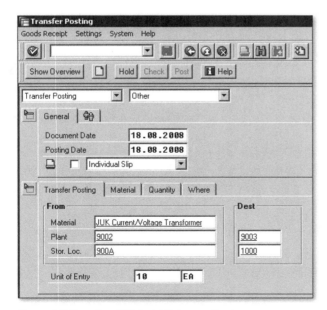

Figure 3.8 Transfer of Material Between Plants

Material Conversion

Company mergers and acquisitions

If your company merges with or purchases another company, there can be issues when the two inventories are consolidated, such as the same material number being used by both companies. Material numbers may also need to be changed if your company converts from an intelligent numbering system to a sequential numbering system for materials. The transfer posting functionality of SAP ERP provides your company with a solution for this situation.

 Example

> An Australian beverage company purchased a Japanese competitor and is working on combining the two product lines. The team working on the consolidation established that both companies were using non-intelligent numbering of materials in SAP, but there are 20 instances where the material numbers are duplicated. The team recommended that the duplicates be changed using the material conversion transfer posting.

 Tip

> Before converting material numbers, review all aspects of renumbering, including the cost of reprinting catalogs, creating new packaging, informing customers, and change-management issues.

Figure 3.9 shows a transfer posting that converts the inventory of one material number to a new material number.

Transfer Posting

Logical movement of material

A transfer posting differs from a stock transfer because it reflects a logical change in material, rather than a physical change. There will be everyday situations in your plant that require a transfer posting in the SAP system.

When material is received at a company's plant, it may require a quality inspection. If the material passes that inspection, it's moved into inventory; if not, then the material is given a status in SAP, reflecting its quality hold.

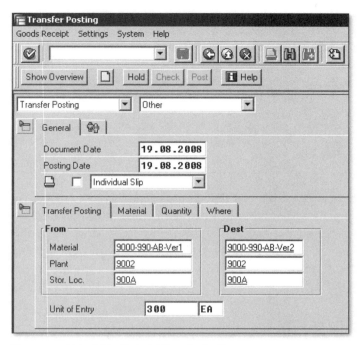

Figure 3.9 Material to Material Transfer Posting

When the material finally passes the quality inspection, the status of the material needs to be changed from being in quality hold to unrestricted stock. In the SAP system, this change in status is achieved by using a transfer posting.

A variety of statuses in the SAP system are provided to help your company with all possible material situations such as the following:

SAP material statuses

> Stock that is assigned to a project

> Stock that is on consignment

> Stock from a vendor that has been blocked from being received into stock

A transfer posting is used to change the status of a material, such as consignment stock to quality inspection stock or project stock to an unrestricted status.

Ex **Example**

A clothing retailer has a distribution center where shipments are received from hundreds of overseas vendors. Before the items are moved into the warehouse and shipped to stores, each shipment from the vendor is assessed for quality. Using the SAP ERP software, each shipment is received into a quality inspection status. A sample of each shipment is taken and the quality checked. After the sample passes the quality inspection, a transfer posting is used to change the status of the items from quality inspection to unrestricted stock.

In this section, we've reviewed the variety of goods movements that are performed every day at your company's plants. In addition to material being received and issued, material is physically moved, and the status can be logically changed. The next section looks at how a physical inventory is performed in the SAP system.

Physical Inventory

A *physical inventory* is a count of what is currently in stock in your company's plant or storage location, compared to what the SAP software indicates is in stock. After a count is performed, you may find that the physical count taken by your staff isn't the same as the amounts in the SAP software. You can run an inventory variance report to see where your counts differ and by how much. The physical count can be taken again for specific variances, or the variance difference can be posted on the SAP system to correct the differences.

Annual physical inventories

Some companies perform a full physical inventory once a year, which is the traditional method. However, your company may need accurate information more frequently. If your company has fast-moving stock, then you may want to consider performing cycle counting, where selected parts of the warehouse or specific products are counted on a more frequent basis.

Physical inventory in the SAP system covers all aspects of the counting material at your company's plants. This includes the yearly inventory, cycle counting, continuous inventory, and inventory sampling.

A physical inventory can be performed on stock that is held in unrestricted, quality inspection, or on blocked status. Physical inventory also can be performed on the special types of stock, such as returnable packaging and consignment stock, at your customer's location.

Material in the plant counted as physical inventory

Physical Inventory Procedures

Before your company's physical inventory can begin, you need to take a number of steps to develop procedures for the count.

If your company has a plant that is complex, identify the different areas in the plant that require counting and develop count procedures that are suitable for each area. This may mean that you have a count procedure for finished goods and a different procedure for raw materials and packaging material. Deciding what to count is very important because counting the wrong materials wastes money and resources.

Physical inventory procedures

When deciding on how and when to perform physical inventories, your company should weigh the effects of any inventory inaccuracies to determine which materials or warehouse sections are more critical than others. Small variances in your company's stock levels of certain materials may have little or no effect on operations, whereas small inaccuracies in the inventory of critical materials may shut down your production. Inventory inaccuracies in finished goods have a negative effect on customer service if deliveries are delayed or canceled due to lack of inventory.

Preparing for the Physical Count

After your company has developed a series of procedures for physical inventory counts, you should complete the following steps before a count takes place:

Getting ready for the physical count

> Complete all SAP transactions that will affect inventory counts, including goods receipts, inventory adjustments, and transfer postings.
> Put away all materials that are being counted in the warehouse.
> Identify material assigned to customer orders that hasn't physically left the warehouse and either label or physically isolate the material from the stock that is to be counted.

> Stop all movements of stock within the warehouse.

> Run the inventory report that shows the items you're going to count, including the quantity of material in unrestricted, quality inspection, and block quantities.

 Tip

Train your physical inventory counters on the process and, in some cases, on how to count specific items. Your company may have items that are difficult to count. If your employees have not been shown how to count the material, the likelihood of errors is high.

After these steps are taken, the SAP count documents can be produced and given to the employees who are performing the count.

Performing the Physical Count

Efficient counts

After the physical inventory count sheets are printed from the SAP ERP software, they can be distributed to the appropriate person for the counting process so the count can begin. Figure 3.10 shows a physical count document that has been printed from SAP ERP.

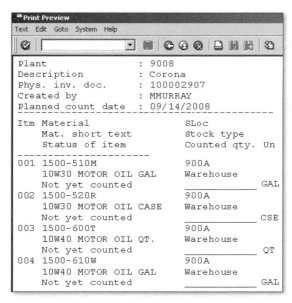

Figure 3.10 Physical Count Document

With more emphasis being given to accuracy of material counts, your company may want to consider training employees on the physical count process in SAP ERP so that the chances of counting materials accurately is improved. Giving employees direct responsibility for counting inventory and resolving discrepancies will significantly improve your company's physical inventory process.

Count Discrepancies

After the count has been entered into the SAP software, you can run a report to see if there are any discrepancies between the count performed by your employees and the stock figures in SAP ERP. Errors can be made by your employees miscounting material or incorrectly identifying material in the warehouse. It's perfectly normal to expect discrepancies.

Simple counting errors

The physical inventory procedures within SAP ERP identify where the material discrepancies occur, but it's is the responsibility of your company's logistics management to decide how to resolve inventory differences. Your company may have designed an auditing process to aid the physical inventory process in investigating the discrepancies.

In the first instance, you may decide to recount the particular materials where a discrepancy was found. The error may be a simple miscount or confusion about what material should be counted. However, if the recount produces the same discrepancy, then a decision must be made on how to rectify the problem.

Recounting

For some discrepancies, an adjustment can be made to the quantity, and then an offsetting adjustment is made if the material is found. Your company could create a variance location to move the lost and found material to and from, as a way of showing the variances without creating adjustments. But a variance location must be closely monitored, and there must be an ongoing procedure for finding the material discrepancies.

Completing the Physical Inventory

The financial impact When all of the counts and recounts are complete, the physical inventory documents can be posted in the SAP system. Any posted document with an inventory differences will cause the stock level to be automatically adjusted. However, always remember that any adjustment in stock levels also causes a financial adjustment. Depending on the monetary value of that adjustment, your company should develop a policy on what discrepancies are investigated and how they are resolved.

 Case Study

> A Canadian medical supply company migrated from a variety of legacy systems to an SAP ERP system. The company had no physical inventory procedures in place due to the batch processing interfaces between the legacy systems. The company had been unable to identify discrepancies between the physical inventory counts and the stock level in the system. The result was that any discrepancies were unknown, and inventory accuracy was below 60%. Customer satisfaction was poor due to delivery dates and quantities that were frequently changed.
>
> After implementing SAP, the company found that its inventory accuracy improved but was still not satisfactory, and delivery dates for customer orders were still being changed. To improve inventory accuracy and customer satisfaction, the company developed a number of procedures that specified how physical inventories were performed and how discrepancies were investigated. After six months of the new procedures, the company's inventory accuracy improved to over 95%.

Now you should have a good idea of the physical inventory process in the SAP system. It's important for your company to carry out regular physical inventories to ensure that the inventory in the SAP system is accurate. If the inventory isn't correct, issues will arise when customer orders are to be fulfilled or when material is to be issued to production orders.

In the worst-case scenario, your company may have a situation where the inventory in the system says items are in the warehouse, but they physically aren't there. This can lead to the inability to fulfill customer orders. Customer satisfaction is extremely important to the competitiveness of your company. You need to have absolute confidence that the inventory on the system is an accurate reflection of the physical inventory in the warehouse.

Accurate inventory is a building block to your company's success. Confidence that customer orders can be fulfilled and that material is available for manufacturing is an important competitive advantage. The physical inventory process in SAP allows your company to achieve inventory accuracy. As important as taking physical inventories, are the procedures that need to be implemented by your company to investigate and process inventory discrepancies that occur.

Summary

This chapter has given you an overview of the inventory management features that are available in SAP ERP. We reviewed the physical and logical movement of material within the plant and how that material is counted to ensure inventory accuracy for your company. SAP IM is a key component in a successful business for the following reasons:

> Replicates your company's logistics structure in the SAP system.

> Goods movements trigger real-time changes in inventory.

> Regular physical inventories ensure accuracy.

> Inventory accuracy provides confidence to ship customer deliveries on time.

The next chapter describes the functions used in SAP Warehouse Management (SAP WM). You'll be introduced to the logical structure of the warehouse as well as the movements that occur within the warehouse and the strategies for the placement and removal of material that ensure an efficient warehouse.

4

Warehouse Management

SAP Warehouse Management (SAP WM) defines the SAP structure and functionality within the warehouse. In Chapter 2, we examined the inventory management structure, which included the plant and storage locations. Your logistics management must determine whether the functionality within the SAP Inventory Management (SAP IM) function is sufficient for your business or whether the added functionality of SAP WM would reduce costs and improve efficiency. This chapter helps you understand the structure and functionality of the SAP WM component.

The SAP WM component is part of the logistics execution functionality. It's a vital part of the SAP ERP functionality for companies that manage thousands of items in their warehouses. Some companies that implement SAP with the SAP IM functionality find that it isn't sufficient to efficiently manage their inventory. Depending on the number of items that they manage and the complexity of their operation, companies may decide that they need the added functionality of SAP WM.

The SAP WM component gives companies a total picture of the warehouse inventory down to the bin level. SAP WM is fully integrated with the inventory management, finance, and sales functionality.

For companies that implement the SAP Supply Chain Management (SAP SCM) business suite, there is added warehouse management functionality called SAP Extended Warehouse Management (SAP EWM). Figure 4.1 shows how SAP WM integrates with the SAP ERP and SAP SCM business suites.

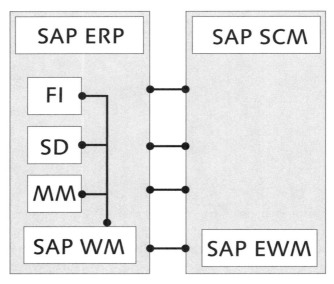

Figure 4.1 Integration Points of Warehouse Management

In the first section of this chapter, we'll review the structure within the SAP WM component.

Warehouse Structure

Structure of the warehouse

This section examines the warehouse structure and helps you understand how the SAP WM component may be more suitable to your logistics function than just the SAP IM functionality.

The lowest level in the SAP IM component is the storage location.

Who needs SAP WM?

If your company uses and stores a small number of materials, SAP WM may be more than you need to run your business efficiently. However, if your plant has a large number of locations where material is stored or placement and removal of materials needs to be efficiently managed, then SAP WM may be more appropriate. There are no set rules for when to use SAP WM rather than SAP IM. The decision should be made by your logistics management with advice from SAP and your SAP consultants.

 Tip

> Before deciding to implement SAP WM, calculate the total expenses and expected benefits to arrive at an objective decision.

Let's take a look at the structure within the SAP WM component.

Warehouse

A *warehouse* is a physically defined area in your plant. It can be an area that encompasses the whole plant, a racking section, a separate carousel system, or any area your company defines.

 Example

> A company that manufactures electronic components uses 4,000 raw materials and sells 6,000 finished products. The raw materials and finished goods are stored in 3 automated horizontal carousels and an area of racking. The company decided to use SAP WM and define each carousel as an individual warehouse but define the racking as a number of separate storage locations that are not assigned to a warehouse.

The warehouse can be assigned to one or more storage locations that are defined in the SAP IM component. This assignment links the SAP WM component to the SAP IM component. By implementing SAP WM, your company can define as many individual locations as required in a structured environment. This is important if your company has thousands of items in a single storage location that need to be moved efficiently.

Storage locations

The warehouse structure is further divided into smaller locations called storage types, sections, and bins. Figure 4.2 shows the warehouses that have been created in SAP. The warehouses 401 through

Storage types, sections, and bins

404 have been created to represent the different storage carousels that have been installed at the company's facility.

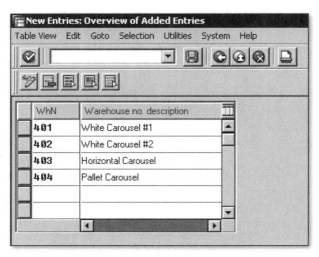

Figure 4.2 Warehouse Entries in SAP

Storage Types

The warehouse can be divided into specifically defined areas, called storage types.

Storage type Search strategies can be configured at the storage type level. These searches can be used by your staff for the variety of different types of stock placement and stock removal that occur. Common storage types in a warehouse can be areas such as cold room, bulk storage, and high racking area.

 **Example**

A company's automated horizontal carousel consists of a series of shelving sections mounted on a horizontal, closed-loop oval track. The company is using SAP WM and has defined the carousel as a warehouse. The company has further divided the carousel's shelves and defined them as storage types.

Figure 4.3 shows storage types created for a warehouse. The figures show the storage types that describe a part of the warehouse. These storage types were created to define the structure of the warehouse. This was carried out in the configuration area of SAP WM as part of the initial implementation. If your warehouse adds additional racking then more storage types may need to be added to the configuration.

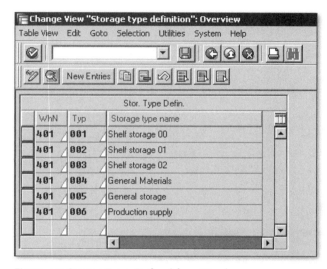

Figure 4.3 Storage Types Defined for a Warehouse

 Tip

Evaluate the addition of each storage type to the SAP system. Sometimes unnecessary configuration can lead to additional workload for your staff. Try to keep the warehouse layout as accurate and straightforward as possible.

Storage Section

The storage type of a warehouse can be even further divided into areas called *storage sections*. This is particularly useful if your company has defined storage types that are large. By dividing the storage type into a number of storage sections, stock placement and removal searches can be more efficient.

One or more storage sections

Ex Example

A company with a number of horizontal carousels has defined each carousel as separate warehouses in SAP WM. Although the company saw no reason to physically divide each storage type, the company logically divided some of the storage types into fast-moving and slow-moving storage sections. The decision was made to logically store slow-moving stock in the same storage section.

 Tip

At least one storage section has to be defined for each storage type.

Figure 4.4 shows a variety of storage sections that have been defined for a number of storage types. Each storage type has to have at least one storage section but can have more than one. The figure shows that storage type 001 has two storage sections defined, 001 and 002. The storage sections in this case are divided between slow-moving and fast-moving items.

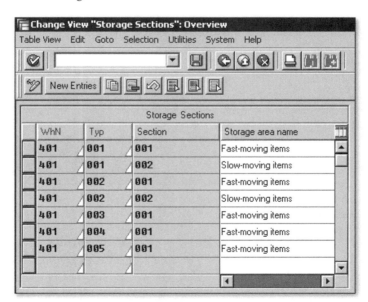

Figure 4.4 Storage Section Defined for Storage Types

Storage Bin

Within a warehouse, the material is physically stored in a storage bin. The SAP WM component is very flexible, and the structure can be changed immediately as your company's storage needs fluctuate. A storage bin doesn't always have to be a physical storage container. A storage bin can be a physical location on a shelving system or a part of a hanging storage system, which is often used to save space in the warehouse.

One or more storage bins

Ex Example

A company has a warehouse with a variety of shelving systems. Each shelving unit has been designated as a storage type, and each shelf designated as a storage section. The company has hundreds of items stored in the warehouse, which vary in size from less than an inch in length to several feet. The company has designated each plastic container on each shelf as a separate storage bin. However, on some shelves, the items are too large for the physical containers. In these cases, the company has marked areas on the shelves with tape and designated each taped area as a storage bin.

Figure 4.5 shows a number of storage bins for storage type 001 in Warehouse 401.

Bin Status Report: Overview

List   Edit   Goto   Settings   System   Help

Bin Status Report: Overview
Warehouse Number 401

Typ	StorageBin	Material	Plnt	Batch	S	S	Sp.Stk No
001	01-01-03	103-400	1000				
001	01-01-04	700-600	1000				
001	01-01-05	107-708	1000				
001	01-01-06	103-700	1000				
001	01-01-07	103-280	1000				
001	01-01-08	700-300	1000				
001	01-01-09	180-600	1000				
001	01-01-10	150-700	1000				
001	01-02-01	108-705	1000				
001	01-02-02	R07270C	1000				
001	01-02-03	R012707	1000				

Figure 4.5 Bin Status Report Showing a Number of Storage Bins

Tip

Storage bins can be created automatically based on a template. If your company has one structured format for storage bins, this can be set up and used to automatically create bins when they are needed.

Quant

Quants stored in a storage bin

Although the storage bin is the smallest container for your material in the warehouse, the material that is placed in the bin is identified differently from other material that is placed in that bin. The unique items that are placed in the bin are called *quants*. Your company may decide that it doesn't need to distinguish between different quants in the warehouse, but the ability to do so is part of the standard SAP WM functionality.

Figure 4.6 shows the details that define an individual quant. The quant information shows where it is stored, storage location 0008, the quantity of the items that comprise the quant, the document that moved the quant into the bin, and the goods receipt date.

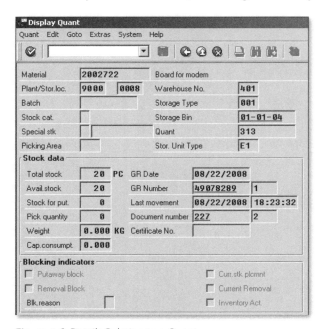

Figure 4.6 Details Relating to a Quant

Example

> Your plant maintenance department orders adjustable wrenches from a
> vendor each month. When the wrenches arrive at the warehouse, they
> are stored in the same storage bin. Each delivery of wrenches moved into
> the storage bin is identified as a separate quant. The storage bin may
> then contain several quants of the same wrenches.

Now that we've examined the various elements that make up the
warehouse structure, let's take a look at the movements of material
within the warehouse.

Warehouse Movements

Movements of stock within the SAP WM functionality are triggered
by either an event that occurred in the SAP IM component, such as a
goods receipt, or an event created within the SAP WM module itself.
This section examines the different events that can occur in the SAP
WM component.

**Automatic or
manual movements**

When items are received at your plant, the SAP software uses the
SAP IM component to move material to the correct storage location.
If your company has adopted the SAP WM component in addition to
the SAP IM component, this functionality can be used to move the
material to the correct area for that item within the warehouse.

However, this is only the case if the item to be moved is flagged as
being stored in the warehouse. If the item isn't flagged as such, then
only the SAP IM component is used to move the item.

**Are materials SAP
WM relevant?**

 Example

> An item that is stored in warehouse number 006 and requires refrigera-
> tion needs to be placed in a storage bin designated for cold storage in
> warehouse 006.

Items that are stored in a particular warehouse can also be moved
among storage types, storage sections, and storage bins. For example,

to fulfill a sales order, items may need to be moved from storage bins in the racking storage type to storage bins in the storage type designated for picking.

Two different types of movements are found in SAP WM.

› Movements that are triggered by other SAP functionality such as SAP IM and shipping that result in picking, packing, and transfers.

› Movements that are internal to the warehouse, such as bin-to-bin transfers or posting changes. The movements inside the warehouse don't affect stock levels, and no information is passed to SAP IM.

Let's review the warehouse movements that occur in SAP WM.

Movements Triggered by SAP Inventory Management

In Chapter 3, we examined the different movements that occur in the SAP IM component, including goods receipts, goods issues, returns, and stock transfers. If SAP WM is implemented by your company, each of the SAP IM goods movements will trigger an SAP WM movement, when the material is stored in the warehouse.

Material is moved in the warehouse by the use of a two-step process: the transfer requirement and the transfer order. The next section describes the functionality that moves materials within the warehouse.

Transfer Requirement

A movement of material in the warehouse, triggered by either an inventory movement or a manual warehouse movement, starts with a transfer requirement. The *transfer requirement* is the planning phase where material is planned to be moved from one warehouse location to another. After a transfer requirement is processed, a transfer order is then used to perform and confirm the move when it's completed.

Figure 4.7 shows a transfer requirement that has been created to move an item into the warehouse. The transfer requirement has been created by the inventory management movement for a goods receipt.

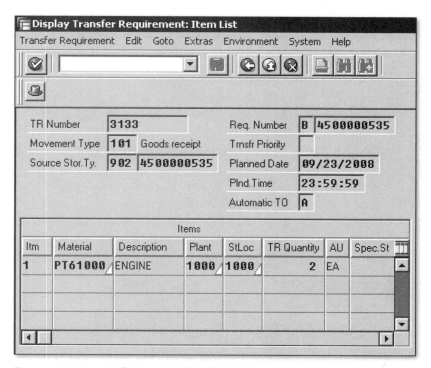

Figure 4.7 Automatically Generated Transfer Requirement

The transfer requirement includes the following information that will help your warehouse staff as the material is moved in the warehouse:

Transfer requirements not always needed

> The material that should be moved within the warehouse

> The quantity of the material to be moved

> The date of when the material should it be moved

> A reason why the material has to be moved

In addition to transfer requirements created by inventory movements, transfer requirements may also be created manually. Material that is stored in the warehouse is sometimes moved between storage types and storage bins; for example, material may have been stored in a temporary location and then needs to be moved to its normal storage bin.

Ex **Example**

At an electrical motor manufacturer, a purchase order (PO) was made for the weekly supply of bearings. The order was received at the plant early, and the bearings couldn't be placed in their normal storage type due to space limitations. The bearings were stored in temporary storage bins until there was enough space. When the bearings could be moved to their normal location, a manual transfer requirement was created to plan the movement.

Figure 4.8 shows a transfer requirement that has been created manually to move items between areas in the warehouse. The transfer requirement shows the material number and the quantity to move. The destination storage bin for removal or placement has not been determined at the time of creation.

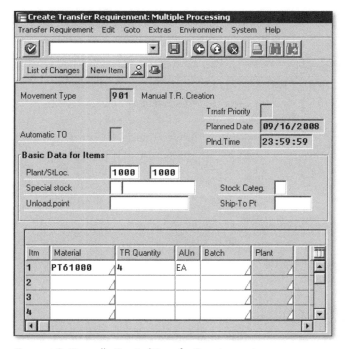

Figure 4.8 Manually Created Transfer Requirement

When the transfer requirement has been created, the next step is to create the transfer order.

Transfer Order

A *transfer order* is used by your warehouse staff to perform the movement of material from one location to another and confirm that movement of material when it's completed. The transfer order can be created from a transfer requirement. The previous section talked about how a transfer requirement can be created automatically because of an inventory movement, or it can be created manually.

Transfer orders perform and confirm warehouse movements

In addition to being created from a transfer requirement, a transfer order can also be created manually or directly from an inventory movement, such as a delivery.

Manual transfer orders

The transfer order contains the information required to perform the movement of materials into the warehouse, out of the warehouse, or from one storage bin to another storage bin within the warehouse.

Figure 4.9 shows a transfer order that is being created from a transfer requirement. The details from the transfer requirement are assigned to the newly created transfer order.

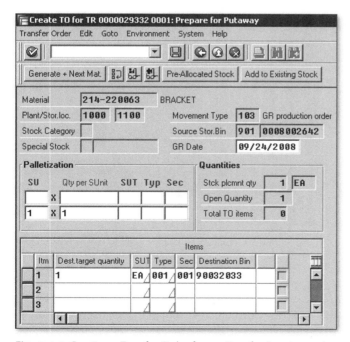

Figure 4.9 Creating a Transfer Order from a Transfer Requirement

Along with creating a transfer order from a transfer requirement, you can also create one manually.

 Example

> After completing a transfer order movement, a warehouse operator finds that the destination bin has material stored in it that should be in the storage bin on the shelf below. The operator informs the warehouse supervisor who creates a manual transfer order to move the items into the correct storage bin.

Figure 4.10 shows a transfer order that has been created manually.

Figure 4.10 Manually Created Transfer Order

Confirming the transfer order   A transfer order is confirmed after the movement of the items has taken place. In many warehouses, the warehouse staff members are given the transfer order document, and they select the items from the source storage bin and take them to the destination bin, indicated on the transfer order document. When the movement of items is complete, the document is then given to a warehouse supervisor. The supervisor confirms in SAP WM that the movement has occurred and if any variances were noted.

Figure 4.11 shows a transfer order that is ready to be confirmed. The confirmation screen shows the source and destination storage bins. The warehouse supervisor can change the quantity that has been moved if the warehouse operator indicated that the amount had changed.

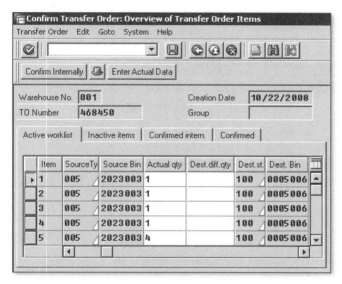

Figure 4.11 Confirmation of Transfer Order

Ex Example

A warehouse supervisor receives a transfer order from a warehouse operator. The operator indicated on the document that although they were supposed to move 10 items from the source storage bin to the destination storage bin, the destination bin could not accommodate all the items. The operator placed only 4 items in the storage bin and returned the remaining 6 to the source bin. The supervisor confirms the transfer order with an actual quantity moved as 4 and not 10 as the document originally stated.

If items are unable to be stored

In some instances, it isn't possible to return the items back to the source storage bin. This may be due to regulatory issues, company policies, or the fact that the source bin has already been replenished. The transfer order does contain information for the warehouse operator about where to place any remaining items, if it's necessary to do so.

On the transfer order there is a line that can be entered to show the operator where to store surplus items. Figure 4.12 shows a transfer order with the source and destination information and also a remainder location, which can be used to store the surplus items. In this example, any surplus items will not be returned to storage bin 900030 in storage type 001 but to storage bin 420301 in storage type 420.

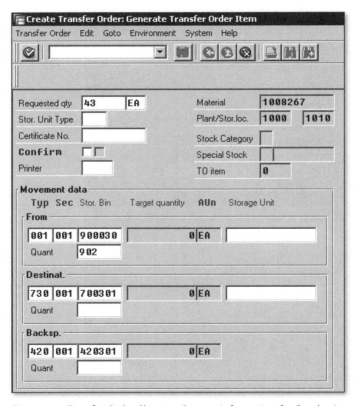

Figure 4.12 Transfer Order Showing Storage Information for Surplus Items

Printing Transfer Orders

Transfer orders can be printed individually or in bulk depending on how your warehouse operates. In a warehouse that does not process many sales orders, movements in the warehouse may be ad hoc, and the printing of transfer orders may be processed when needed.

Transfer orders go to operators to move the items in the warehouse

Figure 4.13 shows an example of a printed transfer order. The printed document can be issued as a document used by the warehouse staff to perform the movement of the material or as a label that can be adhered to the items after the move has taken place. In either case, the document shows the transfer order number, the line item, material number, description, quantity to be moved, and the source and destination storage bins.

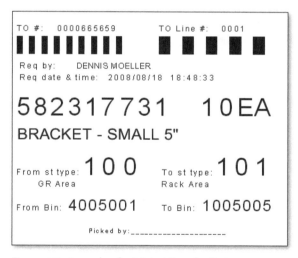

Figure 4.13 Example of a Printed Transfer Order

In warehouses that fulfill a large number of sales orders, wave picking may be implemented, and the transfer orders are printed in bulk.

Wave picking

 Tip

In warehouse operations where there are hundreds of picks to perform per hour, the SAP wave picking functionality can save time and resources.

Wave picking is a warehouse method where multiple customer orders are picked simultaneously. This method is used to improve the efficiency of the overall picking operation because it reduces the time between each warehouse movement. Many warehouses operate wave picking that bulk prints transfer orders for the next hour's picking requirements. The printed transfer orders are given to the warehouse staff members who then perform the movements described on each transfer order.

 Case Study

A Mexican automotive parts distributor implemented SAP software when they were purchased by a German automotive company. Until the implementation of the SAP system, the company had used a best-of-breed solution that included a standalone warehouse management solution. As part of the SAP implementation, the company decided not to activate the SAP WM component but to integrate the SAP application with its existing warehouse solution.

After implementation, the warehouse staff found that the information in their warehouse solution was inconsistent and untrustworthy. The company had underestimated the inaccuracies in their legacy system, and due to the accuracy of SAP software, the problems caused by their legacy system had now been exposed. The subsequent weeks following the implementation of SAP software saw on-time shipping of customer orders to fall to less than 20%. After a number of attempts to improve data consistency in the existing warehouse solution, the company decided to implement the SAP WM component to fully integrate its warehouse function with the rest of the company.

A two-month project was launched to move the warehouse function to SAP WM. The project was completed on time, and after one month of working on the SAP WM system, the on-time shipping percentage had risen to 78%. Six months later, the percentage had reached over 95%.

Summary

This chapter discussed the structure of the warehouse in SAP software and how material is moved around the warehouse. Movements inside the warehouse determine where that material goes, how it gets there, how it is stored, and how it gets retrieved. The transfer requirement and the transfer order are the two documents that move material inside the warehouse, and it's important to know how the processes of each work individually and in combination.

The SAP WM component is important to your logistics operation because it provides the flexibility to adapt to rapid changes in your storage facility. Storage bin creation can be performed in real time, allowing for the constant changes that occur in your warehouse. The SAP WM component gives companies of all sizes the material visibility that they require to efficiently operate the warehouse.

The key points identified in this chapter were the following:

> SAP WM offers a complete solution for companies with complex warehouse requirements.
> The structure is designed to be flexible, allowing for changes in the physical warehouse.
> Warehouse placement and removal strategies offer highly simplistic or highly complex functionality.
> Seamless integration with inventory management is possible.
> High degree of material visibility is helpful to warehouse staff.

The next chapter discusses inbound and outbound logistics in SAP ERP, which will help you understand the goods receipt and goods issue processes.

Inbound and Outbound Logistics

The inbound and outbound logistics function is important to your company because it facilitates purchased material into the plant and ships finished products out to customers. The inbound logistics functionality in SAP software incorporates inbound deliveries, inbound shipments, and goods receipts. The outbound logistics functionality covers the picking and packing of materials as well as the outbound delivery and goods issue.

Inbound shipments from vendors contain the purchased materials that your company requires to do business. The SAP process integrates EDI functionality for you to monitor inbound deliveries.

The SAP outbound delivery process is critical to your business because it is the function that gets finished products to your customers. The efficiencies built into the SAP process allows finished products to be picked, packed, and shipped with the minimum resources.

In the first section of this chapter, we'll examine the inbound logistics function.

Inbound Logistics

Inbound process
starts with a
shipping notification

The inbound logistics functionality is important to your company's supply chain because it offers visibility to incoming deliveries, allowing for detailed planning and therefore greater warehouse efficiency.

The inbound logistics process in the SAP system starts when your company's purchase orders (POs) are processed at the vendor. If your company uses an Electronic Data Interchange (EDI) interface, your vendors can send a shipping notification from which an inbound delivery can be created.

 Tip

SAP software fully integrates with EDI. Implementing EDI is straightforward, and the benefits will produce efficiencies in your inbound and outbound logistics.

Shipping Notification

Documents in EDI

The Advanced Shipping Notification (ASN) is a document sent by your vendor to your company via an EDI interface. Instead of the vendor calling or faxing your purchasing department to tell you a certain PO has been shipped, the vendor sends a shipping notification electronically. The document that is sent is called an EDI 856 Advanced Ship Notice.

 Example

If your company has fully integrated your vendor with EDI, and you require products from a vendor, you have to send an EDI document 850, which is an EDI PO document. This tells the vendor what items you need and where you need the items to be shipped. The vendor receives the PO and sends back an EDI 997 Acknowledgement confirming the receipt. The vendor then sends you an EDI 856 ASN informing you of when to expect the delivery. The vendor fulfills the order and sends an EDI 810 Invoice informing you that the items were shipped, and providing the cost of the items and the delivery information.

When an ASN is received via EDI, this can trigger an inbound delivery to be created in the SAP system. The information from the ASN document is transposed into an inbound delivery. The delivery contains information on the vendor, items, quantities to be expected, and the delivery details.

EDI 856 ASNs create inbound delivery documents

Not all inbound deliveries are created through EDI, and your company may not use EDI with your vendors. If this is the case, the inbound deliveries will be created manually, which is covered in the next section.

Manually Created Inbound Deliveries

Not every company has adopted EDI, so if your company wants to use the inbound delivery functionality, you may want to consider manually creating inbound deliveries. Most vendors will supply your purchasing department with information on when they expect your POs to be delivered. You can use this information to manually create inbound deliveries.

Inbound deliveries created manually

Figure 5.1 shows an inbound delivery that has been created for a PO. The delivery date from the vendor has been entered as well as the items and the quantities expected. The warehouse can use the information on these inbound deliveries to determine workload and where resources would be best used.

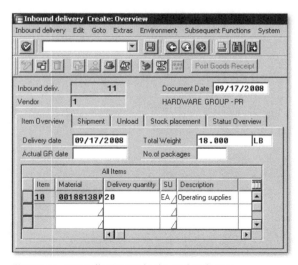

Figure 5.1 Manually Created Inbound Delivery

Inbound delivery documents

Although the details of the inbound delivery need to be entered manually, if not created by EDI, it's useful for your logistics department to have visibility of inbound deliveries.

The next section shows you how your staff can see the inbound deliveries using the Delivery Monitor.

Delivery Monitor

The *Delivery Monitor* is used by your logistics department to display and process open and completed deliveries.

Delivery Monitor shows inbound and outbound deliveries

Your logistics personnel can review deliveries with different statuses in a single list and then perform any further necessary processing. The Delivery Monitor allows your staff to review the following:

> Deliveries that are due for picking or putaway and creation of transfer orders

> Deliveries for which picked quantities or putaway stocks need to be confirmed

> Process deliveries that are due for goods issue or goods receipt

Figure 5.2 shows the options that are available to your company's logistics staff.

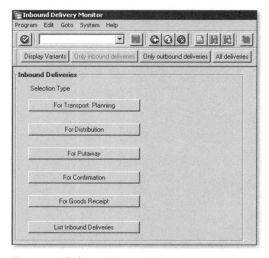

Figure 5.2 Delivery Monitor Options

Your logistics personnel can use the Delivery Monitor to review the particular option required, for example, inbound deliveries. The Delivery Monitor shows all of the inbound deliveries for a certain date for a specific receiving location.

Delivery monitor warehouse workload overview

 Tip

The inbound Delivery Monitor should be reviewed during the day as deliveries arrive. If deliveries are delayed, this can affect production. Communication between transportation and production staff is important if production issues are to be avoided.

Figure 5.3 shows a list of inbound deliveries that are expected on a certain day.

Delivery	Deliv.date	Vendor	Name of vendor
180020520	08/28/2008	108	HARDWARE GROUP
180020522	08/28/2008	108	HARDWARE GROUP
180020550	08/28/2008	108	HARDWARE GROUP
180020551	08/28/2008	108	HARDWARE GROUP
180020560	08/28/2008	12	ITAL EQUIPMENT
180020561	08/28/2008	12	ITAL EQUIPMENT
180020562	08/28/2008	12	ITAL EQUIPMENT
180020563	08/28/2008	12	ITAL EQUIPMENT
180020566	08/28/2008	12	ITAL EQUIPMENT

Figure 5.3 Inbound Deliveries Displayed from the Delivery Monitor

The logistics staff can monitor the number of deliveries for a specific day and make changes to staffing or warehouse equipment based on information from the Delivery Monitor.

Individual deliveries in the Delivery Monitor

In the next section, we'll look at when the inbound deliveries arrive at your warehouse and the goods receipt process begins.

Goods Receipt

Goods receipts are used to record the items that are received from a vendor via a purchase order (PO). The goods receipt is important to your company's business because it moves the items into stock, updating the stock levels and allowing the items to be used in the production process.

Goods receipt updates financials and inventory

Every company has its own procedures for the receipt of material, and these have to be considered when using the goods receipt functionality in the SAP software. If an item is received into stock, the value of the item is posted to your company accounts, which means your company has spent money to have that material in the plant.

 Example

> If your goods receipt process takes three days to complete, your company is spending money on storing materials that are unable to be used. Reducing the goods receipt time means the material can be used more quickly, which saves storage costs.

Faster goods receipt saves warehousing costs

Minimizing the length of time that materials spend in the goods receipt process saves your company money. The processes built into the SAP software can significantly reduce the length of time it takes to get items from the receiving dock into your warehouse.

The goods receipt process can be triggered from the inbound delivery document already in your system or a manually created good receipt document, if no inbound delivery exists.

Goods Receipt from Inbound Delivery

Using the Delivery Monitor, your staff can see the inbound deliveries that are scheduled to arrive at your receiving dock. When items arrive, the receiving staff can review the specific inbound delivery and check the items received against the information in the SAP software. If the received items are correct based on the information in the inbound delivery document, the receiving staff can complete the goods receipt and the stock levels are then updated.

Figure 5.4 shows the stock placement screen of the inbound delivery document. If the delivery details are correct, the receiving staff can select the Post Goods Receipt button to update the stock levels in the SAP software.

Inbound deliveries save time in receiving

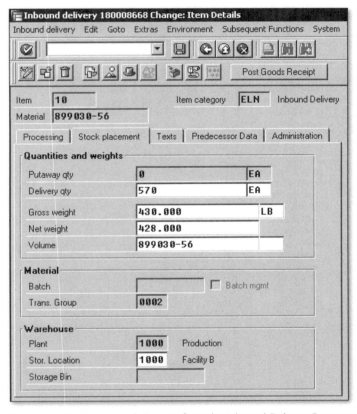

Figure 5.4 Posting a Goods Receipt from the Inbound Delivery Document

Manually Created Goods Receipt

If your company decides not to implement the inbound delivery functionality, goods receipts can be processed manually as the items arrive at the receiving dock. Even if your company does use inbound deliveries, sometimes items arrive where no inbound delivery has been created. In these cases, the receiving staff can manually receipt the items into stock.

Manual goods receipt even with inbound deliveries

If the items arrive from your vendor and have been ordered using a PO, the goods receipt can be processed using the PO number.

Figure 5.5 shows a goods receipt that has been manually created for a PO. The goods receipt document allows your receiving staff to change the delivery total if needed.

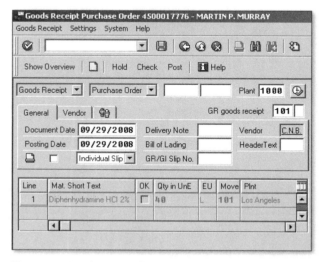

Figure 5.5 Goods Receipt for a PO

Policy for items without POs

On rare occasions, items arrive from a vendor without a PO on the documents, and no suitable PO number can be found in your SAP system. This may be due to a delay in entering the PO in the SAP system, or it can be because of an error by the vendor where the goods were never ordered. In any case, your receiving staff needs a procedure for handling these cases.

Ex **Example**

Some companies will not accept material if there's no PO on the documents or in the SAP system. In these cases, the material will be refused and the delivery not accepted. Other companies will accept delivery of the materials and keep the material in quality or blocked stock until the situation is resolved. In this case, the material will need to be received; there is a movement type in SAP to perform this task.

If your company does decide to receive material without a PO or an inbound delivery, a manual goods receipt is required. Your receiving staff will enter the information for the items and the quantity, which is then posted to the SAP software. Figure 5.6 shows a manual goods receipt for a delivery without a PO.

Manual goods receipts with the item and quantity information

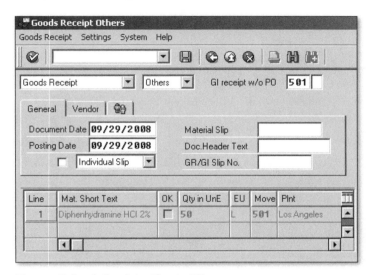

Figure 5.6 Goods Receipt without a PO

Now that you've learned about the functionality in the SAP software that provides a successful inbound logistics function at your company, let's move on to the functionality for outbound logistics.

Outbound Logistics

The outbound logistics functionality is as equally important to your company's supply chain because it offers visibility to the outgoing deliveries, allowing for detailed planning for packing and shipping, leading to greater warehouse efficiency.

Outbound logistics focuses on deliveries to customers

When your customers order items from your company, sales orders are created in the SAP software, and the outbound delivery document is created to facilitate the picking, packing, and ultimate goods issue of the items as they are delivered to your customer.

Outbound Delivery

When one of your customer orders items, a sales order is created that details the items ordered, the quantity, and the delivery date. When that sales order has been created, an outbound delivery document can be created that is used by the logistics department to track progress of the delivery as it works its way through the warehouse.

Outbound delivery contains sales order information

The outbound delivery document is created by the sales, transportation, or logistics personnel, depending on how your company's departments are structured.

Figure 5.7 shows an outbound delivery document created from a customer sales order. The delivery document shows the item and the quantity to be delivered.

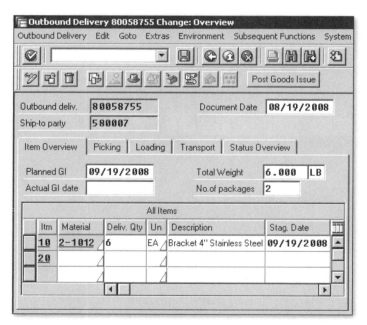

Figure 5.7 Creating an Outbound Delivery from a Sales Order

When the outbound delivery document is created, it can be viewed using the Delivery Monitor, which we discussed in the previous section.

The outbound deliveries can be viewed so warehouse staff can monitor the status of the deliveries and what resources will be needed to pick, pack, and ship the items to the customer.

Delivery Monitor for outbound and inbound deliveries

Figure 5.8 shows a list of outbound deliveries that have been selected from the outbound Delivery Monitor.

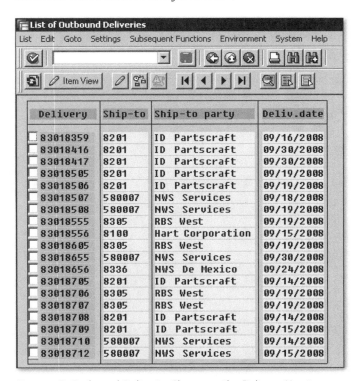

Figure 5.8 Outbound Deliveries Shown on the Delivery Monitor

Picking

The *picking* process involves moving items from a storage bin in your warehouse and staging the quantity in a picking area where the items will be packed for shipping to your customer.

Example

At the warehouse of an Internet company supplying bathroom fixtures, the staff packs and sends 1,500 orders per day. When the staff arrives in the morning, they are given the pick tickets for all the outbound deliveries that will occur the next day. Each pick is taken from a storage bin in the warehouse to the staging area where the packing staff will get the items ready for shipping.

Automatic picking in outbound delivery

However your company facilitates picking at your warehouse, the SAP system can accommodate all instances. Picking can be an automated part of the outbound delivery document, or it can be performed manually as required.

The picking status is updated on the outbound delivery document. When your warehouse staff members have picked the correct quantity from the warehouse and taken it to the staging area, they can update the outbound delivery document to show that the picking has been completed.

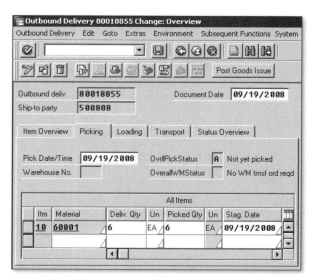

Figure 5.9 Outbound Delivery Showing a Picked Quantity

Figure 5.9 shows an outbound delivery document that has been updated by warehouse staff to show that the picking has been performed. The outbound delivery has been updated to show a picked quantity of 6.

Packing Using Handling Units

Items going to the same customer can be packed into shipping containers or pallets with other items, or by themselves. The SAP software's functionality can help your company with packing material in the warehouse for customer deliveries.

 Tip

If your company uses cartons, pallets, or boxes for finished products, then the SAP handling unit functionality should be used.

The *handling unit* (HU) is a physical item that contains the items to be shipped. The HU is made up of packaging material and one or more items. The HU can be nested, which means that one HU can contain other HUs.

Nested handling units

 Example

At a beverage company, a pallet to be shipped to a customer is made up of 24 boxes. Each of those boxes contained 12 cans of soda. In the SAP software, each box is defined as an HU, and the pallet is defined as an HU that contains 24 boxes, which are also HUs.

When a delivery is ready to be packed, the packing staff can access the outbound delivery document and enter the information about the HU they are creating to ship the items to the customer.

Figure 5.10 shows the packing information that is entered for the outbound delivery. The HU is given a unique number and is updated with the weight of the HU, which includes the packaging and items to be shipped to the customer.

Handling units contain SAP IM information

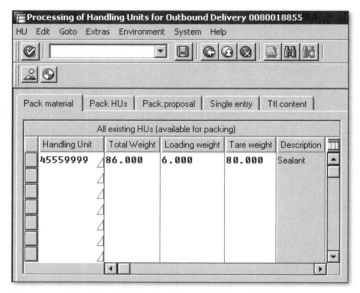

Figure 5.10 Handling Unit Packed for an Outbound Delivery

Goods Issue

Goods issue from
the outbound
delivery document

After the items for the delivery have been picked and packed, they are then shipped to the customer. Your company may use a variety of shipping options, including third-party trucking, postal services, or express shipping companies such as FedEx and UPS. Whatever method is used, as soon as the items have left the facility, the shipping process is complete, and the goods issue should be posted.

The goods issue causes a number of events to take place in the SAP system:

> Inventory stock is reduced by the shipped quantity.

> Financial details are posted to the balance sheet accounts.

> Requirements are reduced by the shipped quantity.

Figure 5.11 shows an outbound delivery that has been fully picked and packed. It's ready for the goods issue to be posted.

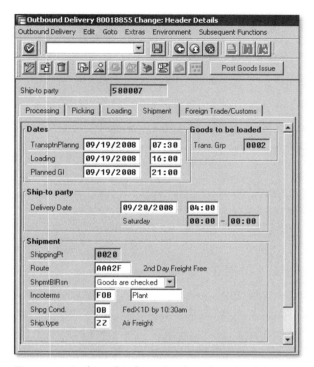

Figure 5.11 Outbound Delivery Ready to Post Goods Issue

 Case Study

An American manufacturer of hand tools was in the process of implementing SAP software and had initially decided to use the shipping processes that it was currently using in its legacy systems. The process that the company used to ship items to customers was rudimentary, where items would be sent to the loading dock in a box with a copy of the sales order. The shipping clerk would check the items against the sales order, tape the box up, and have UPS pick up the boxes at the end of the day. The next morning, the clerk would goods issue the boxes that were shipped the previous evening.

The company implemented the SAP software with this process and found that the benefits they had expected were not being realized. The CIO told the logistics department to use the best practices built into the SAP software and redesign the shipping processes. After three months of the new processes, which included using outbound deliveries and proof of delivery, a survey of customers found that they were significantly pleased with greater tracking of their orders and improved invoicing.

Proof of Delivery

Proof of delivery triggers invoicing

The SAP system allows you to enter a proof of delivery when your customer has received the shipment. This can provide the trigger for the invoice to be generated and sent to your customer.

The proof of delivery from your customer should contain the date and time of delivery as well as any discrepancies with delivered quantity. This information ensures that the invoice sent to your customer is correct and payment should not be delayed.

Shipping companies such as FedEx and UPS provide proof of delivery documentation, which can be entered into your SAP software.

Summary

This chapter has discussed the functionality associated with inbound and outbound logistics. This functionality is important to your company because it provides visibility of your incoming orders, which is vital to your production schedule, and visibility of your outbound deliveries, which your customers are concerned about.

Having greater visibility of your supply chain can help your company minimize costs and maximize customer satisfaction. The best practices built into SAP software can help you with both sides of the logistics process. The SAP inbound and outbound logistics processes are important to the overall success of your company. Efficient movements of inbound materials are critical when your company is operating with low inventory or operating within a just-in-time environment. When material arrives from a vendor, it's vital to move the material to where it is needed.

Equally, the SAP outbound logistics process is important to maintaining an advantage over your competitors. Customers expect on-time and accurate deliveries. Anything less is certain to reduce customer satisfaction and thus reduce any competitive advantage.

There are some key points that you should take from this chapter:

> The Delivery Monitor provides real-time information for your logistics staff.
> EDI functionality is fully integrated into the inbound and outbound logistics function.
> Handling units (HUs) can be used to combine packaging material and finished goods items for shipping.
> Goods issues and goods receipts create the financial records and change inventory levels.

The next chapter discusses product planning, including sales and operation planning (SOP), demand management, and material requirements planning (MRP).

PART II
Product Development and Manufacturing

6

Product Planning

Product planning is important to your company's logistics function because it encompasses the functions that you use to plan the introduction, sale, and manufacturing of items. This chapter discusses three planning functions that your company may use: SAP Sales and Operations Planning (SOP), demand management, and material requirements planning (MRP).

The SAP ERP business suite offers companies a variety of planning options that can be adopted to help create the most accurate production plan possible. The SAP Sales and Operations Planning (SAP SOP) function is designed to give your company a long-term view of production planning based on your company's sales. This functionality can be used with the demand management function, which gives planning resources the ability to manipulate plans in real-time based on information from customers. This gives your company a competitive advantage by understanding its production needs in the long- and medium-term. SAP's MRP function uses the demand and creates the planned orders and purchasing requirements to be used in the manufacture of finished goods for customer orders. After you understand how product planning in SAP systems works, you'll see how important this functionality is in ensuring that customer orders are accurately fulfilled.

Sales and Operations Planning

SAP SOP solution

The SAP Sales and Operations Planning (SAP SOP) solution provides greater visibility of business metrics such as the value of your company's inventory, customer service, resource use, schedule performance, forecast accuracy, order fulfillment, and cash flow. It's especially useful for your long- and medium-term planning because it provides an overall plan for production that will satisfy the level of customer sales from the sales plan and sales forecast. To achieve this, SAP SOP requires cross-functional integration among sales, marketing, manufacturing, and finance. SAP SOP is a powerful component, but requires a significant commitment from your company's stakeholders to adopt the business processes required to drive the functionality.

Because customer service levels are extremely important and can provide a significant competitive advantage, the successful implementation of SAP SOP can result in more accurate deliveries to your customers, reduced inventories, efficient use of warehouse and manufacturing resources, and increased order fulfillment.

Ex Example

Fitting your requirements

Although every company implements SAP SOP in different ways, SAP provides best practices that your company can adopt. The SAP system is delivered with a standard planning process, which allows your planning department to create plans for one organization and its finished products hierarchy. If your company has more complex requirements of SAP SOP, the SAP SOP functionality allows you to develop a structure that can replicate the planning needs of your company.

Standard Sales and Operations Planning

SAP SOP information structures

The SAP SOP solution can be used as delivered or be adapted to fit your company's unique requirements. This is possible because of the environment in which the SAP SOP functionality operates. The underlying technology is based on information structures. These are used in the SAP Logistics Information System (LIS). The information structure is a statistical file that is updated each time a transaction is completed in the SAP software. For a more in-depth discussion on information structures and LIS, refer to the SAP PRESS book, *Understanding the SAP Logistics Information System* (2007).

 Tip

If your company hasn't used SAP SOP before, you can try using the functionality as delivered by SAP. The design SAP supplies is based on best practices.

An *information structure* is a statistical file that contains a number of fields. It's used in SAP SOP to collect data from sales and financial transactions. For example, the information structure for sales and operations planning is called S076. The file can then be used for SAP SOP analyses and plans. SAP delivers a standard information structure that doesn't need to be changed. Figure 6.1 shows the standard information structure for SAP SOP planning.

Information structures

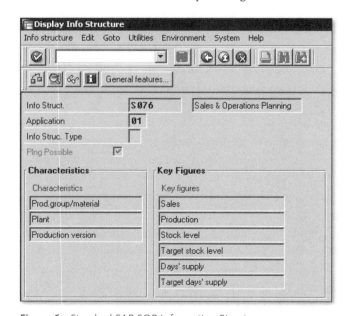

Figure 6.1 Standard SAP SOP Information Structure

The information structure shows that data is collected for product groups (which are described later in this chapter) and by plant. The actual data that is collected, shown in the Key Figures column, includes Sales, Production, Stock level, and Days' supply.

Flexible Sales and Operations Planning

Create an information structure

The standard SAP SOP planning tool uses the SAP-delivered information structure, but if you need greater analysis for your company's planning, you should consider using the flexible SAP SOP planning tools. The data used in flexible planning can be derived using other information structures in the SAP LIS system or by creating a new structure based on your company's requirements.

 Example

> The standard information structure contains stock levels and sales. However, if your SAP SOP analysis previously included information on returns, you need to create a flexible information structure. The new structure will then contain the information you need for your specific analysis.

Master Data in Sales and Operations Planning

Planning hierarchies and product groups

To take advantage of the benefits of the SAP SOP functionality, your company must make decisions on the planning structures—planning hierarchies and product groups—required for successful planning.

Planning Hierarchies

A *planning hierarchy* describes the levels in your organization that you want to plan for. The planning hierarchy can be created automatically by the SAP software or created manually.

Product Groups

Retail companies use product groups

A *product group* allows your company to create a hierarchy of how products are grouped for planning. A product group can contain a number of levels where each level, except the lowest level, can be other product groups. The lowest level is always a material.

Figure 6.2 shows a product group that contains three materials. The product group in this case is a brake kit with three items comprising the product group.

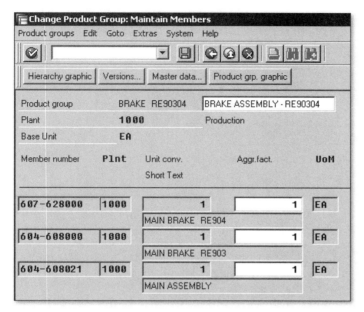

Figure 6.2 Example of a Product Group

Reporting

Four reports can be produced as a result of your SAP SOP function to help your company's planning department:

SAP SOP reports help analyze planning results

> Product group breakdown

> Product group usage

> Material usage

> Planning situation

These reports will now be examined in more detail.

Product Group Breakdown

This report shows detailed information about each of the product groups that you've created.

Figure 6.3 shows the items that are associated with a product group.

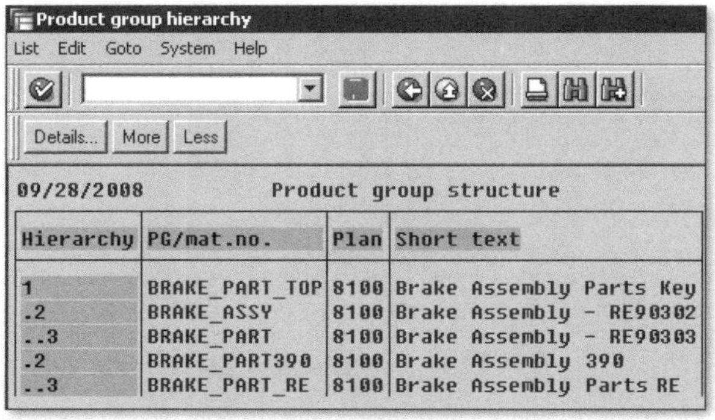

Figure 6.3 Product Group Breakdown Report

The product group is shown in Figure 6.3 as having three levels. The second level has two product groups associated with the product group, and the third and final level shows two materials, BRAKE_ PART and BRAKE_PART_RE.

Product Group Usage

Monitoring usage reports

The product group usage report shows where the product groups are used in other product groups. If your company has a number of products that use similar groups of components, then you may find that the product groups you create will be used in many other product groups.

Figure 6.4 shows a product group usage report showing that the product group BRAKE_ASSY has used a number of other product groups.

Figure 6.4 Product Group Usage Report

Example

In an automotive company, a product group that includes fasteners; bolts, washers, and hex nuts may be used in product groups where the components are used, such as brakes, transmission, engine, and chassis.

Material Usage

The material usage report shows what materials are used in specific product groups. As SAP SOP analyses are refined, this report becomes useful to your staff to see if certain items are members of the wrong product groups.

Figure 6.5 shows the product groups that contain the material BRAKE_ASSY81.

```
Product Group Usage
List  Edit  Goto  System  Help

Details...  More  Less

09/29/2008      Product group structure

Hierarchy  PG/mat.no.      Plan  Short text

1          BRAKE_ASSY81    8100  Brake Assembly 81
.2         BRAKE_ASSY62    8100  Brake Assembly 62
..3        BRAKE_PART_TOP  8100  Brake Assembly Parts Key
..3        BRAKE_ASSY_8    8100  Brake Assembly 8
.2         BRAKE_PARTS     8100  Brake Assembly Parts
.2         BRAKE_PART_PA   8100  Brake Parts PA
.2         BRAKE_PART29    8100  Brake Parts 29
.2         BRAKE_PART762   8100  Brake Parts 762
..3        BRAKE_PART_TOP  8100  Brake Assembly Parts Key
```

Figure 6.5 Material Usage Report

Planning Situation

The planning situation report is useful to measure how the SAP SOP data has been adopted by subsequent planning functions, such as materials production schedule (MPS). The planning staff can use this report to make adjustments to planning groups if necessary and re-run the report.

Production and sales order figures

135

Figure 6.6 shows the SAP SOP evaluation based on a specific product group, BRAKE_PARTS.

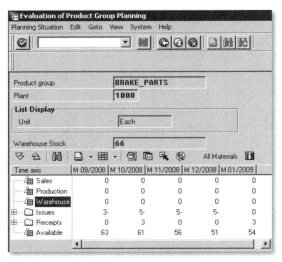

Figure 6.6 Product Group Planning Report

 Case Study

An Australian beverage company completed a business re-engineering project and was implementing the changes recommended from the study. Before the company moved to SAP systems from their existing best-of-breed legacy systems, the company had decided to introduce a sales and operations planning process. After three months of meetings and discussion, the stakeholders were no closer to implementing the new process. A few roadblocks were identified, including the inability of stakeholders to understand the new process, but the main concern for stakeholders was the collection of data, both its complexity and the resources required to build the programs and interfaces needed. SAP was invited to help the group with their task. The SAP team showed the group how the data is collected automatically in the SAP software and how their sales and operations requirements most likely fitted the best practices embedded in the SAP software. The group decided to implement the standard SAP SOP and prepare for the new SAP system by introducing policies and procedures so that the SAP SOP function could be used at the launch.

After three months of using SAP SOP, the group reported that their subsequent planning functions had significantly improved.

The sales and operations planning function is important to companies that want to start the planning process with as much accuracy as possible. If your company doesn't use SAP SOP, then it should consider this functionality when implementing SAP. The functionality uses real data from sales and production to balance the supply and demand for products and product groups that your company manufactures. It's used to take your company's strategic plans and refine them using current data, so they can be used in the subsequent detailed planning process and the demand management functions.

Passing SAP SOP figures to other planning functionality

 Example

> A company using the SAP ERP business suite made a strategic decision to use the SAP SOP function. They had only been using MRP without any long-term planning. The issues that prompted the use of SAP SOP included that some of the production orders were unable to meet customer delivery requirements because the company couldn't get enough raw materials by the time the order needed to commence. The company believed that if it had a better understanding of long-term plans, then it could have pre-empted the raw materials shortage. After SAP SOP was used, the planning department could identify future needs prior to actual customer orders being placed.

Now that we've discussed SAP SOP, let's move on to examine another planning component of SAP functionality: demand management.

Demand Management

Demand planning has enabled companies to more accurately forecast what their customers need. It allows your company to focus on managing demand rather than reacting to it. The SAP demand management function allows your staff to determine requirement quantities and delivery dates for your products. Demand Management uses both planned requirements, from SAP SOP and requirements from your customers, that is, planned sales orders. The demand management function provides inputs for your MRP function.

Demand management identifies potential issues

To use the functionality of demand management, your planning department needs to ensure that each of your products is assigned a planning strategy. A *planning strategy* indicates how your product is manufactured or purchased.

SAP planning strategies

SAP software is delivered with a number of planning strategies that allow your company to use demand management best practices. In the next sections, we'll examine the planning strategies that you can use.

 Tip

Before allocating planning strategies for each material, make sure that the strategies are fully understood because the wrong planning strategy can affect planned totals.

Make-to-Stock Strategy

Stock without customer orders

This planning strategy should be used if your company produces products that are manufactured independently of any customer orders. The production of items without reference to a customer order creates a situation where you'll have to store the items in the warehouse and incur storage charges. Although your company can fulfill customer orders immediately, this has to be weighed against the costs of producing items prior to any sales orders, especially if the unit cost of the items in stock is high.

 Example

A company manufacturing artist canvases advertises that customer orders can be shipped within 24 hours. Because the company manufacturers more than 40 sizes of canvases, the production time for a specific sized canvas could be up to 48 hours. To ensure that the company has enough stock on hand to fulfill its customer orders, the planning department adopts a make-to-stock planning strategy for all of the canvas products.

Figure 6.7 shows the material master record for an item that is being identified as a make-to-stock item. In the master record, 10 has been entered in the Strategy group field for a make-to-stock material.

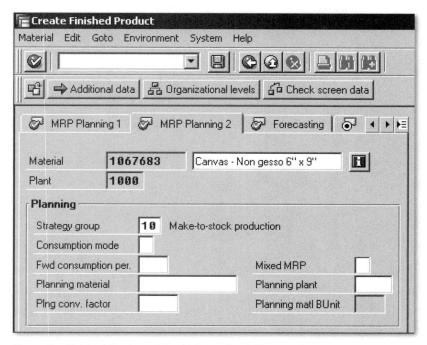

Figure 6.7 Finished Product with a Make-to-Stock Planning Strategy

Not all products that your company manufacturers are make to stock, so let's look at another planning strategy: make to order.

Make-to-Order Strategy

Some items your company sells may be very expensive, so it's not cost efficient to manufacture those items and then store them in the warehouse for an unknown length of time. Also, if items are ordered infrequently, they may sit in the warehouse for months before being ordered by a customer. If you have these types of items, you may need to manufacture them for each specific sales order received and plan accordingly.

Figure 6.8 shows a material master record for an item that is being identified as a make-to-order item. In the master record, 20 has been entered in the Strategy group field for a make-to-order material.

Expensive products should be manufactured when ordered

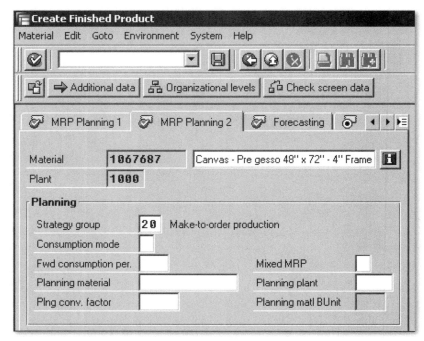

Figure 6.8 Finished Product with a Make-to-Order Planning Strategy

Component items

One key consideration with make-to-order items is that when a delivery date is given to a customer, it must allow for any purchasing lead times of component items.

Ex Example

A manufacturer of art canvases uses the make-to-stock strategy for the majority of its products. However, for the largest of the canvases it manufacturers, it uses a make-to-order strategy because the canvases are ordered infrequently. When an order is received for a make-to-order canvas, the manufacturer has to give a delivery date to the customer that allows for purchasing lead time of the components that are part of the finished product. If the manufacturer wanted to reduce the lead time to the customer, it has the choice to keep the components in stock instead of purchasing them when needed.

In addition to make-to-stock and make-to-order items, there is another strategy that may be applicable for your finished products. In the next section, we'll look at finished products that offer different variants.

Strategy for Configurable Materials

A *configurable material* is a product that your company sells that allows customers a variety of options to configure the finished product. These items can be made to order due to the large number of variations that are possible for the finished product. However, if there are popular variations that are purchased by customers, it's possible to create a make-to-stock strategy for some products allowing quick delivery times.

Configurable materials offer options

 Example

> A manufacturer of commercial elevators has three basic models, but each model has more than two dozen customer selections that can be made, including the finish of the elevator walls, the trim on the control panel, the lighting configuration, and the type of handrail.

Planning for configurable materials can be complex, and SAP software delivers a number of planning strategies that can be used.

Planning strategies with configurable materials

 Tip

> If your configurable materials have a large number of options, be sure that the planning strategy you use is correct for the item. There are a number of strategies for configurable materials, and each can affect the overall planning calculation.

Figure 6.9 shows a configurable material that has been associated with planning strategy 25, for configurable materials.

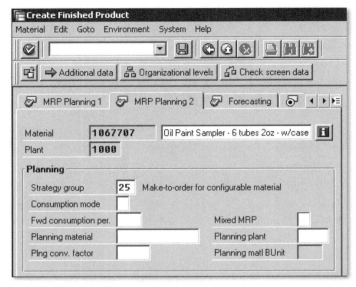

Figure 6.9 Configurable Finished Product with a Make-to-Order Planning Strategy

When your finished products are assigned planning strategies, the planning functionality uses the parameters to determine how the consumption is carried out. For example, if an item has a planning strategy of 30, then the functionality doesn't plan for finished products, whereas a planning strategy of 52 means that planned independent requirements are created. Each strategy has different parameters.

Planned Independent Requirements

Planned independent requirements entered manually or automatically

If your company uses sales and operations planning functionality, it can be used to supply the planned independent requirements for the demand management function.

A *planned independent requirement* is the quantity required for one finished product in a specific period. For example, if your sales force is aware that a customer will place an order for 500 units in May, then you can enter a planned independent requirement for that amount into the SAP software without the sales order being placed. This demand can then be used by the planning function.

If SAP SOP is not used, then the planned independent requirements can be copied from the material forecast or entered manually.

Figure 6.10 shows a manual entry of planned independent requirements for a finished product. The requirements can be entered in days, weeks, or months. In this instance, the daily requirement is entered.

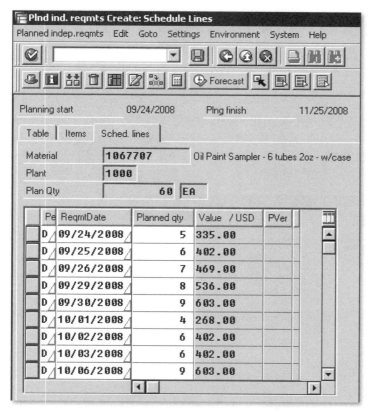

Figure 6.10 Entry of Planned Independent Requirements

In addition to the planned independent requirements, you can also enter customer requirements that have been converted into sales orders. In the next section, we'll talk about those customer requirements.

Customer Requirements

Customer
requirements are
accepted sales
orders

Customer requirements can be entered into the demand management function manually. The requirements are sales orders that have been accepted for processing.

 Example

A customer has made an order for 60 items and a delivery date of November 11th. The planning department can create a customer requirements entry in demand management to reflect the sales order that was taken.

Figure 6.11 shows the manual entry of customer requirements into the demand management system. The entry is made for a sales order that has been entered. The customer requirement can be entered into the demand management function to ensure that the requirements are part of the demand plan.

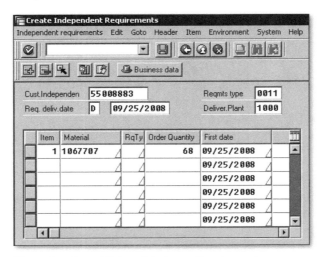

Figure 6.11 Manual Entry of Customer Requirements

After the customer requirements and the planned independent requirements have been added to the demand management function, it's possible to run evaluations, such as the Stock/Requirements List, shown in Figure 6.12.

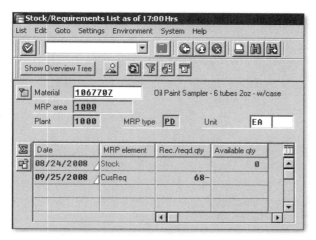

Figure 6.12 Stock/Requirements List Showing Customer Requirements

Figure 6.12 shows the customer requirements that were manually entered and the current stock position. As the demand entered exceeds the current stock position, this leads to production orders being planned to fulfill the demand.

In the next section, we'll look at the SAP material requirements planning functionality. The MRP component is more familiar to those of you who have some planning experience.

Materials Requirements Planning

In the previous sections, we looked at planning tools that help your company have greater visibility of their supply chain. The material requirements planning (MRP) function is vital to your company's ability to ensure that finished goods are available to be delivered to your customers on time and that purchased items are available for your manufacturing process when they are required.

Materials requirements planning (MRP)

The MRP process takes inputs from your demand management function and calculates purchasing requirements to cover this demand. If the requirement is for a component to be manufactured in-house, MRP creates a planned order that can be converted to a production order.

145

Planning with MRP

Planning file contains materials for MRP run

The initial MRP process reviews the planning file, which contains all of the materials that are relevant for the MRP run. The review is followed by a net requirements calculation. This system calculation determines whether the requirements can be fulfilled by the available inventory and any planned goods receipts from production or purchase orders.

Based on the net requirements calculation, the MRP process calculates purchasing proposals to cover any material shortages. The purchasing proposals are calculated using minimum and maximum lot sizes that are found on the relevant material master record.

MRP creates purchase requirements

After the MRP process has calculated the purchasing proposals, the scheduling function calculates when any shortages will occur and if the purchasing proposal needs to be converted to an in-house production order. If this is the case, MRP produces a number of production orders and creates additional purchasing proposals that need to be processed by the purchasing department.

If your finished products in the planning file have a bill of materials (BOM), then MRP explodes the BOM after the purchasing proposals have been created. The resulting dependent requirements are then scheduled as part of the MRP run.

Exception Messages

Finally, the MRP process creates exception messages for your planning staff if the process finds critical situations that need manual input, for example, if the safety stock for a material is exceeded. Exception messages needs to be addressed quickly after each MRP run.

Executing the Planning Run

Single item MRP versus total planning

The MRP process can be run for a single material or a product group; this is called *single item MRP*. The process can also be run for a location, such as a plant, plants, MRP area, or a combination; this is called *total planning*.

Total Planning

For manufacturing companies, running MRP is usually run for the whole plant or series of plants, depending on the structure of the manufacturing operation. The MRP run is set up as a batch job to run overnight, with the planning staff reviewing the resulting MRP list report the next day.

The MRP report for total planning shows the items that have been processed, and your planning staff can review the MRP proposals.

Figure 6.13 shows the MRP list that has been created as a result of the total planning process.

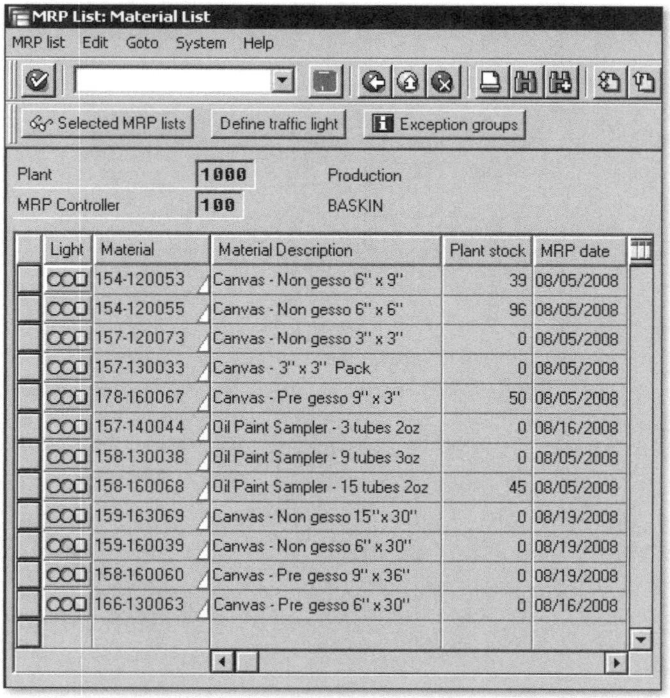

Light	Material	Material Description	Plant stock	MRP date
OOO	154-120053	Canvas - Non gesso 6" x 9"	39	08/05/2008
OOO	154-120055	Canvas - Non gesso 6" x 6"	96	08/05/2008
OOO	157-120073	Canvas - Non gesso 3" x 3"	0	08/05/2008
OOO	157-130033	Canvas - 3" x 3" Pack	0	08/05/2008
OOO	178-160067	Canvas - Pre gesso 9" x 3"	50	08/05/2008
OOO	157-140044	Oil Paint Sampler - 3 tubes 2oz	0	08/16/2008
OOO	158-130038	Oil Paint Sampler - 9 tubes 3oz	0	08/05/2008
OOO	158-160068	Oil Paint Sampler - 15 tubes 2oz	45	08/05/2008
OOO	159-163069	Canvas - Non gesso 15"x 30"	0	08/19/2008
OOO	159-160039	Canvas - Non gesso 6" x 30"	0	08/19/2008
OOO	158-160060	Canvas - Pre gesso 9" x 36"	0	08/19/2008
OOO	166-130063	Canvas - Pre gesso 6" x 30"	0	08/16/2008

Figure 6.13 MRP List for the Total Planning Process

The details in Figure 6.13 show the items processed by the total planning process, and the planning staff can access the details by selecting an individual line item.

Single Item Planning

If your planning staff needs to run MRP for an item before the nightly MRP run, you can run it for a single item. The resulting MRP list shows the details for that specific item.

Figure 6.14 shows the MRP list for a single item.

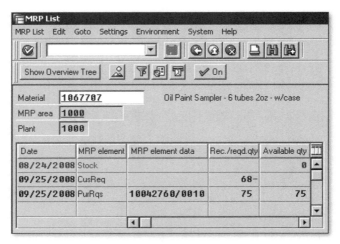

Figure 6.14 MRP List for Single Item Planning

The MRP list shows the current stock position, the future customer requirements, and a purchase proposal to cover those requirements.

The information in the MRP list gives the planning staff the information they need to evaluate the stock position to ensure that all of the customers' requirements are fulfilled. It's important to remember that the MRP function is a tool and can't replace the knowledge of your planning staff. If vendor lead times change, this information needs to be entered into the MRP system so that the proposals can reflect the change.

 Tip

The MRP run is often scheduled as an overnight batch job; however, changes in purchasing, production, or customer orders can happen at any time. Planning resources should remember to run MRP for a single item when required.

This section has shown how MRP can be used to ensure that your customer's orders can be fulfilled. The MRP process triggers either a purchasing proposal or an internal production order to have the component materials available for the manufacture of the items on the customer order.

 Case Study

In the 1990s a Dutch beverage company implemented a MRP software suite as part of a best-of-breed software suite. The software was an off-the-shelf package but heavily customized to fit the company's business. The primary reason for the MRP implementation was to improve the percentage of on-time deliveries for customer orders. Six months after implementation, the company found that the on-time delivery of customer order had slipped from 65% to 57%. A new version of the software was implemented, and after nine months, the percentage had slipped even further to 52%. A consulting firm was hired to find out why the percentage continued to slide. Their report found that the MRP software was working to the company's specification. The report went on to identify three reasons why the software failed to improve the percentage.

> The software program assumed that the inventory level was correct, when in fact the accuracy was less than 60%.

> The software required that the BOM for each item be accurate, but again the accuracy was below 70%.

> The planning staff did not review the proposals from the MRP system. Because the software did not take into account the capacity of the manufacturing facility, the orders passed to manufacturing were often past their due date before they were started.

A new CIO was brought in to lead the implementation of an SAP ERP system (without modification) to replace the aging software. The planning department pre-empted the implementation by cleaning up the BOMs to ensure that the accuracy was as close to 100% as possible. In addition, the warehouse staff improved the inventory accuracy to almost 95% before SAP ERP was implemented.

Three months after go-live, the company saw the on-time delivery of customer orders rise to over 85%.

Summary

In this chapter we've examined how SAP software is delivered with a variety of planning tools to help your company with its overall planning procedures. Although many companies implement an MRP process, many forget that by developing policies and procedures to help with long- and medium-term planning, such as SAP SOP, the data used in the MRP process will be that much more accurate. Your MRP process becomes less reactive, and customer orders are more likely to be fulfilled on time. SAP software provides all of the functionality that your company requires to create a world-class planning process. However, with any MRP process, the knowledge of your planning staff is paramount in making sure that the proposals from MRP take into account the current situation with vendors and plant capacity.

The planning function is an important component of the logistics process. Planning ensures that your company has a good understanding of future requirements. SAP SOP and demand management give a medium- to long-term view that can provide planning information to your purchasing and manufacturing staff. Planning resources and purchases will reduce overall costs. Customer orders will be less likely to be delayed and overall confidence in the company will be enhanced.

Here are some key points to remember about the SAP planning process:

> Sales and operations planning requires input from a number of departments in your organization: marketing, sales, finance, manufacturing, and warehouse.

> Adoption of SAP SOP results in more accurate deliveries to your customers, reduced inventories, efficient use of warehouse and manufacturing resources, and increased order fulfillment.

> Demand management allows your company to react to supply restrictions, changing customer commitments, inventory counts, and factors that can affect demand at any time.

> MRP ensures the necessary materials for production orders are on hand or purchased on time.

> Successful MRP can help to reduce inventory totals, reduce production delays, increase the number of on-time deliveries, and improve customer satisfaction.

In the next chapter, we'll examine the results of the MRP process and look at the SAP manufacturing processes.

Manufacturing Operations

If your company manufactures items for internal use or for sale to customers, then you'll want to examine the SAP functionality that is used to facilitate the manufacturing process. Thousands of companies around the world use SAP software for their production facilities, and this chapter examines the functionality in detail.

The SAP ERP business suite provides a structure that replicates real life, including bill of materials (BOM), work centers, routings, and equipment. SAP ERP gives you the ability to perform capacity checks on your work centers to ensure that bottlenecks don't occur and to check on other essential functions such as work center costing. The SAP production order process provides your staff with visibility throughout each operation. Real-time information enables your staff to react to issues as they arise. The product costing functionality calculates finished goods inventory values. It combines the cost of the direct materials, labor, and the overhead that are consumed when the production order is complete. This gives your company the ability to see the true cost of the products you manufacture as those goods leave the manufacturing facility.

In the first section, we'll talk about the physical items you find in the manufacturing area, such as work centers, and the administration items, such as bills of materials (BOM). In the second section, we'll look at the manufacturing process that you'll see in the SAP system, including production and process orders. Lastly, we'll discuss the topic of product costing.

Manufacturing Structure

Physical and administrative elements

Before we examine the manufacturing process in the SAP software, we need to review the elements that go into making up the structure of the manufacturing operation. These fall under two areas: the physical elements and the administrative elements. The *physical elements* include work centers on the shop floor and are used in the manufacturing process. The *administrative elements* help the manufacturing process, and include BOM and material routings. In this section, we'll look at all of these items that are part of the manufacturing structure.

Work Centers

Not just physical locations

Although a work center is a physical element of the manufacturing structure, it can represent a number of scenarios. A *work center* is either a location at your manufacturing site that contains one or more pieces of equipment, a single or group of employees, or even a production line.

 Example

> In the production of exhaust manifolds for motorcycles, the item passes through a number of work centers that contain equipment to cut and shape the metal. Other work centers later in the process include those where employees manually polish the chrome and wrap the item in protective packaging.

Figure 7.1 shows the work center master record and some of the details that can be assigned. The work center, CAT-4200, in Figure 7.1 is identified as a machine. Other categories include labor, production line, station, and plant maintenance.

Tip

The work center should contain costing, capacity, and scheduling data. If your company can enter accurate data into each work center, this will help provide a more accurate tool for your planning staff.

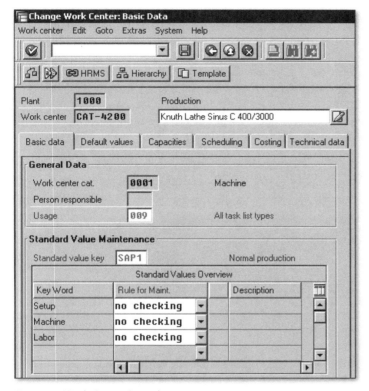

Figure 7.1 Work Center Record

In Figure 7.1, you can see that it's possible to enter data for Capacities, Scheduling, and Costing in their respective tabs of the dialog box.

Work Center Capacity

The work center record allows your staff to enter information about capacity. Data can be added that shows when the work center is used during the working day and the utilization that is normally achieved.

Work center capacity/utilization in the master record

➕ **Tip**

Keeping accurate data on work center capacity can reduce manufacturing bottlenecks.

Ex **Example**

At a manufacturing plant, a drilling station operates from 6AM to 2:30PM; the operator has a 30-minute break during that time. The drilling station therefore has a maximum utilization of 8 hours per day. However, when a one-week study was performed to analyze the true utilization, the drilling station was found to only be used 64% of the 8 hours, due to waiting for items from other work centers. This means the real utilization was only 5 hours and 7 minutes per day.

Figure 7.2 shows the capacity information entered for a work center. In this case, the utilization is 85%, and the operating time for each day is 6 hours and 59 minutes.

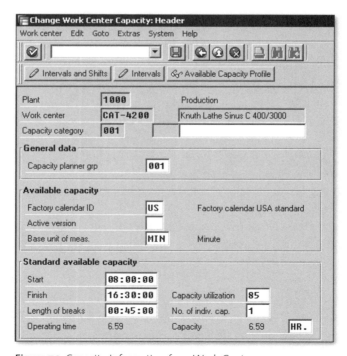

Figure 7.2 Capacity Information for a Work Center

Work Center Scheduling

In addition to adding the capacity of the work center, you should add scheduling information to ensure that production orders are scheduled correctly. The work center record allows your production staff to enter a standard queue time, which is the expected time an order will wait before it's processed at the work center. Your planning staff can also add formulas to calculate the setup and processing times at the work center. SAP provides a set of standard formulas to calculate these times, but your company can create its own formulas based on your manufacturing environment.

Queue, setup, and processing time

 Example

An electronics company manufactures reproduction radio sets. When a production order moves from one work center to the next, it has to sit at the work center until the components used at the work center are delivered from the warehouse. Because of the delay, the work center records include a value for queue times.

Figure 7.3 Work Center Scheduling Data

Figure 7.3 shows the scheduling data on the work center record. In this example, two standard SAP formulas have been entered for setup and processing time. In addition, a 45 minute standard queue time has been entered, with a 20 minute minimum queue time.

Work Center Costing

Product costing is the process of tracking the expenses that are accrued in the production and sale of a finished product. The means collecting information from your raw materials purchases through to the shipping expenses needed to get the finished product to your customers.

In production, product costing can be performed at the work center level. Depending on how your company performs product costing, you may need your finance staff to enter information for each work center that is created in the SAP software. We'll look at the whole topic of product costing later in this chapter.

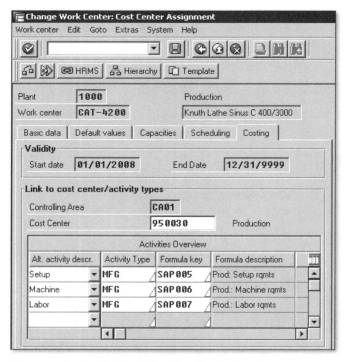

Figure 7.4 Costing Details in the Work Center Record

Figure 7.4 shows the costing information that can be added to your work center records. The work center can be assigned a cost center, and a number of formulas are entered that can calculate the costs based on the time spent on the product at this work center.

 Example

> In terms of manufacturing electronic fans, the components reach a work center that assembles the parts and solders the electronic components. The work center was assigned three activity codes for setup, machine costs, and labor costs. The costs collected at this work center are calculated based on the formulas for the three activity codes and the time spent on setup, as well as the time for machine and labor. The costs collected at this work center are combined with other costs associated with this product.

Now that we've examined the information that goes into creating a work center record, the next item we'll review is the BOM.

Bill of Materials

The bill of materials (BOM) is a list of materials that make up a product. This can be as simple as a wooden shaft and a steel head that go together to make a hammer, or the hundreds of components that are needed to make a laptop computer.

Combined lists of items

The BOM lists the quantities and unit measure of the component items. Before any implementation of SAP software, it's important to ensure that the data in your company's BOMs are as accurate as possible. Errors in quantities and components can lead to production scheduling errors and the inability to deliver your customers' items to them by the promised delivery day.

 Case Study

> The management of a British company that manufactured patio furniture from aluminum tubing and plastic strapping had been informed by its sales representatives that there was an issue with customer deliveries. Further analysis of the sales reps' claims found that the on-time delivery of customer orders had fallen 32% in the previous 6 months on orders that contained plastic wicker chairs. The company found this to be

unusual because the chair had been in production for more than 6 years without any issue.

After further analysis, the company found no logical reason why these sales orders were failing to be delivered on time.

A management consulting company was brought in to examine the issue. In their final analysis, they found an error in the production data. When the company reviewed the BOM and routing for the chair, they found that the BOM called for 16 feet of aluminum tubing when in fact each chair needed 17 feet. This error in the BOM was due to the installation of a new machine saw at one of the work centers in the routing. The way the new machine saw operated caused more scrap pieces than previously, and the amount of tubing required at the work center had increased. Because the BOM was incorrect, this operation in the routing was always requiring extra tubing, which caused longer expected production times. The BOM was corrected to reflect the correct amount of tubing needed for that operation. After the BOM was corrected, the on-time delivery percentage increased.

Text or document BOM items

In the BOM, the items listed are usually component items that make up the final product. However, sometimes they may be text or document items, such as a manual, or nonstock items such as packaging material.

 Tip

BOMs need to be accurate and current to ensure that the manufacturing process is as efficient as possible. An error in the BOM can cause delays in a production order.

Figure 7.5 shows a finished item that has a BOM of three items. The BOM shows the quantity of the component items.

In the next section, we'll look at another administrative element of the manufacturing structure, the routing.

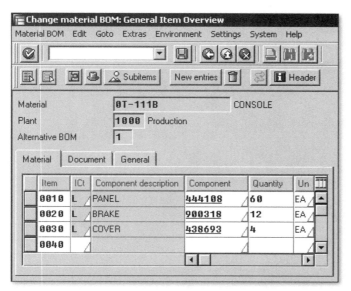

Figure 7.5 Bill of Materials for a Finished Item

Routings

A *routing* is a series of operations that define how an item is manufactured. The routing identifies the work center in which the operation will be performed. The routing is used in a production order for an item because it defines the operations that need to be completed in the order and enables you to plan the production of finished goods.

Planning the production of finished goods

 Example

A routing for a finished item can include operations at work centers, such as drilling, polishing, painting, or assembly. In addition, operations such as quality management or inspections can be included.

 Tip

Material routings need to be accurate and current to ensure that the manufacturing process is as efficient as possible. Errors in the routing can cause delays in a production order.

Figure 7.6 shows the routing for a material that has a number of manufacturing operations and then a final quality inspection operation.

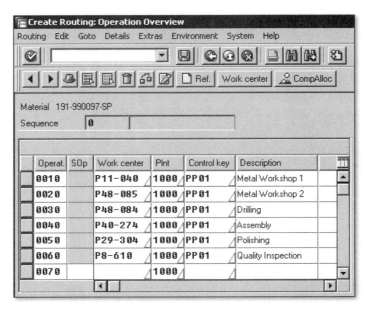

Figure 7.6 Routing for a Finished Product

The routings we've looked at here are specific to regular products that your company may produce. However, if your company makes configurable materials, such as a bicycle where the customer can choose the color, gearing options, type of tires, and so on, then you'll need to use routings that are suitable for those materials. In the next section, we'll discuss that specific type of routing.

Routings for Configurable Materials

Configurable
materials provide
customer choices

If your company manufacturers items where the customer can configure the item to their specification, a different type of routing can be can be used for production. Instead of a normal routing, a superrouting is used, which can contain all of the possible different operations or can be specific to one variant.

Example

A company manufactures a professional mountain bike, which is defined as a configurable product. The customer can select a variety of options, including the finish of the handlebars: brushed nickel, chrome, or a black painted finish. Depending on the option selected by the customer, the routing is different on the shop floor. If the customer wants a chrome finish, the operation is performed in the metal shop; for brushed nickel, the product is sent out for finishing; or for black paint, the operation is performed in the paint booth.

Now that we've looked at the configurable routing that is needed for your configurable materials, we'll examine the resources that you need to complete the operations in the routing. In the next section, we'll discuss the tools that are used in the operations, which in the SAP software are called production resources and tools (PRTs).

Production Resources and Tools (PRT)

Production resources are used in the production of your finished products. They are assigned to the production order based on the routing that is used in that order. PRTs are not just traditional tools such as a torque wrench, but they can also be a drawing or schematic that is used in the production process.

Documents, equipment, instruments, or tools

A PRT can be created in the SAP software as a regular material, a document, or a piece of equipment, which we'll discuss more in Chapter 8 when we look at plant maintenance.

 Example

In the production of a new commercial sound system, the process requires the accurate testing of *transformer impedances*. To do this, the company had to purchase a number of impedance testers to perform the accurate test. Each of the new tools were entered into the SAP software with PRT records so that their use could be part of the planning process.

In addition to those options, your production staff can create a PRT without creating it as a piece of equipment or as a material. The PRT record allows basic information to be entered into SAP so that the PRT can be used in the planning process.

Figure 7.7 shows the basic PRT record that has been entered for a Micrometer. The data shows that it's used in Plant 1000.

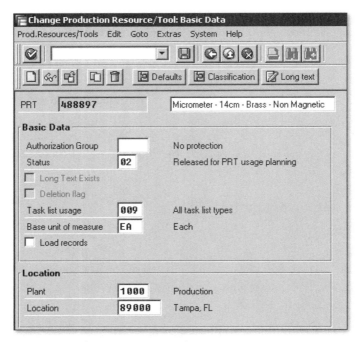

Figure 7.7 Production Resource/Tool Entry

We'll be expanding our discussion of PRTs when we look at the plant maintenance equipment record in Chapter 8.

Now that we've examined the elements that are part of the manufacturing structure, let's turn our attention to the production process and look at shop floor control.

Shop Floor Control

Shop floor functions   Shop floor control covers the operations that occur at your manufacturing location. The manufacturing process requires the production order to create the finished product, but shop floor control covers other aspects of manufacturing such as capacity evaluation. The shop floor functions include production orders, shop papers, and information tools.

In this section, we'll look at the production order and how it's used to facilitate the manufacture of your finished products. In addition, we'll discuss other aspects of the shop floor such as capacity, shop papers, and informational tools such as the Order Info System.

Production Order

The primary function in shop floor control is the production order. It determines the items manufactured the quantity, the duration, the process, and the cost.

Production orders contain the items and quantity

A production order can be created manually, but if your company is using MRP, it's more likely that production orders are created from generated planned orders.

When a production order is created, a number of events occur to ensure that your finished product will be manufactured:

> Routing for the finished product is selected. The sequence and the operations that are defined in the routing are adopted in the production order.

> The BOM is explored. The BOM for the finished product is exploded, and the component items are transferred to the production order.

> Reservations are generated for component items held in stock.

> Costs for the order are created.

> Capacity requirements are generated for the work centers in the routing.

> Purchase requisitions are created for the items not held in stock and for the operations in the routing that are performed by outside vendors.

Tip

Entering manual production orders allows the flexibility to react to customer demands, but caution must be exercised to not delay the manufacture of material for other customer orders.

Figure 7.8 shows the basic information of a production order that has been entered into the SAP software. It shows the quantity of the finished product to be produced, as well as the start date and the expected finish date of the order. The statuses on the order show that it has been released and printed.

Figure 7.8 Production Order

Operations

Operations adopted from routing for finished products

When the production order is created, the routing for the finished product forms the basis of the order. It's the list of operations that need to be performed on the material to create the finished product. As each operation is completed, it's updated in the production order. So, at any time, your production staff can see the progress of the order on the shop floor.

Figure 7.9 shows the operations for the production order. For each operation, the relevant work center is shown with the scheduled start time and date. When the operation has been completed, the status can be updated.

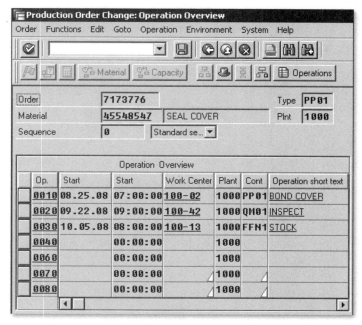

Figure 7.9 Operations for a Production Order

Scheduling

The scheduling dates in your production orders are based on the planned orders that originated in the MRP run. However, if your production staff needs to add production orders manually, then the scheduling dates will be based on the type of order that is entered.

Scheduling dates based on the planned order from MRP

Ex Example

When creating manual production orders, a company manufacturing hand tools determined that orders for different types of tools needed to be scheduled differently. They decided that tools without a BOM needed to be forward scheduled, whereas tools with a BOM needed backward scheduling.

SAP software can be configured to allow your company to determine the scheduling based on the order types it uses.

When orders are manually entered for orders with forward scheduling, the SAP software calculates the scheduled start and finish dates based on the order start date that is entered by your staff. In backward scheduling, your staff would enter the order end date, and the SAP software calculates the scheduled start and finish dates.

Float dates in order scheduled dates

The calculation of scheduled dates is dependent on the information your company enters for float dates, before and after production, as well as release periods and the factory calendar for the plant.

Capacity Requirements

Capacity requirements calculated for each operation

The production order generates the capacity requirements for the work centers, but you can manually assign capacity if necessary.

 Example

> An operation in a production order has the lathe work for a material to be performed by the Knuth DM1000A lathe. However, the production staff knows that lathe is due for preventive maintenance. To ensure the work gets completed, your staff can move capacity in the production order to the two Knuth Turnado 230 lathes in the same work center.

Inspection Lots

Inspections at regular intervals

Inspection lots are sometimes required when the items progress through the production process. Checks on quality or specification may need to be performed after certain operations.

 Example

> A company that manufacturers flat panel monitors for government agencies are required to provide test data for components during the manufacturing process. After each operation where a component is added to the finished product, an inspection must be performed and documented to comply with requirements.

Planned inspections are maintained in the routing of a material so they will be carried through into the production order. However, the SAP software allows your staff to enter unplanned inspections into the production order if required.

Planned or unplanned inspections

Ex Example

Due to quality issues on the production line, the quality management department could ask the production staff to enter a series of unplanned inspections. The inspections can be inserted in a number of operations of production orders to investigate the cause of the quality issues.

Figure 7.10 shows an inspection lot that has been created from a production order. The inspection is based on specifications that are particular to the finished product in the production order.

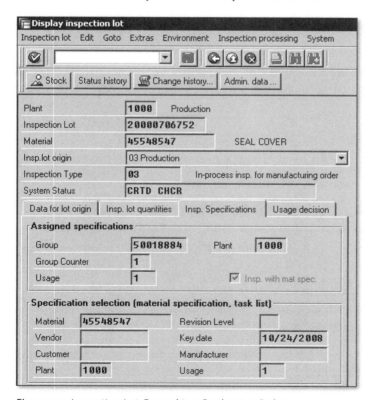

Figure 7.10 Inspection Lot Created in a Production Order

Now that we've looked at the various elements of the production order, we're ready to move on to how production orders progress with confirmations.

Confirming a Production Order

Confirming operation completion

When a production order operation has been completed, the status needs to be updated in the production order by way of a confirmation.

 Tip

> It's important that confirmations occur as close to the end of the operation as possible so that the information is accurate for planning purposes.

When an operation is confirmed, the information on the quantity of material, work center, and resources is recorded in the production order.

Confirmations trigger other transactions

When your production staff updates the production order via a confirmation, a number of other transactions are triggered:

> Updating order data such as quantities, dates, and status

> Backflushing components in the order

> Automatic goods receipt of materials

> Updating costing information

> Capacity reduction in the work center

> Updating excess or missing quantities of materials in the order

> Updating the usage counter for PRTs used in the operations

 Example

> An order for 50 specialty brackets goes through a number of operations before completion. At the end of each operation, the production staff enters a confirmation in the production order. The confirmation records the quantity that is completed at the end of the operation. On the last painting operation, 3 brackets were dropped and damaged. The confirmation of that operation noted that the completed quantity was 47 because 2 brackets were reworked, and 1 was sent for scrap.

Figure 7.11 shows a confirmation of actual data for a production order. The confirmation in this instance is to show that setup has been started. The date and time of the confirmation as well as the person who enters the confirmation has been identified.

Figure 7.11 Confirmation of an Operation in a Production Order

A confirmation can trigger other events to occur, such as goods movements.

Backflushing

When a confirmation is made in a production order, this can trigger a backflushing movement. *Backflushing* is an automatic goods issue of materials that were used in the operation but were not previously issued to the production order. It's especially useful if your company has orders where the precise amount of material used in operations varies or where operations call for bulk material where the exact quantity required in the operation can't be obtained.

Backflushing records material used in the order

Tip

Delaying the confirmation of an operation that contains backflushing will delay the backflushing process. Inventory issues can arise when material that is expected to be in stock isn't in stock because it has already been consumed by backflushing but as yet not been processed.

 Example

In the production of a specialty coating, an operation in a production order calls for 2 kilograms of yellow pigment. However, the pigment is stored in 55-gallon drums. The 2 kilograms are taken from the drum on the shop floor, and the amount is backflushed in the SAP system when the operation is confirmed.

Automatic Goods Receipt

Goods receipt of finished products triggered by confirmation

For some companies, it's important to have the finished product in stock as soon as the last operation is complete. If that's the case for your company, SAP functionality allows you to post the goods issue when an operation is complete.

The operation where you can post goods issue doesn't have to be the final operation in the production order. If you have a product that can be quality inspected in the warehouse, then the product can be moved to stock as soon as the final manufacturing operation is complete.

 Example

A custom automotive parts manufacturer supplies engine parts to racing car teams in the United States and Europe. The company receives orders for parts that need to be manufactured and shipped within two days. To ensure the items are shipped the moment they hit the warehouse, the company automatically goods receipts the items after the last manufacturing step. This is one operation before final inspection so that the shipping department can prepare the packaging prior to the items arriving in the warehouse.

In this section, we discussed confirming operations in the production order and how that can trigger other events. Following on from order confirmation, we'll look at order settlement in the next section.

Production Order Settlement

When your production orders are completed, you can settle the costs associated with the production order. The settlement or offset between the planned costs of the finished goods and the actual costs is collected by the production order.

Offset between actual and planned costs

If your company predetermines the costs of your finished goods, then the actual costs will be equal to the planned costs, and there will be no settlement.

A *settlement rule* is assigned to each of your production orders, and this contains the information that determines the cost receivers where the order is settled. These can include a cost center, an internal order, a material, a sales order, a project, and a network.

Settlement rules determine order settlement

If your costing department requires more than one cost receiver for production orders, the settlement rule can determine the percentage of the costs to distribute to each of the cost receivers.

Figure 7.12 shows the settlement for a production order that is split between two different cost receivers, one for material and the other for a project.

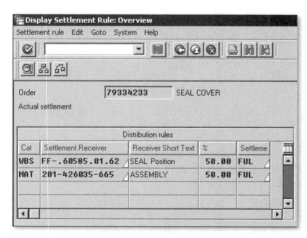

Figure 7.12 Settlement of a Production Order

In the next section, we'll look at the shop papers that can be printed as part of the manufacturing process.

Printing Shop Papers

Time tickets, confirmation slips, pull lists, control tickets

When a production order is being processed on the shop floor, paperwork often needs to be printed. This may occur when an order arrives at a work center or a particular operation is to be performed.

The shop papers can consist of a variety of standard SAP documents, such as pull lists and control tickets, or can be documents that are specific to your manufacturing department or industry. The documents can be set up to print at a specific printer on your shop floor.

> **Ex** **Example**
>
> On the shop floor of a manufacturing plant, a production order for an electric wheelchair covers seven work centers. When the item arrives at each work center, a document is printed at the work center printer that describes the operation to be performed. In addition, at Kanban locations, a Kanban label is printed on a Zebra label printer. When the item arrives at the last work center, a goods issue slip is printed.

Figure 7.13 shows a production order that will have an object list printed at Printer PRT90040455, but no other document will be printed for the production order.

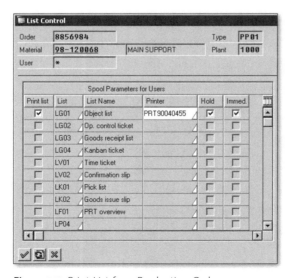

Figure 7.13 Print List for a Production Order

Next, we'll examine the Order Info System. This is a very useful tool for your production staff as they monitor the production orders on the shop floor.

Order Info System

The Order Info System is a tool that allows your production staff visibility of the production orders on the shop floor. In addition, your staff can also view planned orders that have yet to be converted.

Order Info System reports on planned and production orders

The Order Info System has options that your staff can select from, including displaying a range of production orders, PRTs, operations, purchase requisitions, purchase orders, sequences, capacities, and goods movements.

Figure 7.14 shows the Order Info System displaying a number of order headers specific to a manufacturing plant. Each individual order can be accessed by drilling down from the header information on the report.

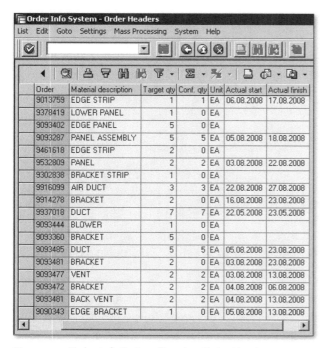

Figure 7.14 Order Info System Showing Order Headers

We've now looked at the functionality that encompasses shop floor control. The production order is the driver that takes a variety of components and manufactures the finished goods. In the next section, we'll look at how that finished item is costed.

Product Costing

Product costing determines costs incurred

Product costing is the SAP functionality that calculates finished goods inventory values by combining the cost of the direct materials, labor, and the overhead that are consumed when your company produces a finished product. The direct material costs are calculated based on the finished product's BOM, whereas the labor and the overhead costs are allocated using routings. This is also described as *cost of goods manufactured* (COGM). When the costs involved in sales and administration are added to the COGM, this becomes the *cost of goods sold* (COGS).

To calculate the COGM or COGS, your costing staff can create a material cost estimate that is based either on a quantity structure or without a quantity structure. Cost estimates with a quantity structure are used for items with standard prices and don't take into account any orders. Cost estimates without a quantity structure are more frequently used for items with little or no quantity structure.

Cost Estimate with a Quantity Structure

Quantity structure includes BOM and routing

This method is used for planning costs and setting prices for items without taking into account any order information. To perform this costing, the item needs to have a BOM and a routing.

Your finance or product costing staff can create a cost estimate for a material when the details have been created for the BOM and routing.

Figure 7.15 shows a cost estimate created in the SAP software for an item. The figure shows the items and quantities from the BOM. The cost estimate shows a total for the item, based on the quantity structure.

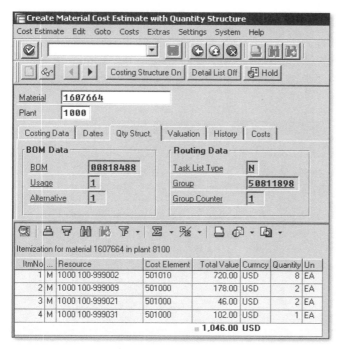

Figure 7.15 Cost Estimate for a Finished Product

When the costing has been completed for an item, your costing staff can then analyze the data against the current material price. If appropriate, the material master record for the finished product can be updated with the new cost estimate.

In Figure 7.15, the cost estimate has been calculated at $1,046. However, in the material master record, the standard price has been entered as $1,023, as shown in Figure 7.16. Based on the cost estimate, it's vital to update the standard price of your material to the cost estimate because this reflects the cost of manufacturing the material.

Compare cost estimates to standard prices regularly

 Tip

Review of the cost of materials manufactured should regularly occur to indicate what products are costing more to manufacture than the price you can sell them for.

Your costing staff can copy the new cost estimate to be the new standard price in the material record.

Figure 7.16 shows the transaction where the cost estimate is transferred as the Standard price in the material master record for the finished product.

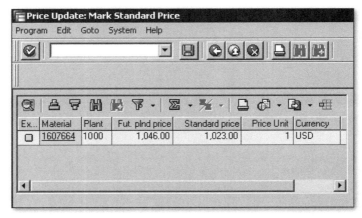

Figure 7.16 Updating the Standard Price from the Cost Estimate

Your costing staff can also create cost estimates for items that your company uses that don't have quantity structure. In the next section, we'll look at estimating costs for those items.

Cost Estimate without a Quantity Structure

Cost estimates of
raw materials

If your company needs to create cost estimates for raw materials or new items, these won't have BOMs or routings, so a cost estimate has to be made without a quantity structure.

The costs must be entered manually by your costing staff. The cost estimate can include a number of elements such as materials and work centers.

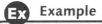 **Example**

A new, finished product has been designed, and the item hasn't had the BOM or a routing entered into the SAP software. To complete costing, a cost estimate without a quantity structure can be performed.

Figure 7.17 shows the entry of costing data for a finished good that does not have a quantity structure. A total for each cost entry is calculated based on quantity, and an overall cost estimate is calculated.

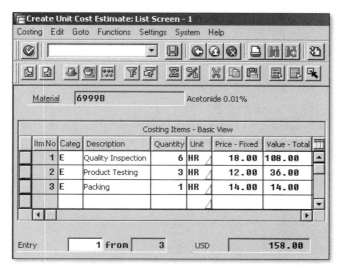

Figure 7.17 Cost Estimate without a Quantity Structure

In this section, we've looked at the product costing estimates that can be created for items that have a quantity structure and those that don't have a quantity structure. It's important to regularly check the cost estimates against your material prices to see if adjustments are needed.

Summary

In this chapter, we looked at the manufacturing operations that are found in the SAP software. You've likely recognized that the manufacturing structures in the SAP system probably resemble your own manufacturing environment.

There are a number of points to highlight from this chapter:

> Information in routings and BOMs needs to be accurate and current for successful manufacturing.

> Capacities of work centers should be calculated so bottlenecks don't occur in the manufacturing process.

> Production orders should be created from your MRP runs.

> Each operation within the production order should be confirmed as soon as it's completed to ensure accurate information.

> Product costing calculates finished goods inventory values and tells you if your product is profitable to manufacture.

In this chapter, you've seen that the shop floor control processes are driven by the production order. The order pushes the product through the manufacturing process from raw material to a finished item.

Product costing is important to your business because it ensures that the costs you expend in the manufacture of a product are reflected in the price of a material. Regular reviews of the cost estimate against the material price makes good business sense.

In the next chapter, we'll examine the maintenance processes when we look at the SAP plant maintenance (PM) component.

8

Plant Maintenance

Plant maintenance is an integral part of the logistics function, and it's fully integrated with other components in SAP, including materials management and production. Every company that has a manufacturing operation has implemented some level of plant maintenance to keep their operation at optimum efficiency.

The SAP plant maintenance (PM) component covers three areas of maintenance: inspection, prevention, and repair. The inspection process allows your staff to identify the condition of the equipment at the time of inspection. The preventive maintenance process is used to keep items at their optimum operating condition. This SAP process gives your company the opportunity to ensure that equipment is in optimum condition. Failure of equipment on the shop floor can lead to delays in production and ultimately delays in customer shipments. Using the SAP preventive maintenance function will improve competitive advantage over time. Lastly, the repair process is required when equipment needs to be restored to its optimum operating condition. This functionality assists your staff in reducing downtime of

Inspection, prevention, and repair

equipment, but with the use of preventive maintenance, breakdowns will be kept to a minimum.

This chapter helps you understand the importance of the PM component and how it is highly integrated with other SAP logistics functions. In the first section, we'll look at the structures within PM, including equipment and functional locations.

Maintenance Organization Structure

Technical objects   Before we examine the PM process in the SAP software, we need to review the technical objects that are found in the PM function. These fall under two areas: functional elements and equipment. It's important to the success of your maintenance function that the information loaded into the technical objects is as accurate as possible. Let's look at the first of the technical objects, the functional location.

Functional Location

Maintenance tasks occur here   The functional location is a location in your plant where a plant maintenance task occurs. It can be a location where a piece of equipment is installed and used. There are three distinct functional locations that you can consider when planning your PM structure.

Functional

When you consider a location that is deemed functional, you should identify the location that defines a function, such as a drill shop or spray cabinet.

Process Related

A process-related functional location can be defined as a location that describes a process. For example, a building may be defined as a fabrication or welding.

Spatial

A functional location that is a spatial location describes the physical location rather than the function that is found there. For example, a spatial location may be a laboratory or an office.

 Tip

> Your maintenance staff members are key to identifying these functional locations and the development of functional hierarchies.

One feature that SAP software offers with respect to functional locations is that you can create a functional location hierarchy if your PM structure requires that definition.

Create functional location hierarchies

The highest level of the hierarchy can represent a building or plant. The lower levels can include paint shops or fabrication shops, and the lowest levels can include functional locations found at the fabrication and paint shops.

Each of the functional locations has a record in the SAP software, and each can contain an individual maintenance history.

Functional locations have individual maintenance histories

 Example

> A fabrication shop has a number of functional locations that are structured as a hierarchy so that maintenance information is kept on various areas of the fabrication shop. The first level of the hierarchy identifies the two areas of the fabrication shop, the turning area and the cutting area. The metal in the shop is either cut by bench saws or cutting torches. This represents the next level of the hierarchy. The cutting torches used in the cutting area are either plasma cutting systems or oxyacetylene cutters. These two functional locations represent the next level of the hierarchy. Finally, the lowest level of the hierarchy describes the cutting systems used in the plasma and gas areas.

Figure 8.1 illustrates the hierarchy that is described in the example. In your company you may find that your maintenance personnel have identified a number of hierarchies like this example where they want information at the various levels.

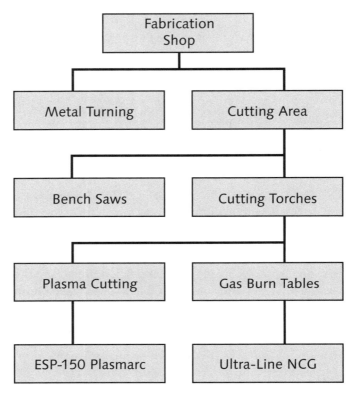

Figure 8.1 Example of a Functional Location Hierarchy

Functional locations as fixed assets   When your maintenance personnel add a functional location, they can include a variety of information that is relevant for the functional location. If the functional location is a fixed asset in the SAP system (i.e., individually shown on the company's financial balance sheet), the asset number should be entered into the record. Other financial information, such as a cost center, can also be entered for the functional location.

The functional location can contain one or more pieces of equipment, which can be added to the functional location record.

Figure 8.2 shows the organization structure information that has been entered for functional location 9903-003-GB-03.

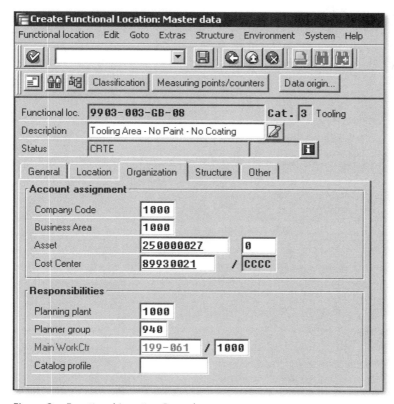

Figure 8.2 Functional Location Record

Now that you've seen the functional location, let's look at the other technical object, the equipment record.

Equipment

In your company's manufacturing area, there will be many pieces of equipment, such as a bench saw or a lathe, that are used in a variety of operations on the shop floor. Each piece of equipment can have its own record that contains relevant information and can collect maintenance information over a period of time.

Equipment records aren't only relevant to the PM component. Equipment records are also used in materials management (MM), customer

Assign equipment to a functional location

Equipment records used in other components

185

service (CS), production planning (PP), and quality management (QM).

A number of different equipment record types have been created in the SAP software so that all of your company's equipment can be entered. These types include production resources and tools (PRTs), machines, and test equipment.

 Tip

> When creating an equipment record, make sure you have all of the information regarding purchase date, vendor, serial number, and so on. These details are important when considering warranties and service of the item.

The record that you create for your pieces of equipment can include specific details on the individual item, such as serial number and information on the usage.

 Example

> A company uses a number of temperature gauges in its manufacturing process. The gauges are used on the line for 60 days and then have to be calibrated. The equipment records for the gauges are created so that the usage information is entered. When the usage is close to 60 hours, the gauge is scheduled for calibration.

Figure 8.3 shows an equipment master record that has been entered. The record shows detailed information on the machine, including the manufacturer, the serial number and the date of startup at the plant.

Permits

U.S. permits issued by state, county, or city

Some types of equipment require a permit to be obtained for them to be used. These can include permits concerning fire and hazardous materials for national, state, county, or city requirements. The SAP system gives you the ability to enter those relevant permits into the equipment record.

Figure 8.3 Equipment Master Record

 Example

At a Los Angeles manufacturing company, several welding stations are situated in a building with a number of acetylene cylinders. State of California regulations require that all businesses with pressurized tanks more than 1.5 cubic feet and greater than 150 pounds per square inch, obtain an air tanks permit from the Department of Industrial Relations.

Tip

As environmental issues become more prevalent in industry, keep abreast of local and national laws that may restrict the use of certain chemicals or equipment. Having the correct permits can save your company significant time and money.

Figure 8.4 shows an equipment record that has been assigned a number of permits for its operation.

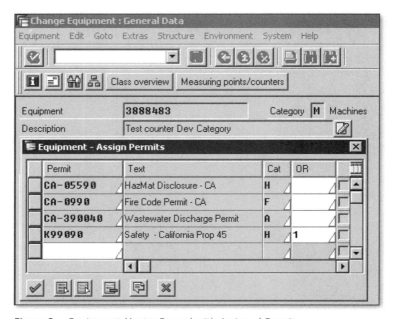

Figure 8.4 Equipment Master Record with Assigned Permits

Counters and Measurement

Counters or measuring points

Equipment master records can be documented to indicate the condition of the items your company uses. This can be achieved through counters or measurement.

Counters are used for pieces of equipment that have to be maintained after a certain number of cycles or rotations.

 **Example**

An airline has a number of Bombardier Dash-8 series aircraft. They have identified the propeller housing as an individual piece of equipment. When a propeller is fitted to an aircraft, each hour it's in operation is recorded, and at 9,000 hours, the propeller housing is removed from the aircraft and overhauled.

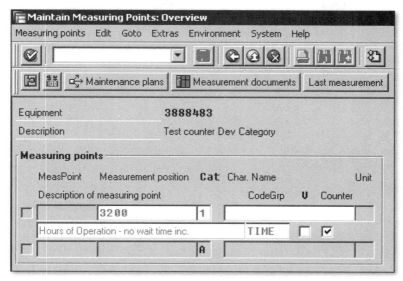

Figure 8.5 Equipment Record with Counter Information

Figure 8.5 shows an equipment master record that has a counter set to 3,200 hours.

Measurement readings can be made to ensure a piece of equipment is within operational tolerances. The equipment master record is annotated with the measurement. The measurement that is taken is a snapshot and only valid for that specific moment.

Tolerances as a range or single value

 Example

> The coolant from a plating machine is checked to ensure that it's still functioning to maximum efficiency. The plating machine has a measuring point entered on the equipment master record that indicates the maximum temperature allowed before the machine needs maintenance to change the coolant.

Figure 8.6 shows a measuring point of 5422 flight hours for a Dash-8 Aircraft. Depending on the number of flight hours, the aircraft will be required to undergo one of a number of maintenance checks.

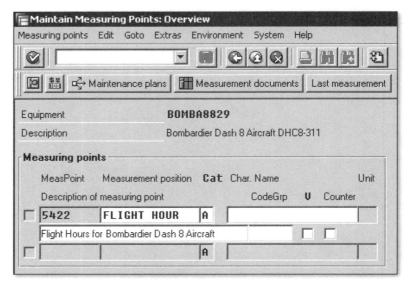

Figure 8.6 Measurement Point for an Equipment Record

Measurement Documents

Manual or
automatic update of
measurement
documents

When a measurement is taken for a technical object, a measurement document can be created to record the value. The document can also record any variance, the date and time the measurement was taken, and the person responsible for taking the measurement.

 Example

During a line check for an aircraft, the maintenance staff records a number of measurements relating to various technical objects that are part of the aircraft. The measurements are recorded on measurement documents and entered into the SAP software manually or automatically.

The measurement document in Figure 8.7 shows that a manual measurement of flight hours was taken for measuring point 5422, as shown in Figure 8.6.

Figure 8.7 Measurement Document for Measuring Point 5422

In this section, we've looked at the technical objects you'll find in the PM component. Now that you understand the capabilities of functional locations and equipment, let's discuss the preventive maintenance functions your company can implement.

Preventive Maintenance

Preventive maintenance is a schedule of planned maintenance that is focused on preventing equipment breakdowns and failures. The goal of any company's preventive maintenance program is to prevent the failure of equipment before it actually occurs, causing the loss of finished product and customer delivery delays. A world-class preventive maintenance program ensures equipment reliability by replacing equipment components before they fail, all the while ensuring maximum efficiency at the lowest cost.

Preventing unexpected equipment failure

In this section, we'll look at how a preventive maintenance program is created in the SAP system and the elements that can be found in preventive maintenance. We'll start with the functionality of the task list and its importance in PM.

Maintenance Task List

Sequence of maintenance operations

The maintenance task list is a sequence of operations that are used in the maintenance of a functional location or piece of equipment. The task list is usually provided by the manufacturer of equipment as part of a maintenance manual. However, this isn't always the case, and your maintenance staff may have developed their own lists of operations for the maintenance of your manufacturing equipment.

 Example

> The Lincoln Electric Pro 25 plasma cutter is supplied with an operations manual that includes two sections on routine and periodic maintenance. These list the operations, mostly visual inspections, which should be performed to ensure safe operation. However, many companies would expand upon the operations listed in the manual for preventive maintenance purposes.

Equipment, functional location, or general maintenance lists

The three types of task lists that can be used in preventive maintenance are the general maintenance task list, the equipment task list, and the functional location task list.

General Maintenance Task List

This type of task list isn't specific for a functional location or piece of equipment. It's used to identify the operations for maintenance tasks that are performed on the shop floor.

 Example

> A set of operations is required before the calibration of any tool is performed in the laboratory. The task list for these operations doesn't change whether the item to be calibrated is a gauge, tool, or a piece of equipment. It's defined as a general maintenance task list.

Figure 8.8 shows a general maintenance task list for laboratory work not specific to a functional location or piece of equipment.

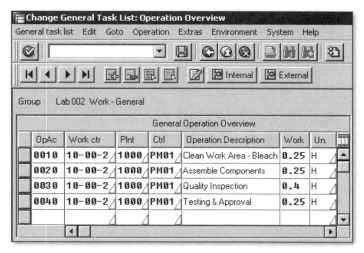

Figure 8.8 General Maintenance Task List

Equipment Task List

Maintenance of your equipment is important to your manufacturing operation. Each piece of equipment requires a task list for your maintenance staff to follow when preventive maintenance is required. The equipment task list contains a sequence of operations that are specific to a type of equipment. If your company has a number of pieces of equipment that have the same type or model, then the same task list can be used for those items.

Contains operations specific to equipment type

 Example

A metal fabrication company uses a dozen Lincoln Electric DC series multiprocess welding machines. The company uses the welders in the manufacturing of a number of finished products. The company uses the same task list for preventive maintenance for all of the DC series welders.

Figure 8.9 shows a task list for a piece of equipment. The task list shows the sequence of operations to maintain a cutting station.

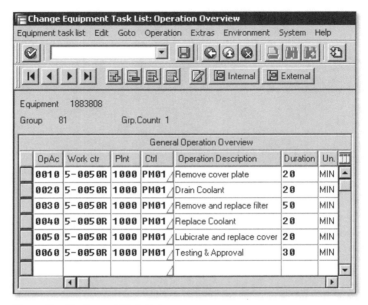

Figure 8.9 Equipment Task List

Functional Location Task List

Preventive maintenance can be performed at functional locations. At these locations, a process is performed, such as spray painting in a spray cabinet or welding in a welding shop, for which you can use a task list that contains the operations required for the preventive maintenance.

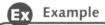 **Example**

> A beverage company has a number of storage tanks that are used to store finished product. Each of the tanks and associated pipework is defined as a functional location. The preventive maintenance plan schedules a cleaning of the tank, pipework, and the pumping equipment after every 17 cycles. The maintenance is performed by means of a task list for each functional location.

Figure 8.10 shows a task list for a functional location. The task list shows the operations that are required for periodic cleaning of a storage tank.

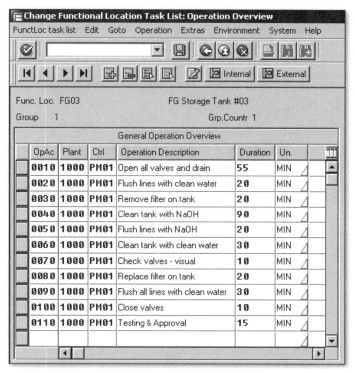

Figure 8.10 Functional Location Task List

Now that we've discussed the task lists that contain the operations used in preventive maintenance, let's consider preventive maintenance planning.

Maintenance Plans

To ensure that your shop floor equipment is operating at optimum efficiency, your plant maintenance department likely implemented a preventive maintenance program. The schedule of maintenance can be dictated by manufacturer's recommended periodic checks, requirements by local or state government, or even by environmental factors, such as the conditions that the equipment operates in.

Reducing unplanned breakdowns

Tip

Make sure that your maintenance staff works with the production staff in developing the maintenance plan. The maintenance plan should have a minimum impact on the production schedule.

 Example

The Bombardier aircraft manufacturer issues a list of recommendations when certain components of its Dash-8 aircraft need to be maintained. However, some airlines in colder climates have increased maintenance of some parts due to increased stress on those parts by the environment.

Maintenance plans based on cycles or elapsed time

A single-cycle preventive maintenance plan can be created in the SAP software for simple maintenance of technical objects where the maintenance is performed after a number of cycles, operations, or elapsed time.

 Example

Airlines that operate the Bombardier Dash-8 aircraft are recommended by the engine manufacturer, Pratt Whitney, to perform a preventive maintenance overhaul of each engine after an elapsed time of 7,000 hours.

Figure 8.11 shows a simple preventive maintenance plan, 8148, for a functional location. The maintenance plans call for the replacement of an air filter after every 1,000 hours of operation. The sequence of operations to be performed by the maintenance staff can be found in the task list attached to this maintenance plan. This maintenance plan causes maintenance orders to be created when the plan is scheduled.

You should create a preventive maintenance plan for each piece of equipment and functional location that requires maintenance. After the plans have been created, the preventive maintenance schedule can be created. We'll look at maintenance scheduling in the next section.

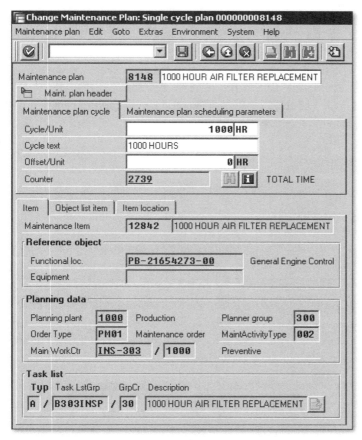

Figure 8.11 Preventive Maintenance Plan

Maintenance Scheduling

Before any scheduling can occur, the counters entered into the maintenance plans for the technical objects need to be set. This means that
the number of cycles or total hours of use should be entered into the
plan. If this doesn't occur, the scheduling functionality assumes that
the number of cycles or number of hours is zero. For this reason, it's
important when implementing the PM component that the correct
values are recorded just prior to being loaded into the SAP software.

Usage figures

Call Horizon

0% call horizon
creates immediate
maintenance call

The scheduling functionality uses a call horizon in conjunction with the counter to determine if a maintenance plan is to be scheduled. The call horizon is a percentage figure. If the call horizon is set to 100%, the plan isn't scheduled until the counter has reached the maximum number of cycles or time elapsed. The call horizon percentage can be changed depending on your plant maintenance department.

Ex | **Example**

In the maintenance plan for the replacement of an oil filter is every 40 days, the call horizon is set to 80%. The plan operates a 24/7 plant. The counter in the maintenance plan is reviewed by the scheduling functionality to determine if the maintenance plan needs to be scheduled. In this case, the scheduling will occur after 32 days instead of 40, which is the maximum allowed.

Figure 8.12 shows the Maintenance Plan 8148, to replace an air filter after 1,000 hours of operation. The Call horizon for this plan has been set at 75%. This means that the plan will be scheduled after 750 hours of operation.

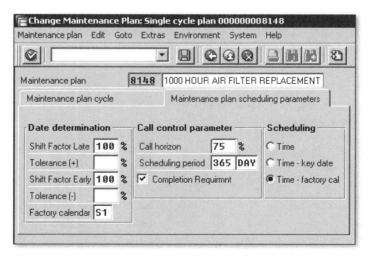

Figure 8.12 Maintenance Plan with Call Horizon Set at 75%

Scheduling the Maintenance Plan

The scheduling functionality in the SAP software can provide your maintenance department with a timetable of the maintenance that needs to be performed in a given period. The schedule includes plans that are due to be processed in a specified date range. The interval between scheduling runs can be set by the maintenance department.

Developing a maintenance schedule and plan

Figure 8.13 shows the scheduling function where the maintenance department creates the schedule for the next 10 days (Interval for Call Objects).

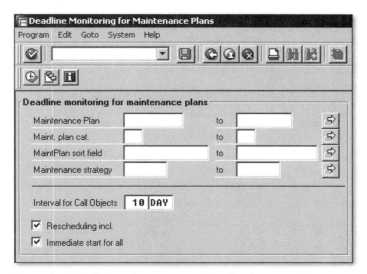

Figure 8.13 Scheduling of Maintenance Plans for the Next 10 Days

The scheduling function reviews all of the plans on the system for those that are due to be worked on based on the interval entered. The resulting maintenance schedule is then available for your maintenance staff to review before any maintenance orders are created.

It's best to review the resulting maintenance schedule because the maintenance department may not have enough capacity to complete the preventive maintenance in the time allocated. The scheduling function allows simulation of the maintenance plans, which allows your staff to amend the start dates of the planned maintenance as required.

Simulate maintenance schedule to show capacity

Ex **Example**

A maintenance department schedules the preventive maintenance for a normal workweek. The resulting schedule is reviewed and illustrates that there are four maintenance plans that use the same resources all on the same days. The maintenance staff then reviews the four maintenance plans to determine the priority in which they should be scheduled.

Figure 8.14 illustrates a simulated maintenance plan schedule. The schedule shows that a number of plans are due to commence on the same day, which may mean that capacity or resources are an issue.

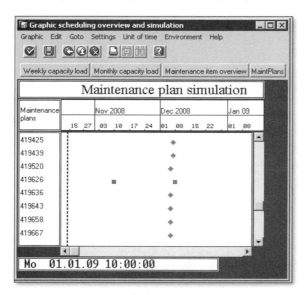

Figure 8.14 Simulation of a Maintenance Plan Schedule

After the maintenance department has scheduled the plans based on capacity, then the maintenance plans can be released and maintenance orders created, which will be discussed in the next section.

In this section, you've seen how to create a preventive maintenance schedule for the technical objects at your company's location. In the next section, we'll look at how the maintenance plans are processed as maintenance notifications and maintenance orders, along with unplanned maintenance that occurs periodically.

Maintenance Processing

In this section, we'll examine the functionality that is used to perform maintenance on the technical objects at your plant. The two functions we'll look at are the maintenance notification and the maintenance order.

Maintenance processed through notifications or orders

Maintenance Notifications

Maintenance notifications are used when there is a malfunction with a technical object. If one of your drilling station operators finds a problem with a drill, the operator reports the issue with a maintenance notification.

Report problems, request maintenance, or document activity

 Tip

Production staff should be trained to notify maintenance as soon as an issue is found with equipment on the shop floor. Failure to create a notification quickly can lead to a breakdown and production delays.

A notification can also be created when there is a requirement for maintenance without a malfunction being reported, for example, if an operator requires a new dust cover for a drill station.

 Example

In the warehouse of a beverage company, each warehouse area has a computer and label printer. The computer keyboard is covered with a silicone protective cover to keep out dust. An operator noticed a tear in the cover and created a maintenance notification for a replacement, although the issue was not an actual malfunction.

Figure 8.15 shows the creation of a maintenance notification due to a malfunction. In this notification, the operator requires a torque wrench to be recalibrated by maintenance personnel. The maintenance department creates a maintenance order to perform the work.

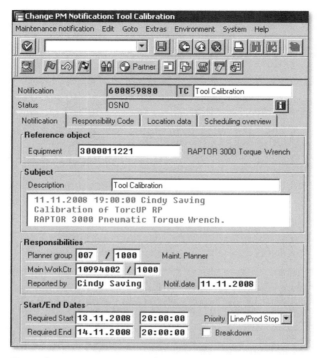

Figure 8.15 Maintenance Notification

Company-specific policies on maintenance notifications and orders

The maintenance notification can also be used as an activity report on the maintenance activity that has been performed to maintain a technical object, which could be from a scheduled maintenance plan or a miscellaneous maintenance item that didn't require a maintenance notification. Your plant maintenance personnel will have policies in place that help determine the requirements for maintenance notifications and orders.

Ex **Example**

A manufacturing company has a Maxisaw MX370FA cold saw on the shop floor. It has a four-gallon coolant tank that requires periodic checks to ensure that the coolant level is above minimum. Instead of creating a maintenance plan, the maintenance department checks the coolant tank when attending to other equipment close by. If the coolant requires adjustment, the maintenance staff members enter their activity into a maintenance notification.

Figure 8.16 shows the entry of a maintenance activity for a printer dust cover that did not require a maintenance order.

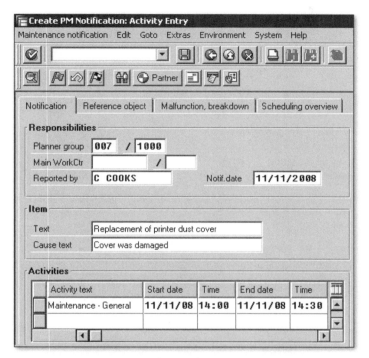

Figure 8.16 Maintenance Notification for Maintenance Activity

Now that we've examined maintenance notifications, you need to see how these notifications can be converted into maintenance orders.

Converting Notifications to Maintenance Orders

A maintenance notification created due to a malfunction of a technical object or for unplanned maintenance has to be converted to a maintenance order to ensure that the maintenance work can be planned, assigned, and executed.

Converting notifications to orders or assigning to an existing order

The maintenance order can be created directly from the notification, or it can be created in the background.

Figure 8.17 shows the creation of a maintenance order from the no-tification 10006919. The information from the notification is trans-ferred to the order.

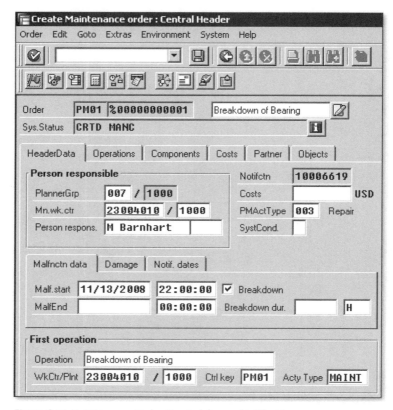

Figure 8.17 Maintenance Order Created from a Notification

Maintenance Orders

Creating maintenance orders without notifications

The maintenance order contains the details by which a maintenance task can be performed. The maintenance order can be created from a notification, from a preventive maintenance plan, or directly.

The maintenance order contains details of the tasks to be performed, including the dates, resources, and scope. The order also contains all of the financial details needed for account assignment and settlement of the costs involved with performing the tasks in the order.

Availability Checks

After the order has been created, a check is performed to ensure that any materials needed for the maintenance to be performed are in stock. If not, a purchase order (PO) is created for the missing items. If the materials are in stock, and the tools are available, the order can be released for processing.

Maintenance orders processed only after release

 Example

> A maintenance order is created to repair a Maxisaw MX370FA cold saw. The parts needed included an overload protection switch for the coolant pump. This part wasn't in stock, and a PO was placed with Maxisaw for the spare part. The maintenance order could not be released until the part was received at the plant.

Scheduling

After the maintenance order has been released, it should be scheduled. The scheduling functionality reviews the basic dates that were entered in the maintenance order and uses the scheduling type assigned, which is normally forward or backward scheduling. Based on the available capacity of the resources required for the order and the availability of the materials needed, the start and finish dates for the order are calculated.

Forward or backward scheduling

 Example

> A maintenance order was created to replace a broken bearing guide on a band saw. The date the order was to start was December 4th, but the spare parts had to be purchased from the manufacturer. Therefore, the scheduling function calculates that the order won't commence until the parts arrive at the plant, which is scheduled for December 11th.

Completing the Order

After the spare parts arrive at your plant, and your maintenance staff performs the tasks assigned in the order, the order is then complete.

Flagged complete only if all tasks are completed

The completion confirmation process allows your maintenance staff members to enter all of the information that is relevant to the work they performed. There are a number of entries that your staff should make:

> Enter total time spent on maintenance order.

> Enter material used, including unplanned material.

> Enter measurements and counter readings.

> Enter technical data, including cause of malfunction, location of any damage, and testing information.

Figure 8.18 shows the completion confirmation entered for maintenance order 11000700. The actual number of hours spent on the order (Actual Work) was 7 hours. A description has been entered regarding the cause of the malfunction.

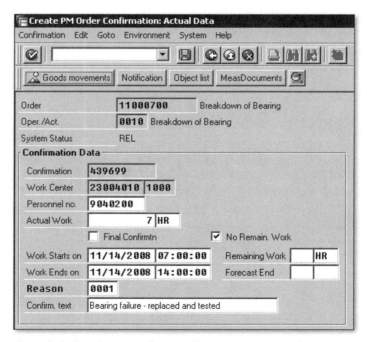

Figure 8.18 Completion Confirmation for a Maintenance Order

Subsequent to the time and materials having been entered for the maintenance order, the final costing of the order can be calculated.

 Case Study

An American manufacturer of hand tools for the automotive industry was operating on an in-house software system that did not include PM. The system used by the maintenance department was a standalone PC package purchased eight years ago. The maintenance software wasn't interfaced with the in-house software and contained its own inventory levels for items that the maintenance department frequently used.

A preventive maintenance plan was implemented where the maintenance personnel inspected the equipment on the shop floor on a periodic basis. However, the software didn't allow for equipment cycles to be entered and ran the preventive maintenance with elapsed time as the driver.

Over the period that the software was in place, the maintenance department had to deal with a number of issues. The primary concern was that the equipment was failing due to infrequent maintenance. This was primarily due to equipment being checked at the time suggested by the software, which was often weeks after the number of maximum number of cycles between maintenance checks had been exceeded. Despite constant modification of data on the software system, the preventive maintenance plan was only checking 65% of the equipment prior to it exceeding the recommended time between maintenance.

When the company was then purchased, the new owners wanted to bring the new acquisition onto an SAP software instance already in operation. The plant maintenance department lobbied to be the first phase of conversion but had to wait over a year before it was converted to the SAP software. In the year waiting to move from the legacy system, the plant maintenance department recorded 412 breakdowns of equipment on the shop floor with more than 60 occurrences of the line being stopped due to equipment failure. After the SAP system was implemented for PM, an improved preventive maintenance plan was developed. In the six months following implementation, there were only 52 breakdowns, and only 3 resulted in line stoppages.

In this section, you've seen how the maintenance order is used to perform the maintenance work that has been identified in the notification or via the preventive maintenance plan.

Summary

This chapter provided an overview of the SAP PM functionality. Although each plant maintenance department has some uniqueness, the functionality of the maintenance notification and maintenance order will ensure that your maintenance department works as efficiently as possible. Preventive maintenance is extremely important in any company because it's key to reducing costs. Keeping your equipment running at optimum efficiency and reducing downtime due to breakdown saves money, helps ensure that customer deliveries are on time, and keeps customer satisfaction high.

In this chapter, we've thoroughly examined the SAP PM functionality. Here are some key points to remember:

> The maintenance structure gives your company the flexibility to create equipment and three variations of functional locations: spatial, process-related, and function-based.

> Preventive maintenance is vital to keeping equipment operating; it reduces breakdowns and optimizes production capacity.

> Operating on a maintenance plan provides the best use of resources, and integration with production ensures no loss of capacity.

> Notifications are key to informing the plant maintenance department of equipment issues on the shop floor.

> Maintenance orders collect the costs of maintenance to equipment, which is vital in considering major equipment overhauls or replacement.

In the next chapter, we'll follow with an examination of the SAP functionality that is used in quality management. Quality plays an ever-increasing role in the supply chain, and SAP provides your quality function with the tools to provide a world-class quality operation. We'll examine the planning function, as well as quality notifications and inspections.

9

Quality Management

Quality management (QM) is an integral part of the logistics function and in SAP it's fully integrated with complementary components, including materials management (MM), plant maintenance (PM), production planning (PP), customer service (CS), and SAP Transportation Management (SAP TM). QM is important to the inventory staff, inspecting incoming material as it arrives, and for manufacturing operations where quality of in-process items are checked during manufacturing process, and finished goods are inspected before they reach the warehouse. Figure 9.1 shows the integration points between QM and other SAP components.

The SAP QM component covers the three areas of planning, notifications, and inspections. The quality planning function allows your quality department to plan inspections for goods receipts from vendors and production, work in process, and stock transfers. A quality notification can be used to request action be taken by the quality department. This may be to review an internal problem, an issue with items from a vendor, or a customer complaint. The quality inspection is the physical inspection using specifications defined in quality planning.

Quality maintenance

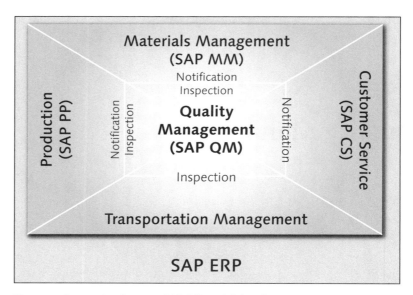

Figure 9.1 Integration Between SAP QM and Other Components

The QM component is an integral part of the wider logistics function. Production planning (PP), SAP Transportation Management (SAP TM), and materials management (MM) are fully integrated with SAP QM. It's possible for each material that your company uses to be relevant for QM. This allows materials that are sent from a vendor to be subject to quality inspection when they arrive at your facility.

Quality inspections can also be a part of the SAP production process. In a production order, an operation can be specified as a quality inspection, where in-process material is checked against specific requirements. If the material passes the inspection, then it continues to the next operation.

QM is also integrated with the SAP TM function. A quality inspection can be performed on finished products that are part of a delivery before leaving the facility to the customer. In addition, the customer service department can create a notification for quality issues reported by customers.

This chapter will help you understand the increasing importance of QM in the supply chain and how it is highly integrated with SAP logistics functions. In the first section, we'll look at the structures that are used in QM, including the inspection characteristic, inspection method, and catalog.

Quality Management Structure

In the SAP QM component, you need to understand a number of master data records before we examine other quality functionality. These include catalogs, inspection characteristics, and inspection methods. So, let's start with the catalog.

Master data

Catalog

A *catalog* is used to describe defect items, tasks, and activities in quality notifications. A number of catalogs are predefined in the SAP software, but your company can define its own when necessary. For example, SAP predefined catalogs include Activities, Defect Types, Tasks, and Defect Locations. Each catalog can contain code groups, which in turn contain codes.

Managing quality information

Code Groups

A *code group* contains a number of codes, which are related in some fashion. For example, a code group called Paint Finishes might include codes such as satin, eggshell, gloss, semi-gloss, and flat.

Related codes

Code

A *code* is a descriptive item that combined with other codes is assigned to a code group. For example, in the code group Metal Finishes, the codes might include chrome, brushed nickel, and bronze.

Lowest level of the catalog

 Example

> A predefined SAP catalog, Defect Locations, has a code group called QM Defect Locations. The code group has a number of codes assigned to it that describe the location. These include organization, purchasing, and contract.

Figure 9.2 shows the Defect Locations catalog, Code Group, and the associated Codes.

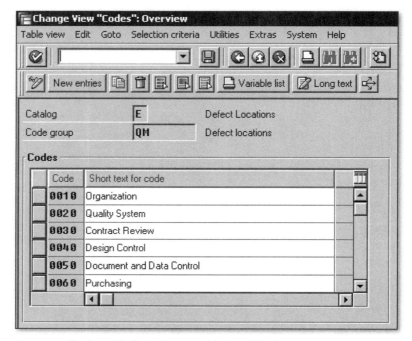

Figure 9.2 Catalog with Code Group and Assigned Codes

Selected Set

Selected set

Selected set is used at a plant to include a number of codes that can be assigned from different code groups. A selected set is useful because it can select a small number of codes from a code group, if the code group has a large number of codes that aren't needed.

 **Example**

> The Paint Color code group has 70 codes assigned, but at plant 1000, they only use 5 of those codes. So at plant 1000, a selected set is created to just contain those 5 codes.

Figure 9.3 shows a selected set for Plant 1000, which contains codes from two Code Groups: QM and QMS-ISO.

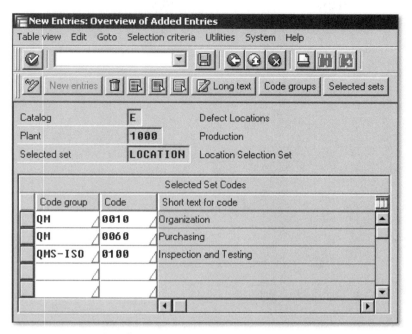

Figure 9.3 Selected Set for Plant 1000

Inspection Characteristic

The inspection characteristic can be used in quality inspection plans to describe a characteristic of the item that is being inspected as part of a quality inspection.

Inspection characteristic

 Example

An inspection characteristic, RCC-C01, is created to describe the color characteristic of a material when it's inspected by the quality department.

Figure 9.4 shows an inspection characteristic for the color code of items when they are inspected.

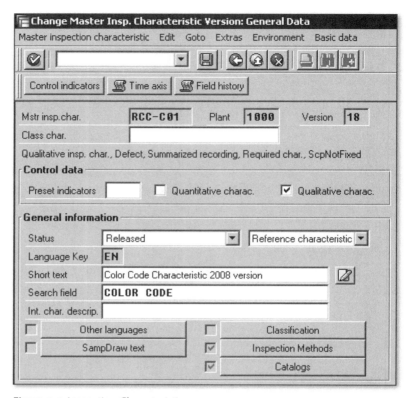

Figure 9.4 Inspection Characteristic

Now that we've looked at the basic data elements used in QM, let's move on to examine the planning function in QM.

Quality Planning

The quality inspection plans define how an item is to be inspected. The plan also determines how the inspection is to take place, the item characteristics to be inspected, and all of the required test equipment relevant to the inspection. The two main concepts we'll discuss in this section are the role of the material specification and the inspection plan.

Material Specification

Inspections of an item can be performed using two techniques, inspection plans or material specifications. Your quality department will decide on the preferred method. The advantage material specifications have over inspection plans is that material specifications are valid for the item across the company, while inspection plans are plant-specific. If your company approaches quality differently from plant to plant, then inspection plans may be more suitable for your company.

Companywide material specifications

 Tip

To ensure that your materials are inspected correctly, make sure the material specification includes all of the relevant inspection characteristics.

The material specification contains a number of inspection characteristics that have been assigned. For example, Figure 9.3 shows the inspection characteristic RCC-C01 for color. That characteristic can be added to a material specification.

 Example

A purchase order was made for a 55-gallon drum of flame retardant epoxy resin. When the drum arrives from the vendor, it is visually checked at the receiving dock for any signs of external damage.

After the visual check, a quality inspection is performed. The epoxy resin has a material specification with a number of characteristics that are used to check whether the item passes quality inspection. The inspection checks the viscosity, specific gravity, and cure shrinkage. While these quality tests are performed, the drum of resin remains in a quality inspection status.

Figure 9.5 shows a storage tank that has a material specification assigned to be used in quality inspection. The material specification has three characteristics that can be checked each time the item arrives at the plant. Because the three are all visual checks, no testing or inspection equipment is required.

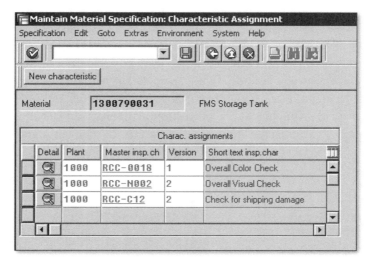

Figure 9.5 Material Specification

Inspection Plan

Inspection plans describe how a quality inspection should be performed. You can use an inspection plan to define which characteristics are to be inspected in each operation and what test equipment is to be used in the inspection process.

Ex **Example**

> An inspection plan used for inspecting the process material includes operations such as visual checks and measurement checks.

Figure 9.6 shows an inspection plan that contains a number of operations to be completed as part of the inspection.

Work centers and tools

The operations describe each stop of the plan. Your quality staff can define work centers where the inspections are performed and the sequence in which they are to be performed. If a tool should be used for the inspection at one specific operation, that can be added to the operation as well.

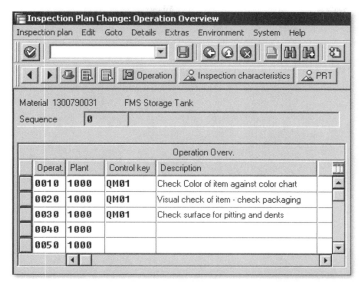

Figure 9.6 Inspection Plan

Inspection characteristics can be assigned to the operation. A *characteristic* may be a quality test on a chemical, such as viscosity or pH value, or be a physical test such as checking the color or checking that the serial number is visible. Inspection characteristics give more definition to the quality operation, so the more inspection characteristics an operation has, the more accurate the inspection will be. For example, if an inspection calls for a quality check with only one characteristic, viscosity, this isn't as accurate as an inspection with the three characteristics of viscosity, density and tensile strength.

 Tip

When purchased material arrives from a vendor, the inspection needs to include all operations that are required to make a quality usage decision.

Figure 9.7 shows the inspection characteristics assigned to the inspection plan operation. The quality inspection team reports against these characteristics when inspecting an item.

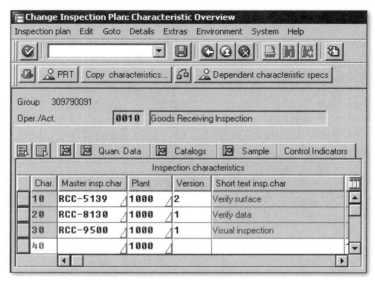

Figure 9.7 Inspection Characteristics for an Inspection Plan Operation

Now that we've looked at the planning of quality inspections with respect to the inspection plan and the material specification, let's move on to review the functionality of the quality notification.

Quality Notifications

Internal or external quality issues

The quality notification records a quality problem that is either instigated by a customer against one of your products or by your company against the product of a supplier. A notification can also be raised internally at your company to report a quality issue. You can assign a quality notification to an existing QM order to create a new order for the specific notification.

Customer Complaint

Quality notification

Periodically, all companies receive complaints from customers about products. Each of these complaints needs to be investigated to determine whether or not it's a quality issue. After that issue is determined, a quality notification can be created to review the customer's complaint.

Tip

If you receive a notification of a quality issue from a customer, you should make this a top priority to resolve. Keeping customer satisfaction high is a competitive advantage.

Ex **Example**

A customer calls a customer service department to report that 90% of the last delivery of automotive exhaust systems was damaged. This was only found when the packaging material was unpacked, which suggested that the damage was caused in production or warehousing. To investigate the customer complaint, a quality notification is created.

Figure 9.8 shows a quality notification for a customer complaint. The complaint was raised because a product failed to pass the customer's inspection process at goods receipt.

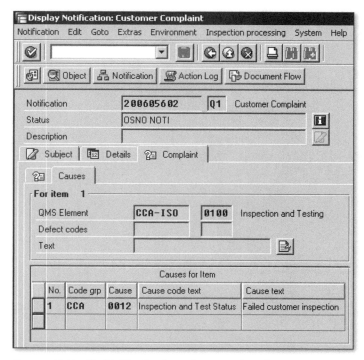

Figure 9.8 Quality Notification for a Customer Complaint

Complaint Against a Vendor

Damaged items from suppliers

There are occasions when a supplier sends your company items that are damaged, items that fail goods receipt inspection, or items that fail during use in the manufacturing process. In these cases, you can create a quality notification that relates to a complaint against a vendor.

Case Study

At the receiving dock, items get a visual check as they're received from the trailer. One of the receivers notices damaged packaging and removes the packaging to find a damaged item. More items are removed from the trailer showing the same damage. The receiving staff then calls the quality department to inform them of the issue. Because of this, a quality notification is created to investigate the issue further with the vendor.

Figure 9.9 shows a quality notification for a complaint against a vendor. In this case, 8 out of the 10 received items are damaged, as shown in the Subject Long Text field.

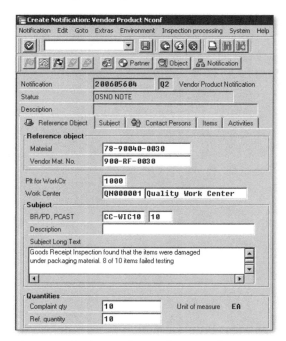

Figure 9.9 Quality Notification for a Complaint Against a Vendor

Internal Problem Report

When quality issues arise either in the manufacturing process or when items are in the warehouse, a quality notification can be created. This internal problem report should identify the items that need inspection and the issues that should be checked.

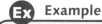 **Internal problems**

Ex Example

In a manufacturing plant, items are received into the warehouse from the production line. At the final assembly work center, items are visually checked. In one batch of items, an operator finds some color issues and creates a quality notification due to the problems found.

Figure 9.10 shows a quality notification for an internal problem. In this instance, the items have two defects shown in the Text column: Missing Holes and Paint Color Issue.

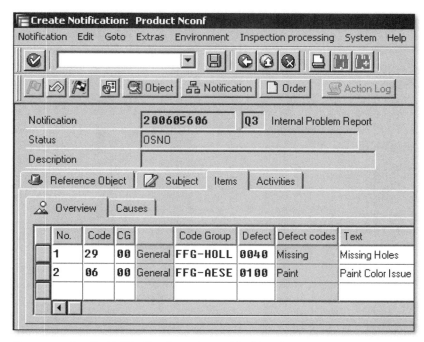

Figure 9.10 Quality Notification for an Internal Problem Report

Notification Monitoring

Standard reports   A number of standard reports can be viewed by the quality department to monitor the status of the notifications. The reports include monitoring of the different types of quality notifications.

Figure 9.11 shows the report for the quality notifications based on internal problem reports. The report shows the Completed, Processed, and Outstanding notifications for each material. This report can be run for a specific date range.

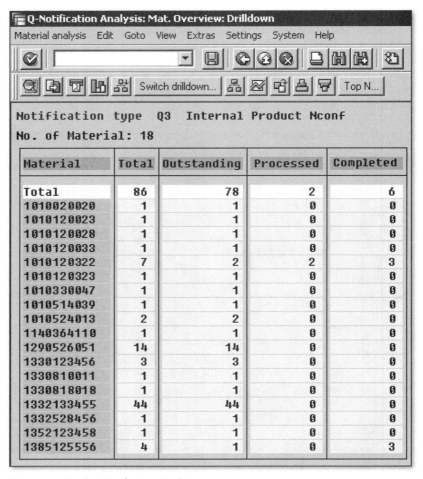

Material	Total	Outstanding	Processed	Completed
Total	86	78	2	6
1010020020	1	1	0	0
1010120023	1	1	0	0
1010120028	1	1	0	0
1010120033	1	1	0	0
1010120322	7	2	2	3
1010120323	1	1	0	0
1010330047	1	1	0	0
1010514039	1	1	0	0
1010524013	2	2	0	0
1140364110	1	1	0	0
1290526051	14	14	0	0
1330123456	3	3	0	0
1330810011	1	1	0	0
1330818018	1	1	0	0
1332133455	44	44	0	0
1332528456	1	1	0	0
1352123458	1	1	0	0
1385125556	4	1	0	3

Figure 9.11 Quality Notification Analysis

Case Study

A Dutch chemical company that manufactured a number of paper-making products had been using a variety of quality systems to track testing in the production process and for the receipt of raw materials from suppliers.

The company manufactured chemicals only to a customer's specification. The product was inspected only for the tests required by the customer. If the product failed inspection, it was reworked, stored, or scrapped.

The company was purchased by a large European petrochemical company and was tasked with producing finished goods that could be sold to any number of customers rather than one specific customer.

The company developed a number of products that incorporated its customer's products but found that customer complaints increased. A consulting company was brought in to review the quality process and offer recommendations.

The consultants identified a number of areas of concern. They found that the quality department had not developed sufficient testing plans for the products. This led to the product being only partially tested in production and insufficient testing carried out when the finished good was received in the warehouse. In addition, there was no testing of the product prior to delivery to the customer, and often the product was already out of tolerance for some customers by the time it shipped.

The consultants also raised concerns about the inability for quality systems to interface with each other and the company's production and warehousing systems.

The parent company was using SAP software at other companies but had not scheduled an implementation for this company for another year. To ensure that the quality department would be successful in the interim, the parent company introduced a number of changes in the process that mirrored the best practices used in the SAP QM component.

In this section, we've looked at the different types of quality notifications that your quality department can issue. In the next section, we'll examine quality inspections.

Quality Inspections

Quality department inspections

An inspection is a snapshot of the quality of an item at one specific moment in time. A *quality inspection* occurs when members of the quality department inspect items as determined by the inspection planning functionality.

An inspection is based on one or more inspection lots. A *lot* is a request to inspect a specific item or a quantity of that item.

Inspection Lot

Inspection lot function

The inspection lot function allows an inspection of your company's product or a specific quantity of that product. The product can be a finished product or a raw material. You can also create inspection lots for technical objects.

Inspection lots can be created manually or be created automatically by the SAP system. A number of events can trigger an automatic inspection lot.

Most inspection lots are automatically triggered by either a goods receipt or a goods issue. But other events, such as the creation or release of a production order, the creation of deliveries, or a stock transfer, can trigger an inspection lot.

Ex Example

A company's primary vendor for raw materials closes, so the company needs to find a replacement. They decide to assess three new vendors. The quality department checks all incoming deliveries from the three vendors. To ensure that all material was checked, the quality department has inspection lots automatically created each time a goods receipt from any of the three vendors is processed.

Creating inspection lots

Inspection lots can also be created manually. If your quality department doesn't trigger the creation of inspection lots from certain events, it will be necessary to manually create them.

Ex Example

A company overhauls its production line and installs new equipment. The quality department is involved in the overhaul and is confident that the finished products will pass customer inspections. To check their assumptions, the quality department manually creates inspection lots for the product as it leaves the end of the production line.

Figure 9.12 shows the manual creation of an inspection lot for a goods receipt from Vendor 1610. The inspection lot has an assigned specification.

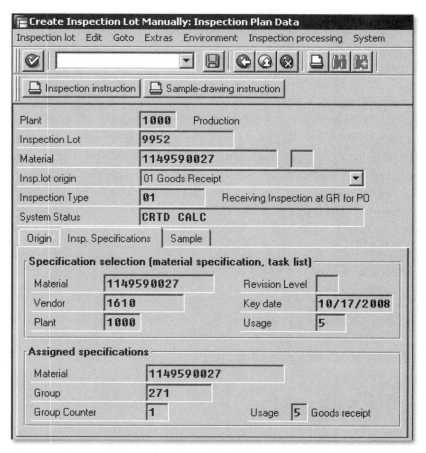

Figure 9.12 Manual Creation of an Inspection Lot

Assignment of an Inspection Specification

Inspection specifications

Inspection specifications can manually or automatically be assigned to an inspection lot. A specification can be a material specification or a task list.

It's important to assign a specification because it can record the inspection that takes place. If no specification is assigned, then the inspection lot can only record the defect that occurred.

In the case of the automatically assigned specification to an inspection lot, this can only take place for a material with only one specification. If the material has more than one specification, it becomes a manual selection for quality personnel to make.

Figure 9.12 shows the Inspection Lot 9952 with a specification assigned to it.

Sample Size

Quantity of the lot for inspection

After the inspection specification has been assigned to the inspection lot, the system calculates the correct sample size. The item that will be inspected may have information on its master record that is used by the system to calculate the correct sample size. For example, on the material master file, the quality department can enter information that allows them to enter a manual sample size in the inspection lot.

The resource that is inspecting the item can amend the sample size with the actual quantity that was sampled as part of the inspection.

Figure 9.13 shows the sample size for Inspection Lot 9952. The inspection lot size (Insp. Lot Qty) is 40 items, but the actual quantity sampled (Actual Lot qty) was manually reduced to 36. This may be due to some items not being available to be inspected.

Now that we've looked at how an inspection lot is created and the information that it contains, let's examine how the results of the inspection are recorded.

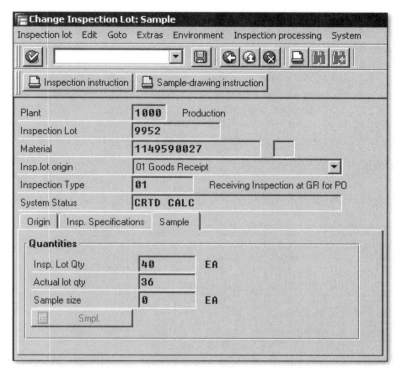

Figure 9.13 Sample Size for the Inspection Lot

Recording Results

When the inspection takes place, you need to record the results for each of the inspection characteristics. When the inspection lot is being processed by your staff, they will inspect the item's one characteristic. After the inspection of each characteristic, they will enter the results into the inspection lot. This is completed for each of the characteristics in the inspection lot.

Results are recorded

You can enter the results for each inspected item or for the items as a whole. If your staff enters the results for the whole inspection lot, they will indicate how many items of the lot were approved or rejected.

Ex **Example**

An inspection lot for 10 exhaust systems need to be inspected for a number of characteristics, including surface finish, dents, scratches, and weight. The quality department has required that the items need to be tested individually, but the results should be entered as a summary. The results recorded indicate the number of exhaust systems that are approved and those that are rejected out of the lot of 10.

Figure 9.14 shows a recorded result for a number of characteristics for an inspection lot. In this example, only three of the four characteristics were tested, but at each test, the items were approved.

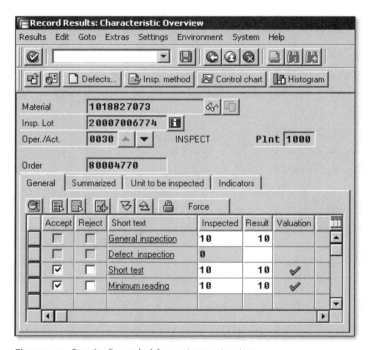

Figure 9.14 Results Recorded for an Inspection Lot

Digital Signature

Digital signatures can be used for recording the results of an inspection lot as well as confirming a usage decision, which we'll examine later in this section.

If your company is used to using digital signatures or if this is something you want to consider, SAP software provides a digital signature tool for approvals.

More than results can be recorded, and in this next section, we'll look at reporting defects found during an inspection of materials.

Defects Recording

Characteristics can be given as a value or recorded as a defect. A defect is recorded when an item does not meet the specifications in the inspection lot. Then, you can create a quality notification when a defect is recorded in the inspection lot.

Characteristics results

 Example

The quality department inspects an inspection lot for 10 items received from production. The items fail a visual inspection characteristic, and because no value could be recorded, the result gets recorded as a defect.

Figure 9.15 shows two characteristics for an inspection lot. The items in the inspection lot have failed both characteristics and caused a defect to be recorded for both.

Figure 9.15 Defects Recording for an Inspection Lot

229

When any defects have been entered for an inspection lot, and the lot is then processed, a usage decision may have to be made on the inspection lot. In the next section, we'll look at the usage decision.

Usage Decision

Accepting or rejecting a material

After the inspections have been completed for the inspection lot, a usage decision can be made as to whether the material can be accepted or rejected. After the quality department has made a usage decision, the inspection is technically closed. After the usage decision has been made, it can't be reversed.

Figure 9.16 shows the Usage Decision for item 595907720. The inspection has been completed, and the usage decision has been made to reject the lot and send the items back to the vendor.

Figure 9.16 Usage Decision for an Inspection Lot

Example

> Let's say that 20 items from a vendor are received. In this case, the staff
> on the receiving dock creates a quality notification, which forms the basis
> of the inspection lot. At the end of the inspection, the quality resource
> indicates that the usage decision concludes that the items aren't accept-
> able, and they should be sent back to the vendor. When the usage deci-
> sion is entered, the inspection lot is closed.

Now let's examine a subject that may relate to your industry—the use
of quality certificates.

Quality Certificates

Some industries and companies use quality certificates to certify the
quality of the items. The certification may indicate some physical or
chemical properties that are required by your customer when you are
shipping products or by your company for incoming deliveries.

Certifying specific properties

Incoming Certificates

Your company may require quality certificates for certain items you
purchase, such as chemicals that are required to be within certain values. The quality certificate can be sent with the product or in advance.

The quality certificate should show the range that the characteristics
should fall within and the actual value that was recorded.

 Example

> A company purchases 55-gallon drums of Pigmented Acrylic Lacquer
> from a supplier. The company requires the lacquer to have certain charac-
> teristics and requires that a quality certificate accompany the shipment.
> The certificate has to show that the test results on the batch of lacquer in
> the drum are within the specified tolerances.

Figure 9.17 shows an example of a quality certificate for a 55-gallon
drum of etching lubricant. The material has a number of characteristics that were tested, and the results are on the quality certificate.

Figure 9.17 Quality Certificate for Incoming Delivery

Outgoing Certificates

If your company manufactures items that require quality certifications, the SAP system provides a range of options to ensure compliance. An outgoing certificate can be created for an inspection lot, delivery, or batch.

The certificate can be printed and sent with the items in the delivery or electronically sent ahead of time.

Tip

If your customer requires a quality certificate for the materials you ship, ensure that the certificate is sent ahead of time or sent with the shipment. If the certificate isn't sent, the customer may reject the shipment, which may reduce customer satisfaction.

Now that we've reviewed the need for quality certificates, both inbound and outbound deliveries, we'll move on to examine reporting that can be found in the QM component.

Reporting

A variety of standard reports in the SAP software can be used by your quality department to monitor trends in notifications, lots, and defects.

Quality management reports

The reports are based on information that is directly collected from the quality transactions that are performed each day.

Material Defect Report

Material that fails inspection can be from a vendor or produced internally. One key report that should be of interest to your quality department is the material defects report. This can be executed for any time period. The report shows the number of times this item has been in defect.

Fails inspection

 Example

The quality department reviews the defects report each month to track what items are frequently failing. The failed materials that are above a certain standard deviation are subject to increased inspections.

Figure 9.18 shows a standard defects report. The report was pulled for the previous six-month period and shows all items that had more than 50 failed inspections over that period.

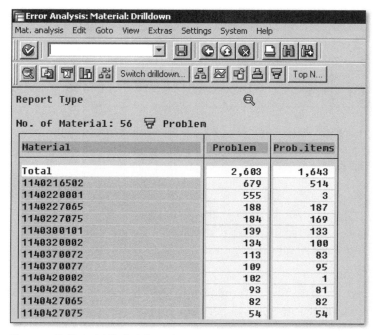

Figure 9.18 Material Defect Report

Vendor Defect Report

Defective material from vendors

Instead of reporting on the materials that were defective, the reports can also show the frequency of failed material by vendor, which can inevitably affect your production schedule. By looking at inspection lots for goods receipts, your quality department can pinpoint vendors who are supplying goods that frequently fail inspection.

Monitoring of these figures can help your company work with vendors to improve the quality of material. If the material your company receives improves, this will help with the availability of material for your production schedule and ultimately the delivery time to your customer.

Figure 9.19 shows the defect report of material by vendor. The report shows the number of defects per vendor over the past six months. The top 10 vendors with the largest number of defects are shown.

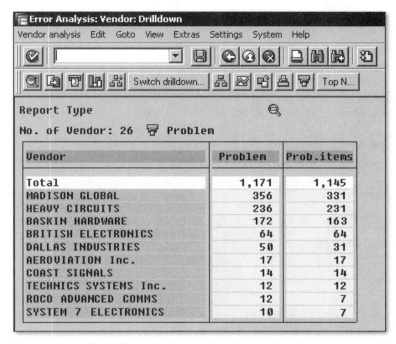

Figure 9.19 Vendor Defect Report

Customer Defect Report

The customer defect report is very important with regard to customer satisfaction. This shows the defects that were found on inspections for outbound deliveries. This is extremely important to monitor because it not only shows what materials are failing inspection but also to which customers. An outbound delivery that fails an inspection will probably be delayed. This creates a domino effect because if the shipment is delayed, you have failed to provide on-time delivery, which erodes customer satisfaction.

Customer satisfaction

Figure 9.20 shows a customer defect report for the previous 12 months. There have only been 6 customers whose deliveries have failed inspection.

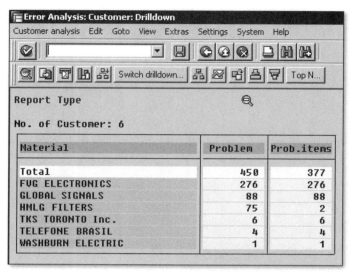

Figure 9.20 Customer Defect Report

A number of standard reports can be used to review the QM function. Your quality department members should review the available reporting in the SAP software to ensure that they can successfully monitor all aspects of quality within your company.

Summary

As you've seen in this chapter, the SAP QM component is a vital part of your company's logistics function. It's fully integrated with other SAP components such as MM, PP, and SAP TM.

There are a number of key things to remember from this chapter.

> Quality planning is important because it determines how an item is to be tested. If an item isn't correctly tested, the item may either fail inspection when it's perfectly acceptable to the customer, or it may pass inspection when the incorrect tests have been performed on it. This leads to probable rejection by the customer and customer dissatisfaction.

> Quality notifications are useful to the quality department because they give customers and other areas of the company an opportunity to indicate when a quality issue has occurred. Although notifications of a quality issue from a customer are unfortunate, they can help to identify a problem with production, warehousing, shipping, transportation, or perhaps even with the way in which the product is tested. Notifications from within the company greatly help the quality department because the problem has not yet reached a customer.

> The inspection process is the key to the success of the QM function. Inspections must be accurate to ensure that the correct usage decision is made, and the items sent to the customer are within the specifications required.

In the next chapter, we'll look at the sales order management function, including sales orders, shipping, and billing.

PART III
Sales and Service

10

Sales Order Management

The SAP sales and distribution (SD) component is the part of logistics that provides functionality to supports your customers. This includes providing quotations to your customers, receiving sales orders, shipping finished goods, and billing the customer. SD is highly integrated with the finance (FI), costing (CO), materials management (MM), and production planning functions.

Figure 10.1 shows the integration points between the SD component and other SAP components.

The SAP sales structure is flexible so that you can create the organization you require to have an efficient sales force. Your company's sales structure is likely to change as it reacts to the market.

The ordering functionality in the SAP software allows your sales team to react to customer requirements, such as inquiries. Customers expect a prompt reply to their requests, and the SAP functionality provides the ability to quickly respond, giving your company a competitive advantage.

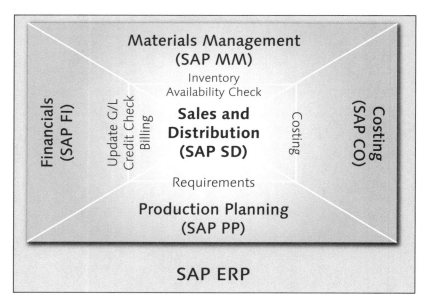

Figure 10.1 Integration Between SAP SD and Other Components

The SAP shipping process is integrated with the SAP Transportation Management (SAP TM) function. It has the functionality to provide accurate, on-time deliveries to customers in a cost-effective manner.

The final section in this chapter looks at the SAP billing process. It's important to ensure customer's orders are delivered on time, but it's equally as important to ensure your company receives payment within the time specified. The SAP accounts receivable functionality provides the processes that will assist your staff in obtaining timely customer payments.

In this chapter, we'll initially look at the components that you can find in the sales structure and then follow up with an examination of the ordering process, shipping, and finally the billing process.

Sales Structure

Every company that sells products or services to customers has a sales structure that should be designed to provide maximum benefit to the customer at the lowest cost. The organizational structure in the sales component provides your company with the ability to do just that.

Levels of the sales structure

Let's look at the elements that go into making up the sales structure, starting with the highest level of the structure, the sales organization.

Sales Organization

The sales organization is the highest level of the sales structure. On the financial side, a sales organization is a legal entity and assigned to one company code, so the accounting for the sales organization isn't dispersed across various companies.

Legal entities

On the logistics side, a sales organization can sell products for more than one plant, and a plant can have more than one sales organization selling its products.

Depending on the structure of your company, you may only have one sales organization defined. Some companies have many sales organizations.

One or many sales organizations

 Example

A North American company has three plants: Dallas, San Diego, and Atlanta. The company has three sales organizations in the United States: Eastern, Central, and Western. However, the sales organizations aren't limited to sell products from the plants in their region. The Central sales organization sells products from the Dallas and San Diego plants, whereas the Eastern sales organization sells products from Atlanta and Dallas. The Western sales organization only sells products from the San Diego plant.

Figure 10.2 shows sales organizations that are assigned to company codes. In this example, each company is assigned to one company code.

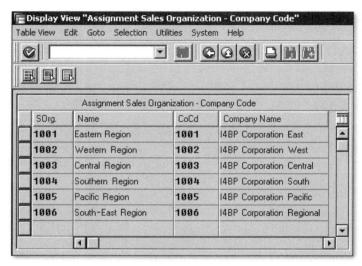

Figure 10.2 Sales Organizations Assigned to Company Codes

Now, let's move on to the importance of distribution channels that are created for each sales organization.

Distribution Channel

Distribution channels get products to the right customers

Distribution channels are important to your company's sales function because they focus your sales force on getting the right products to the right customers at the right price. The choice of distribution channels depends on the products you manufacture or services you sell. If you are a company that manufactures parts for other companies, you may have distribution channels that are simply for direct sales, wholesalers, and distributors. This may be completely different if you are a retailer. Your channels may distinguish among discount stores, direct mail, Internet, chain stores, and department stores.

 Tip

> The sales organization is a flexible entity that needs to change as the market changes, so remember that the initial distribution channels and divisions you decide upon will most likely change over time.

A good distribution channel strategy will help your company increase sales, improve sales and marketing coverage, and reduce your costs across the sales function.

Ex Example

A small firm that manufactured specialty cat food was purchased by a large multinational pet care company. The new owners wanted to increase sales coverage for the cat food and overhauled the manufacturer's sales distribution channels. The new channels included national grocery stores, national pet stores, independent and regional pet stores, mass merchandisers, and Internet sales.

Figure 10.3 shows the seven distribution channels that have been created for one sales organization.

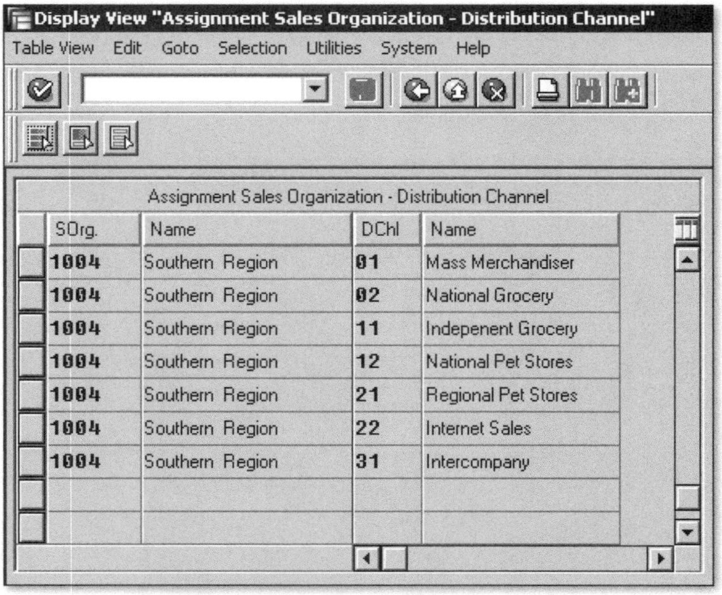

Display View "Assignment Sales Organization - Distribution Channel"

Table View   Edit   Goto   Selection   Utilities   System   Help

Assignment Sales Organization - Distribution Channel

SOrg.	Name	DChl	Name
1004	Southern Region	01	Mass Merchandiser
1004	Southern Region	02	National Grocery
1004	Southern Region	11	Indepenent Grocery
1004	Southern Region	12	National Pet Stores
1004	Southern Region	21	Regional Pet Stores
1004	Southern Region	22	Internet Sales
1004	Southern Region	31	Intercompany

Figure 10.3 Distribution Channels for a Sales Organization

In the next section, we'll look at the sales divisions that can be created within a sales organization.

Sales Division

Structure of resources in the sales organization

For each sales organization, there can be one or many sales divisions. The role of the sales division can be to structure the sales resources within the sales organization. This can identify a group of resources to be dedicated to one group of customers or products independent of the distribution channel.

Ex Example

A small computer company's sales organization has five distinct distribution channels: national, international, local, Internet, and mass merchandising. However, the company wants to distinguish between different parts of its sales organization. To do this, it has created three divisions representing the regular products it sells, the services it sells, and specialty order items that it manufactures. The company therefore creates new divisions; merchandise, services, and specialty sales.

Figure 10.4 shows a sales organization that has been split into four divisions representing its business.

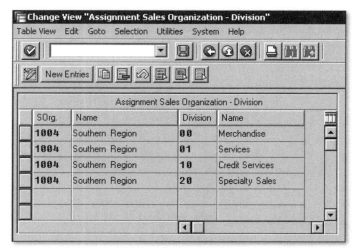

Figure 10.4 Divisions in a Sales Organization

When your company has defined the structure of your sales function, you can map this out in the SAP software.

Figure 10.5 shows the assignment of the sales organization to distribution channels and divisions. If your sales function decides that a certain distribution channels isn't relevant for a specific division, then that linkage doesn't need to exist in the SAP software. This combination of sales organization, channel, and division is called a distinct sales area.

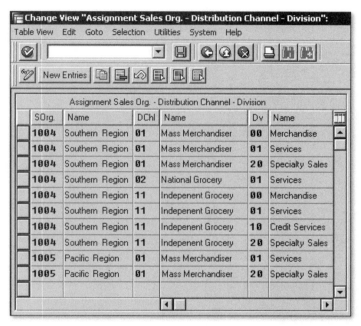

Figure 10.5 Assignment of Sales Organization, Distribution Channel, and Division

Now let's move on to the sales offices within your company's sales department.

Sales Office

If your company operates nationally, a sales office can be defined as a regional branch office. It can be the physical location of the office, or if your sales teams operate from a central location, it can represent the area that they operate in.

Regional branch

Example

A company manufactures items that are sold in department stores across North America. The sales force sells to national department stores and independent stores. The company uses strategically located sales offices for sales to the independent department stores.

Figure 10.6 shows the assignment of sales offices to sales areas.

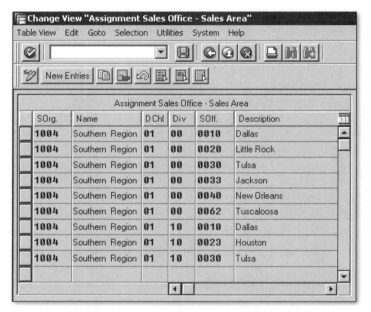

Figure 10.6 Assignment of Sales Offices to Sales Areas

In the next section, we'll talk about sales groups within the sales office.

Sales Group

Sales office divided into sales groups

Depending on the size of your sales department, your company may operate a number of sales groups within each sales office to focus on a certain customer or group of customers. A sales group can consist of one of many sales resources.

Ex Example

A company that manufactures children's toys has a sales office for the state of Florida. Within the sales office, the company created a number of sales groups assigned to smaller territories within the state. Each sales group contained several employees who concentrated on customers within the sales group territory.

Figure 10.7 shows the sales groups defined for the sales offices 10 and 20. In this example, the sales groups have been identified with the team lead's surname.

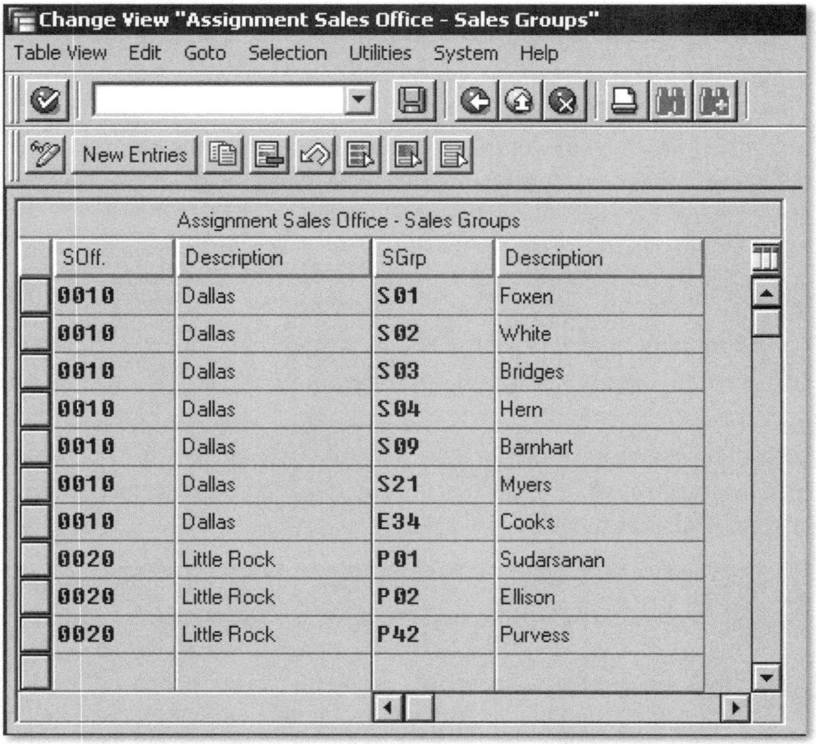

SOff.	Description	SGrp	Description
0010	Dallas	S 01	Foxen
0010	Dallas	S 02	White
0010	Dallas	S 03	Bridges
0010	Dallas	S 04	Hern
0010	Dallas	S 09	Barnhart
0010	Dallas	S 21	Myers
0010	Dallas	E 34	Cooks
0020	Little Rock	P 01	Sudarsanan
0020	Little Rock	P 02	Ellison
0020	Little Rock	P 42	Purvess

Figure 10.7 Sales Groups Per Sales Office

In this section, we've discussed the structure of the sales department in the SAP software. Not every sales department is the same, but the

SAP software design allows your company to use the functionality it needs to develop the most efficient sales structure. The flexibility of the SAP sales structure allows you the implement changes to your sales department when they are needed.

In the next section, we'll look at the sales ordering process and how your customers and business partners are defined in the system.

Sales Ordering

Inquiries, orders, contacts, and returns

The sales ordering function covers a number of business transactions, including customer inquiry, quotations, sales order, sales order contracts, credit memos, and returns.

The customer is the driver for these functions and, as part of the SAP implementation, your company will need to convert your customer data from your legacy systems to the SAP system. Let's look at the structure of the customer master record.

Customer

Customers or business partners, such a vendors

Your company associates with business partners, whether they are customers or vendors. Sometimes a vendor can also be a customer. If you are implementing SAP software, you'll need to convert your customer database from your legacy system to your new SAP system. In this section, we'll go over some of the important aspects of the customer master record.

 Example

> A company manufactures a variety of hand tools that are used in heavy industry. A vendor that supplies the company with steel 1/8-inch Round A-2 drill rods may also be a customer for the finished goods that company makes.

General Data

The general data information on the customer record doesn't depend on the company code the customer is assigned to. General data information includes the customer name, address, and telephone number.

Customer master record has many parts

Figure 10.8 shows the general data for a customer. The data are the same for every company code.

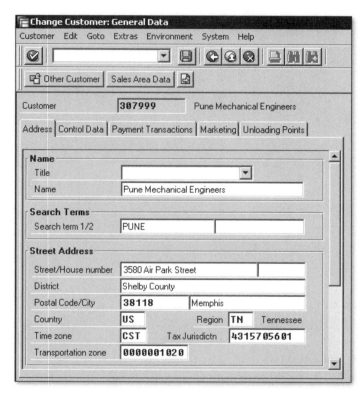

Figure 10.8 General Data in the Customer Master Record

Sales Area Data

There will be specific data for each sales area that the customer is assigned to. The data between sales areas may differ in price, shipping conditions, or delivery information.

Data varies between sales areas

Figure 10.9 shows the data for a customer for a specific sales area.

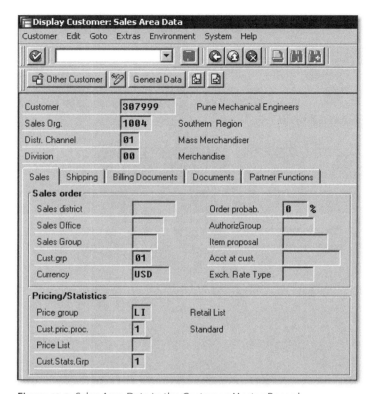

Figure 10.9 Sales Area Data in the Customer Master Record

Partner Functions

Ship-to, sold-to, bill-to, and payer

If a customer is owned by a larger corporation, or the customer owns other companies, the orders your company receives may be placed not by your customer but from one of its partners. There are many partner functions; the more common ones are sold-to party, ship-to party, bill-to party, and payer.

 Example

> Your company supplies hand tools to a customer in Vera Cruz, Mexico. However, the company in Vera Cruz doesn't have a purchasing department, so all its orders are placed by its parent company in the United States. In addition, your company doesn't have an accounts payable department at that location, and all invoices are paid from another company location in Mexico City.

Tip

Customer records must be updated on a regular basis. Having the wrong fax number, delivery address, or partner information can lead to delays in deliveries and delays in accounts receivables.

Figure 10.10 shows the partner functions for a customer. The customer uses a different partner for the bill-to party and the payer.

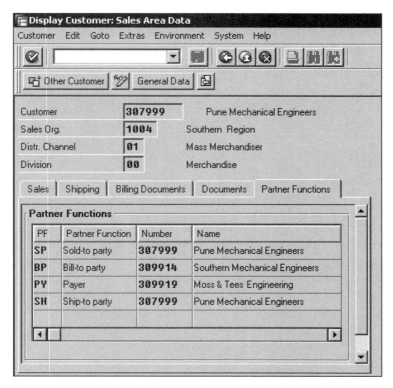

Figure 10.10 Partner Functions in the Customer Master Record

Now that we've looked at the customer master record, let's move on to the sales ordering processes, starting with the customer inquiry and quotation.

Customer Inquiry

Availability, price, and delivery time

Customers often shop around for the best deal. They will contact a number of vendors to find out whether the items they want are in stock, the cost, and the delivery time.

This inquiry is important to you as a vendor because it's your company's chance to win business. Establishing new business is important to your company's growth. If the inquiry is from an existing customer, it's important to keep customer satisfaction high. Customer service is often more important to a customer's purchasing decision than price alone.

Figure 10.11 shows a customer inquiry for three items.

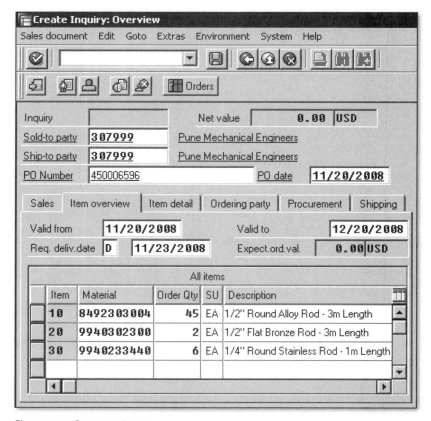

Figure 10.11 Customer Inquiry

The inquiry shows when the customer's purchase order (PO) is valid for and the required delivery date. From here, it's your sales department's task to reply to the inquiry with the best price and conditions possible.

 Tip

> Ensure that your sales team responds to the customer inquiry before it expires. Don't lose business due to not responding to customers.

The next section shows the response to the inquiry in the form of a quotation.

Customer Quotation

After the inquiry has been received by the sales office associated with the customer, the team can work on a response. The resulting sales document is a quotation that is sent back to the customer with the best price and conditions offered by your company.

Quotation in response to customer inquiry

 Example

> A customer sends an inquiry for three items that the customer hasn't purchased before. The customer isn't a large purchaser, but the inquiry may indicate more purchases in the future. The associated sales office wants to encourage further inquiries, so they offer the customer a discounted price for the items with favorable payment terms that are normally reserved for priority customers.

Figure 10.12 shows the customer quotation for the inquiry that was shown in Figure 10.11. The quotation shows the best price for the items on the original inquiry and the payment terms required for that price.

If the customer decides to accept the quotation, it can be converted to a sales order. The next section looks at the sales order document.

Converting quotations to sales

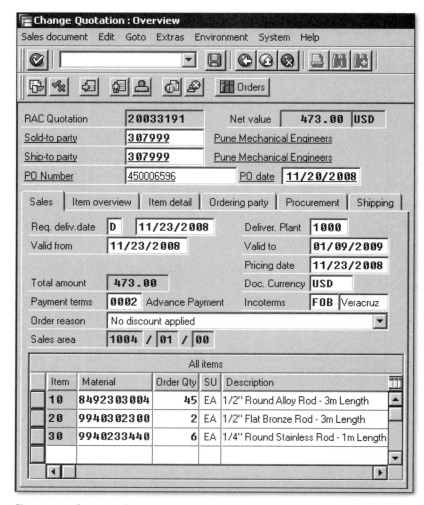

Figure 10.12 Customer Quotation

Sales Order

The sales order is the agreement between your company's sales organization and the customer. The document specifies the items to be delivered, the quantity, and the date of delivery of the items to the customer.

Ex **Example**

A customer calls your sales department and wants to order 20 precision
hand tools. The customer wants to purchase the items at the agreed-upon
contract price, but instead of waiting the normal 3 weeks for delivery, the
customer wants them in 7 days. Your sales department checks availability
and can only supply 17 of the tools by the delivery time specified. The
customer accepts the quantity, and a sales order is created for 17 items
at the contract price to be delivered in 7 days.

Figure 10.13 shows a sales order that has been created from the customer quotation.

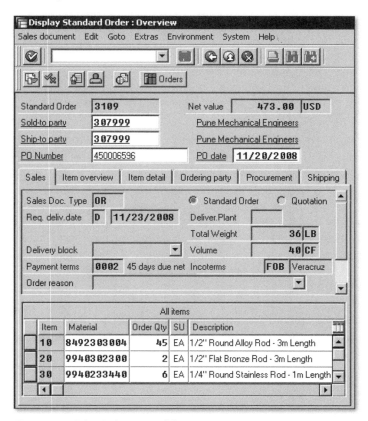

Figure 10.13 Sales Order Created from a Quotation

Some customers require that their items be delivered at certain times, and this can be created in the SAP software using a scheduling agreement, which we'll look at next.

Scheduling Agreements

Creating multiple deliveries over time

The scheduling agreement is similar to the sales order in the sense that the customer orders a range of items, price and conditions are agreed upon, and a delivery is arranged. The scheduling agreement differs from the sales order in the respect that it schedules the deliveries to the customer over a period of time, specified by the customer.

 Example

> A customer wants to place an order for 60 forklift trucks. However, they require that the trucks be delivered to their new plant on a number of specified dates, as their new plant become operational. To achieve this, your company creates a scheduling agreement where you and the customer set the delivery dates, which are entered into the SAP software.

Figure 10.14 shows the scheduled deliveries for a line item on a scheduling agreement. The customer has requested a quantity of 90 to be delivered over a period of 12 months. The specific delivery dates and quantities have been entered into the scheduling agreement.

The next section looks at how you can set up different contracts with customers, including master contracts, quality contracts, and value contracts.

Contracts

Outline agreements

Contracts with customers are outline agreements for products or services within an agreed period of time. There can be several types of contracts that your sales department can create: master contracts, value contracts, and quantity contracts.

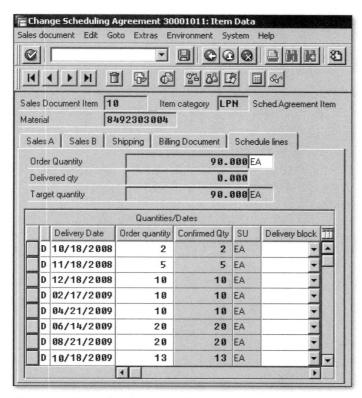

Figure 10.14 Scheduling Agreement Line Item

Master Contract

The master contract contains information that can be used when new contracts are set up with a customer. The master contract is set up with just header information such as contact and billing data.

Master contract manages other contracts

 Example

> A customer has been purchasing a number of items on a few occasions but now has decided to enter into a number of contracts for a variety of items. The sales department sets up a master contract that can be referenced each time a new value or quantity contract is created.

Figure 10.15 shows a master contract that has been set up for customer 307999.

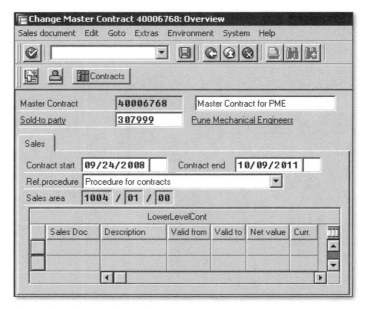

Figure 10.15 Master Contract

 Tip

Having contracts with customers means that they are more likely to return to you to purchase more material.

After the master contract has been created, any of the other contracts can use the master contract as a reference.

Quantity Contract

Volume discounts encourage quantity contracts

A *quantity contract* is established when you reach an agreement with a customer that the customer will purchase a certain number of items over a given period of time. This is likely to occur if the customer needs to have a confirmed source for items over a given period. Customers are more likely to enter into quantity contracts when your company offers volume discounts.

> ### Ⓔ🅇 Example
>
> A customer has approached a sales office with a view to purchasing 600 rolls of stainless steel wall covering that your company manufactures. The customer has offered to have the items delivered over a period of time but is unable to schedule any deliveries. The sales office had already created a master contract with this customer and will create a quantity contract when the customer agrees on a price.

Figure 10.16 shows a value contract for customer 307999 with one line item for Material 8492303004. The customer has agreed to purchase 400 items in the period that the contract is valid.

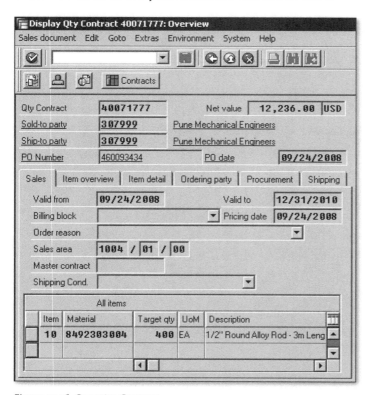

Figure 10.16 Quantity Contract

Value Contract

Discounts for customers who spend a certain amount

A *value contract* is similar to a quantity contract in the respect that the customer is purchasing items over a given period of time. The difference is that the customer isn't contracting to purchase a specific number of items but to spend a certain agreed amount.

> **Ex Example**
>
> A customer purchased quantities of stainless steel rods from your company on a number of occasions. The customer has been taken over by a competitor, and its yearly budget for stainless steel has been reduced. To continue purchasing from your company, the customer has indicated that there is a budget for stainless steel purchasing. They negotiated with your sales office to spend their budget at your company for a discount on all finished items. A value contract is then created for the amount the customer can spend over the next year.

Figure 10.17 shows a value contract for an item and the total value the customer intends to spend over the period of the contract.

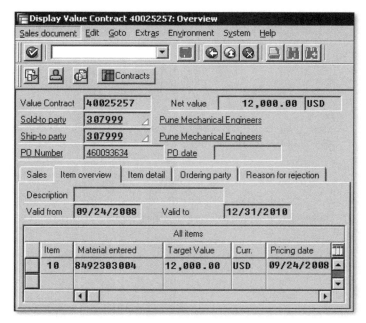

Figure 10.17 Value Contract

Release Orders

When a customer has a contract in place, either a quantity or value contract, the customer can submit an order with reference to that contract. The order value or quantity total is then reduced from the contract total. If the order exceeds the total specified in the contract, your sales department can configure the system to allow or disallow further orders.

A customer orders against a contract

Now that we've looked at the contracts that can be used with your customers, let's move on to the final sales document your sales department will deal with, which is the credit memo.

Credit Memo

Sometimes, a customer will want to return items to you because they are the wrong items, they failed inspection, or they aren't required. Depending on your company's return policy, you may require the customer to obtain a Return Material Authorization (RMA) number, or you may allow customers to return items without an RMA. When the returns are processed, a credit is issued to the customer in the form of a sales document called a *credit memo*.

A request for credit for a customer

Credit memos can also be processed if the customer has been charged a price that is in excess of the agreed amount, if a discount has not been applied, or if the customer has been charged for freight when the order included free shipping.

The financial aspects of the credit memo are processed by the billing function, similar to invoice processing.

 Tip

> Although credit memos are negative income, they should be processed quickly. Customers are more favorable to companies who process refunds quickly.

The opposite of a credit memo is a debit memo, which can be created if your sales department has undercharged a customer for items on the sales order.

Ex **Example**

A customer made an order to take advantage of a 10% discount that your company was offering for purchases over $1,000. The offer was advertised to end on July 7th. The customer's order was made on July 6th and shipped on July 12th. The invoice was sent to the customer for the full amount and didn't include any discount. The customer contacted the sales office to dispute the invoice, and the sales office agreed. A credit memo was created for the 10% discount that should have been applied to the invoice.

Figure 10.18 shows a credit memo request for a two line item order. Both line items were rejected by the customer: one Ordered in Error, and the other Reject for Credit.

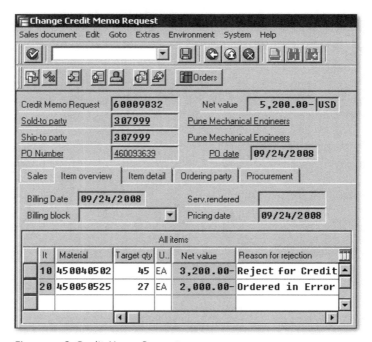

Figure 10.18 Credit Memo Request

Now that we've looked at the sales order process, let's go on to look at the SAP shipping functionality.

Shipping Processes

The shipping function covers the process from when the material is picked in the warehouse until it's received at the customer. In this section, we'll discuss the shipping process in the plant, and in Chapter 12, we'll examine the transportation process that integrates with shipping.

The first part of the shipping process is packing items prior to the delivery leaving the plant.

Packing

After the order has processed, the items have to be removed from stock. The picking process is completed in the warehouse, and the items are staged ready for delivery. In some instances, the items need to be packed before a delivery can be processed.

Packing before delivery

Customers can request to have special packing or transportation cartons. Often items are shrink-wrapped on pallet for easy transportation. SAP functionality can help your company with packing items for customer deliveries using handling units.

A handling unit (HU) is a physical item that contains the items to be shipped. The HU is made up of packaging material and one or more items. It can be nested, which means that an HU can contain other HUs.

 Example

At a beverage company, a pallet to be shipped to a customer is made up of 24 boxes. Each box contains 12 cans of soda. In the SAP system, each box can be defined as an HU, and the pallet can be defined as an HU that contains 24 boxes, which are also HUs.

 Tip

The use of HUs is appropriate for companies that use packaging material to hold finished product for shipping to your customer.

After the items have been packed, they can be shipped to the customer. In the next section, we'll examine outbound deliveries.

Outbound Delivery

Outbound delivery contains sales order information

The outbound delivery document is created by the sales, transportation, or logistics personnel for a customer order. The specific functionality of the outbound delivery has been discussed in Chapter 5, so we'll do a quick recap.

An outbound delivery can be created for the delivery of a single sales order or for a number of sales order deliveries that are grouped together.

Figure 10.19 shows an outbound delivery document created from a customer sales order. The delivery document shows the item and the quantity to be delivered.

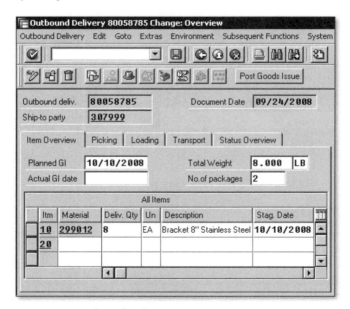

Figure 10.19 Outbound Delivery

When the outbound delivery has left the plant, the delivery can be goods issued, which we'll discuss in the next section.

Goods Issue

The goods issue takes place when the outbound delivery has left the plant. The goods issue completes the sales order process by reducing the inventory stock, reducing any outstanding requirements, and posting the details to the balance sheet accounts.

Reduces stock level and posts to financial accounts

After the goods issue has processed, the next stage is the billing process. We'll discuss that functionality in the next section.

Billing Function

The billing function creates the invoices that are sent to your customers. The invoices are based on the items that have been shipped or services that have been performed. The information is posted to the system using the goods issue function. The billing function also processes the credit and debit memos that have been issued to a customer.

The final part of the sales process

There are a number of ways to create billing documents, such as invoices, and we'll look at those in this first section.

Billing Processes

The billing process can be executed by three methods: individual billing documents, collective billing document, and invoice splits.

Individual Billing Documents

The individual billing document is created for each delivery. This isn't necessarily equivalent to one billing document to one order because a sales order could have been separated into a number of distinct deliveries.

One invoice per delivery

 Example

A customer orders three items and requires them to be delivered at the same time. However, one of the items is available in advance of the other two items, and the sales office offers the customer the items on a separate delivery. The customer accepts the offer, and two deliveries are created for the one order. The invoice process is configured to create one billing document per delivery, and two invoices are created for the one order.

Collective Billing Documents

One invoice for many deliveries

In the collective billing process, the deliveries that would have been individually processed as invoices are combined to produce a single invoice. If this billing process is required by your accounts receivables department, then a single invoice will be created for deliveries that have the same customer, sales organization, and billing data.

The invoice contains any number of unbilled deliveries that your customer has as long as the data on the deliveries allows the consolidation to occur.

This method is more appropriate if you bill your customers on a periodic basis, for example, monthly.

 Example

> A customer has three orders with your company. Because of availability issues and delivery dates, six deliveries were created for the orders. At billing time, all of the orders had been delivered, and the billing process combined the six deliveries to a single invoice.

Invoice Splits

The SAP system allows your customers to receive separate invoices for items despite being on the same delivery. The system allows your sales staff to create rules that split the invoice depending on certain values that the customer requires.

 Example

> A customer has requested that its sales order with 16 line items be invoiced with several invoices that contain items of a similar characteristic, instead of one invoice. This invoice splitting can be achieved in the system to allow multiple invoices for the one delivery based on specified characteristics.

Now that we've looked at the billing processes, let's examine methods used to create billing documents.

Creating Billing Documents

Several methods can be used to create billing documents, including automatic processing of the billing due list, manual processing of the billing due list, and manual conversion of selected documents.

Automatic or
manual billing
documents

Figure 10.20 shows the billing due list that has been executed for a certain period. The list shows a number of unprocessed billing documents.

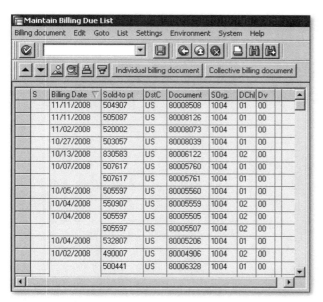

Figure 10.20 Billing Due List

Automatic Billing

The automatic billing process runs as a batch job and can be performed on a periodic basis. This is an effective way of running the billing process if your company has to regularly process large numbers of billing documents.

Manual Billing

Manual billing allows your accounts receivable staff to run the billing process when it's needed. If your company requires invoices to be created as soon as possible after the goods issue, then manual billing is more suitable.

Manual Conversion

There are occasions when your accounts receivable department needs to create billing documents on an ad hoc basis. For example, a customer might call to obtain a credit, and the sales department needs to process a credit memo immediately.

Figure 10.21 shows a manually created invoice. The invoice was created from a line item on the billing due list.

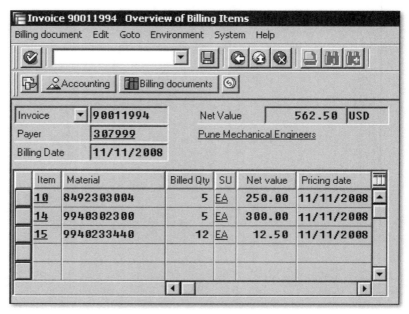

Figure 10.21 Manually Created Invoice from Billing Due List

The invoices are printed and sent to customers, or they can be transmitted to your customers by the method agreed upon. On receipt of the invoice the customer should pay within the specified period: 30 days, 45 days, and so on.

In the next section, we'll look at standard reporting that can be found in the billing functionality.

Reporting

There are many reports to assist your billing department with the billing process. We'll look at a couple of standard SAP reports that you should find useful.

Standard SAP reports in the billing process

Accounts Receivable Report

This report is a financial report but is useful in giving an overview of the outstanding billing documents that have been issued to your customer with no payment received.

Figure 10.22 shows the overdue documents that have been sent to customer 307999. The overdue balance is more than $148,000. This information is important to your accounts receivables staff to determine if further action needs to be taken against this customer.

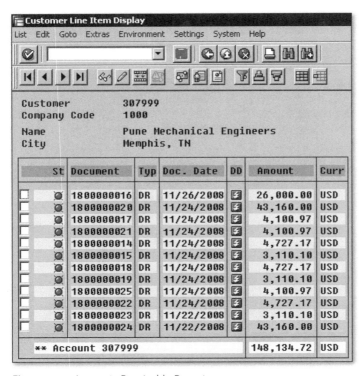

Figure 10.22 Accounts Receivable Report

Account Balances

The account balances report shows the sales to a customer and the payments they make during a financial year. The report shows the information per financial period. The report will instantly show you if there is an outstanding balance on your customer's account.

 Tip

> Obtaining payment from customers is key to the success of your company. Even if you make the best and cheapest MP3 player in the world, your company will never be successful unless it receives payment from customers.

Figure 10.23 shows the customer balance for each period of the 2007 financial year. The report shows the sales in Period 8 and the payment in Period 9.

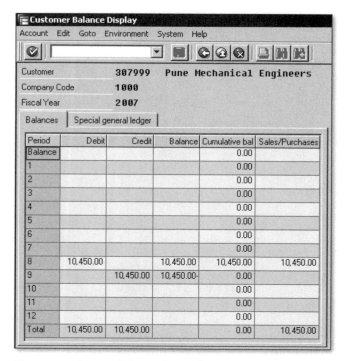

Figure 10.23 Account Balances Report for a Customer in a Fiscal Year

Many other reports can be accessed by your staff in the SAP software.

 Case Study

A clothing company based in Puerto Rico had grown very quickly through the use of offshore manufacturing and the need for large U.S. brand-name stores to have private labeled clothing at a low cost. The clothing company had originally used spreadsheets and low-cost computer accounting packages to run the business. With the dramatic increase in regular sales at the company, they have been implementing more complex software to keep pace with their increasing sales. In a period of three years, the company's sales had grown by 4,000%. Sales order were still being taken by telephone or fax, and the sale details were hand-written on cards and then transposed into the latest software package to be installed.

At the end of 2005, the company was using a different software package for sales, accounting, production, warehouse, and shipping. Due to the high level of manual data entry, sales orders were commonly entered incorrectly. Interface issues with accounting, sales, and warehousing had caused stockout situations, and customer deliveries were often considerably late.

The company saw a downturn in the number of orders in the first quarter of 2006. A survey of customers revealed that dissatisfaction with delivery dates, inaccurate orders, and incorrect billing had led customers to look for other suppliers, especially in China and Vietnam.

The company decided to correct the situation with a two-phase strategy. The initial phase was to put into place companywide business processes that replaced the disjointed procedures operated by different departments. The second phase was to implement the core SAP functionality: finance (FI), SD, MM, and PP. The accounting and sales functions were a priority to recover from some of the customer dissatisfaction regarding sales orders and billing. The SAP core functionality was implemented at the end of 2006.

A subsequent customer survey at the end of the second quarter of 2007 noted that customer satisfaction levels were substantially higher than the levels of the first survey, and customer orders had risen above the levels at the end of 2005.

Summary

This chapter discussed the functionality associated with sales order management. The sales function is extremely important to your company, and the sales teams are always looking to create sales for your company. It's important that the business processes are in place to make the operation from customer inquiry to customer delivery seamless and efficient.

This chapter introduced you to the sales structure that can be used in the SAP software. Your company may structure itself differently to every other company, but the SAP SD component allows you to configure the organization so that it can meet its objectives.

Key points to remember from this chapter:

> The sales order is the document that captures the requirements of your customer. This document can affect purchasing, production, shipping and accounting decisions, so it's important that is contains the most accurate data possible.

> The shipping process has been discussed in other chapters but is a vital piece of the sales function. Accurate customer deliveries are the key to achieving customer satisfaction. If orders aren't delivered on time, satisfaction will diminish, and customers will be looking to your competitors to take your place.

> Billing is the interface between the sales and the accounting functions. The invoice is directly related to the customer delivery, while the goods issue process moves information from the sales component to accounting. Although billing can be called an accounts receivables function, it's an important part of the supply chain.

In the next chapter, we'll discuss the customer service (CS) component, which focuses on the functionality that exists to service your customers. CS functionality covers service agreements, warranties, and processing of service orders.

11

Customer Service

The customer service (CS) component contains the functionality that your company needs to process the services you offer your customers. The services can be for warranties offered with your products or warranties purchased by your customers. The CS functionality includes the ability to receive requests from customers to provide maintenance. Providing service to your customers for either warranties or repairs is important for a number of reasons. Providing excellent customer service helps your company develop customer loyalty. In addition, customers are more likely to purchase from companies that have a high level of customer satisfaction. In turn, this makes your company more competitive and leads to increased sales. Unless your company manufactures a unique product or provides a unique service, there will always be competition from other companies. Your company needs to ensure that it can distinguish itself from the competition. Excellent customer satisfaction is key to beating out the competition, and world-class customer service is an important factor in keeping customers satisfied.

The SAP CS component is fully integrated with other logistics functions such as sales and distribution (SD), plant maintenance (PM), finance (FI), and costing (CO).

Figure 11.1 shows the integration between CS and other SAP ERP components.

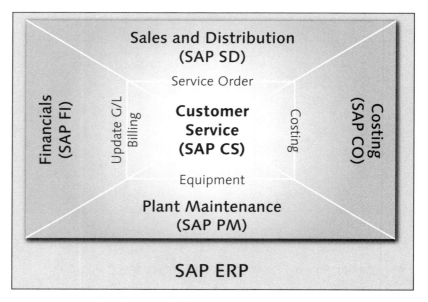

Figure 11.1 Integration Between SAP CS and Other Components

The SAP CS function provides processes, such as service agreements, that you can enter into with your customers. This ability to create contracts gives your company the advantage of increasing revenue and increasing customer satisfaction. This, in turn, can produce sales opportunities.

The SAP warranty process makes the repair of customer items under warranty very efficient. Customers require quick turnaround of warranty items, which can improve customer satisfaction.

The SAP service order process is flexible in that it can be created from a notification or entered directly. The process allows your service department to rapidly respond to customer service requests.

The CS component is an integral part of the SAP logistics function. It's also an important element in your company's attempts to improve customer satisfaction.

In this first section, we'll look at some of the structures that you'll find in the CS component in the SAP ERP business suite.

Service Structure

When a customer calls regarding maintenance of an item, the service can be performed on a variety of objects. The service item may be a material, a piece of equipment, or a functional location. We'll now take a look at these serviceable objects.

Material

Finished goods that are sold to your customers can be serviceable or nonserviceable. If your company manufactures disposable plastic pens, it's unlikely that you'll be providing service. However, if you manufacturer pneumatic power tools, the service of items will be an important part of your company's business.

Serviceable or nonserviceable

Serialized Materials

Finished goods that are sold can be serialized, or identified by a serial number. However, this isn't necessary for all finished goods, and it's up to your company to decide what items, if any, are serialized.

Serial numbers uniquely identify finished items

 Example

A company manufactures one model of vacuum cleaner for consumers. Each vacuum cleaner has a unique serial number that identifies it from another. Inside the vacuum, some components, such as the motor and power supply, are also serialized so they can uniquely be identified.

 Tip

Serial numbers are important in the customer service process, and it's important that your company identify all materials, purchased and manufactured, that require serialization.

Figure 11.2 shows the serial number information of a material that has been sold to a customer. The record shows the Customer and the Sales Order line item that contained the item.

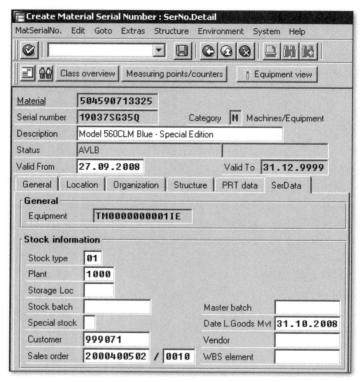

Figure 11.2 Serial Number Information for a Material

Equipment

Equipment can be sold to a customer

A piece of equipment is a machine or installed technical object. Equipment may be sold to a customer. In Chapter 8, we looked at a piece of equipment that is used by your company at your plant and is maintained by your company's plant maintenance department. Now we need to consider a piece of equipment that has been sold to one of your customers. In this case, the equipment is serviced by your staff, and requests for service are received in the CS component.

> **Ex** **Example**
>
> Your company manufactures elevator systems for the building industry. Each of your custom systems contains hundreds of items, and the system as a whole is described as a piece of equipment. The system is sold to a customer, and the information regarding the customer is held on the equipment master record. All service information is collected in the equipment record.

Figure 11.3 shows a record for a piece of equipment that is installed at a customer. The record shows the customer number and the sales order that it was sold on.

Figure 11.3 Customer Equipment Record

Functional Location

In the CS component, you can consider a functional location that is at a customer's facility. The functional location can be where a piece of equipment is installed and used. As noted in an earlier chapter, there are three distinct functional locations: functional, process-related, and spatial.

Functional location at a customer's facility

> **Functional**
>
> A site that is deemed functional is described as a location that performs a function, such as a drill shop or spray cabinet.

> **Process Related**
>
> A process-related functional location can be defined as a location that describes a process. For example, a building may be defined as fabrication or welding.

> **Spatial**
>
> A functional location that is a spatial location describes the physical location rather than the function that is found there. For example, a spatial location may be a laboratory or an office.

Ex **Example**

> A customer has several pieces of equipment that it has purchased from your company. These items are located in a functional location that is situated in the customer's manufacturing plant. The customer has requested service for the equipment, and your company has defined the functional location for information collection purposes.

Figure 11.4 shows a functional location that is at a customer's facility.

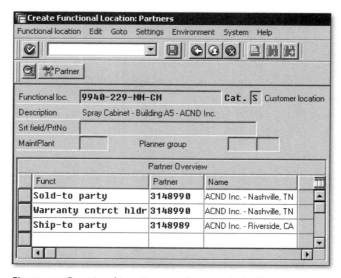

Figure 11.4 Functional Location at a Customer's Facility

Installed Base

An installed base can be created in your system to service items that are located at a customer's facility. An installed base can include materials, equipment, or functional locations, and can be created from the information in a sales order. If your customer buys items to install in a specific location, an installed base can be created to include all of the items from the sales order.

Materials, equipments, and functional locations

 Example

> A customer places a sales order for spray systems for its new spraying facility. The items are delivered to the customer's plant and installed. The items from the sales order are used to create an installed base, which is then used to record information for the individual components.

Figure 11.5 shows the equipment that comprises an installed base at a customer's facility.

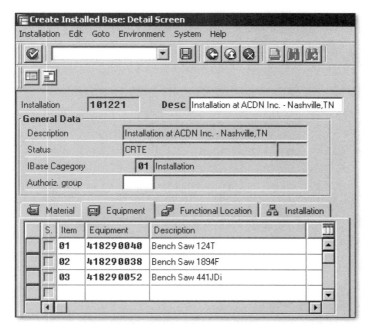

Figure 11.5 Installed Base with Three Equipment Records

This section has shown you the structures that your company will use in the CS function. In the next section, we'll look at service agreements that your company will enter into with your customers to maintain items at their locations.

Service Agreements

Long-term or short-term service agreements

Service agreements are made by your customers in the same manner that they make orders. The service agreement is a commitment by your company to service items either at a customer's facility or at your company (for items that they ship to you for repair).

Service agreements can either be long-term or short-term. Long-term agreements are in the form of maintenance contracts and warranties, whereas short-term agreements are made for one-off service needs.

 Tip

> Long-term agreements will tie customers to your company for a longer period. This can increase revenues and chances to improve customer satisfaction.

Service agreements are beneficial to your company because they ensure that the customer is purchasing services from you and not a competitor. It also gives your company the ability to keep customer satisfaction at a high level. But this can also turn into a negative if the customer perceives that your company isn't providing good service.

Service Contract

Service contract is a service sales document

A service contract is a sales document that is created in the same way as other sales contracts. The contract is for a service, similar to a sales order for a finished product.

Inquiry

The process of a customer purchasing a sales contract is similar to other sales processes. The customer can create an inquiry for service. Your customer may have items that require service and aren't covered by any warranties. Instead of creating an order for a one-time service call, the customer may decide to purchase a service plan that covers one or more items for a specified period of time.

 Tip

> Your customer service staff should reply to customer inquiries as soon as possible to increase the chances of winning the business and giving a good impression to the customer.

The inquiry may cover items that your company did not manufacture or sell to the customer.

Inquiry for items not sold by your company

 Example

> A company has a variety of service contracts for personal computers, printers, and other office equipment. Some of these contracts are due to expire, and the customer wants to combine the separate contracts to one service provider. To obtain the best price for the new contract, the customer has provided several service providers with a service inquiry.

Figure 11.6 shows an inquiry from a customer for an office equipment service contract. The customer's inquiry is only valid until January 23rd, 2009. After that time, the customer won't entertain a quotation from this inquiry.

Quotation

After your company has received an inquiry, you can create a quotation to reply to the customer. However, because the customer is requesting a service contract, this may not be an item that has been offered by your company before. In that case, to reply to the inquiry, a new service item must be costed and created in your system.

Quotation for services not provided before

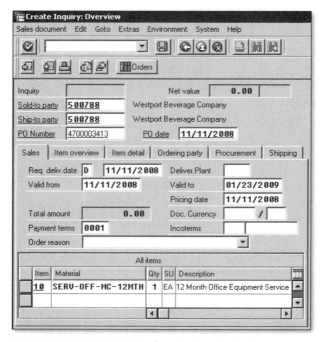

Figure 11.6 Customer Inquiry for a Service Contract

 Example

The customer inquiry is for a 12-month service contract to maintain the equipment used in spraying cabinets. Your company didn't sell the serviced equipment to the customer, and the items are not ones your company normally services. To complete a quotation to the customer, your sales and service departments need to cost the work to be performed to give an hourly rate. In addition, an estimate of how many hours of work are expected over the period of the contract is required.

Service Contract

Service contract specifies the level of service

The service contract is the agreement for your company to provide service to a customer for an agreed period of time. The service contract will cover a specific item or items and specify the service level offered. This may be a 24 hours, 7 days a week remote support, or on-site support guaranteed within 3 hours.

284

The billing of a service contract may be different to a sales order. Many service contracts offer periodic billing, where the customer is billed the same amount per month over the life of the contract.

Ex Example

A customer signs a service contract for a year with your company. The contract specifies that service will be on-site, and your service technicians will be available between 8 AM and 8PM, Monday through Friday. The contract specifies that the regular monthly payment will cover up to 100 hours of on-site support, and any hours above that will be billed at an agreed-upon hourly rate. The contract covers office equipment at their headquarters location. A list of the equipment and their serial numbers has been submitted to your service technicians. Each month, the numbers of service hours are collated and if the total is below 100 hours, the customer is billed the contract rate. If the total exceeds 100 hours, the additional hourly charges are added to the monthly charge billed to the customer.

Figure 11.7 shows a 12-month service contract for the maintenance of office equipment.

Figure 11.7 Service Contract

Quantity Service Contract

Service contracts based on number of service hours per month

Some service contracts are based on quantity contracts. The service contract is for a certain number of service hours at a set price. After the number of service hours exceeds the number of hours on the contract, additional hours can be purchased via another contract or individual sales orders.

Ex Example

A customer is reluctant to purchase service contracts for its six plasma cutters because they have not required any significant maintenance since purchase. However, the manufacturer's warranties on the cutters have expired, and new service agreements with the manufacturer are cost prohibitive. After rejecting a quotation from your company for a service contract, the customer has approached your sales office to inquire about entering into a quantity contract for service hours. The customer would like to sign a contract for 50 hours to investigate whether a service contract is required.

Figure 11.8 shows a quantity contract for a service line item. The contract is for 100 hours for the next year. Based on the net price, the hourly rate is calculated at $212.00.

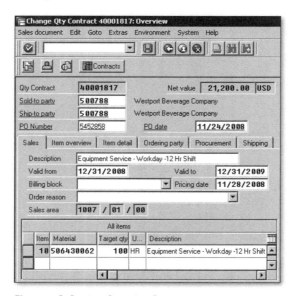

Figure 11.8 Service Quantity Contract

Service Order

A short-term agreement between your company and a customer can be made by issuing a service order. This is generally a one-time service need by the customer.

Ex Example

> A customer purchased a lathe from a company 10 years ago. The warranty expired after the first year, and the customer entered into a service agreement for 5 additional years. After the service agreement expired, the lathe was stored and not used. The customer has decided to sell the lathe but requires a service to be performed so it can be inspected and repaired ready for the sale. Because this service is a one-time request, a service order is created.

Figure 11.9 shows a service order for a customer. The order has three operations to be performed.

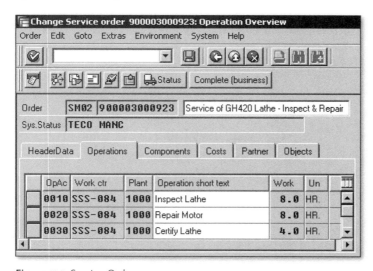

Figure 11.9 Service Order

Now that we've looked at service orders and long-term sales contracts that can be established with your customers, let's examine warranties.

Warranties

Valid for a period of
time with conditions
and requirements

When your company sells an item to a customer, you may offer a warranty with the product. This may be included with the price of the product or purchased at the time of sales order. In addition, your company may sell items through distributors, and the warranty is with the consumers who don't purchase the items directly through your company.

Ex **Example**

Your company manufactures vacuum cleaners, and each is sold with a 90 days parts and labor warranty. As a manufacturer, you sell vacuums through a number of distribution channels, including directly to the customer, through retailers, and through national distributors. The warranty you offer on each vacuum is valid despite the method of sale to the consumer.

Figure 11.10 shows a warranty that has been created with two services.

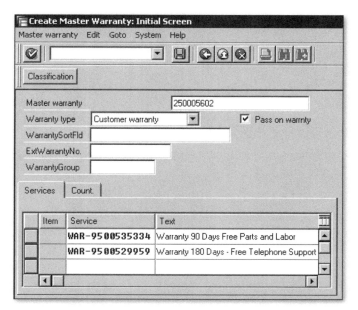

Figure 11.10 Master Warranty

Warranty Counter

A warranty counter is used to determine when a warranty has expired. When your company issues a warranty with a product, the terms usually include conditions. These conditions may use one or many warranty counters.

A warranty counter defined in time or cycles

 Example

> A warranty issued by the manufacturer of an office photocopier has conditions that allow free parts and labor for the first 180 days or 10,000 copies. The copier has a mechanical counter inside the machine to count copies, and the 180-day condition can be considered to be a warranty counter also.

Figure 11.11 shows the counter that is used for the 90-day free parts and labor element of the warranty.

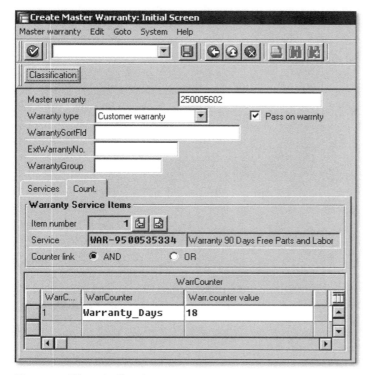

Figure 11.11 Warranty Counter

289

Warranty counters start at various times

Each warranty counter can commence at a different time, depending on how your company manages warranties. A warranty counter can start when an item is goods issued from a sales order, when an item is installed at a customer, or when the piece of equipment is used for the first time.

In this section, we've looked at the range of sales agreements that are found in the CS component. The next section examines the service processes that your service department will use, including service notifications, repair orders, and warranty claims.

Service Processing

Service notifications, service orders, and repair orders

When your customers call with requests for service or warranty claims, your service department has a number of processes that can be used, including the service notification, service order, and repair order. The first process we'll look at is the service notification.

Service Notification

The service notification is a key element in processing service issues with your customers. Issues with a piece of equipment at the customer's site will result in a call to your company informing you of an issue. This can be directly entered into the system as a service order or a repair order. However, if the issue isn't clear to the customer or to your sales department, then a service notification should be created that contains all of the information that your technicians need to investigate.

Ex Example

> A customer has a service agreement with your company for the service of a number of drilling stations. A customer representative has called with a description of the issues but does not know the cause. To ensure the information is gathered correctly, a service representative opens a service notification and enters the information relayed by the customer's representative. Your service technicians can read the information in the service notification to investigate the error before visiting the customer site.

The service notification can contain information such as customer tests performed or diagnostics on an item. This information can be added to the notification for your technicians.

Service notifications include customer observations or tests

 Tip

A service notification from a customer should be dealt with quickly because any delays could reduce customer satisfaction.

Figure 11.12 shows a service notification that has been reported by a customer. The notification shows the date and time that the malfunction occurred.

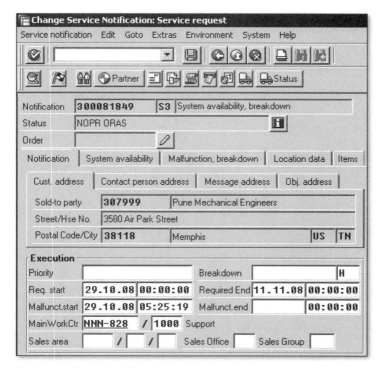

Figure 11.12 Service Notification

The service notification can result in a sales order being created for the customer's service need. The next section looks at a notification document that is created to record information.

Activity Report

Activity report just contains documentation

An activity report is created to collect information for maintenance or service that has been performed, and no further processing is required. These actions will be purely service tasks that aren't a result of damage to or failure of the equipment. The activity report is a service notification that just contains documentation on the service performed.

 Example

> A service technician is at a customer site to perform a repair. While the technician is there, he is told that one of the drill stations may have a low coolant level. The technician checks the drill station and finds that the coolant level is within tolerance. On the technician's return to his service center, he creates an activity report to document the activities performed.

Figure 11.13 shows an activity report that has been entered to document a visual inspection on a drill station. The activities that were performed are entered into the report.

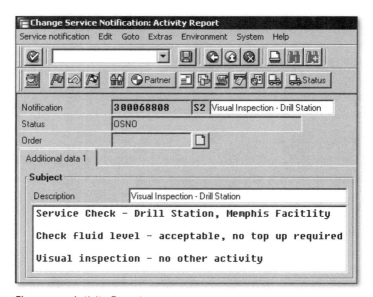

Figure 11.13 Activity Report

In the next section, we'll examine the types of service orders that your customer service department processes for customers.

Service Orders

When a customer has placed a service order, the tasks that need to be performed on the technical object may require parts and technical resources. The service order allows planning to be performed. The order is scheduled to allow maximum efficiency of your company's service resources. Using service orders means that tasks can be monitored and costs assigned where appropriate.

Contains tasks to be completed

The service order can be created from the service notification or directly without a notification.

 Example

A service order has been created for an out of warranty service that is needed on a plasma cutting tool. The service technician has a number of tasks to complete, and the number of hours has been estimated. The service order hasn't yet been scheduled for completion.

Figure 11.14 shows a service order to maintain a drill station at a customer site. The individual tasks have been entered on the service order.

Figure 11.14 Service Order Tasks

Special service orders

A number of special orders can be created depending on the services your customers require and the types of technical objects they have.

Calibration Order

If your company sells items that require periodic calibration, then calibration orders will be created to facilitate this task. The order will contain the tools or equipment that needs calibration. The calibration order is created by using a special order type for calibration.

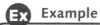 **Example**

A customer purchased a number of flowmeters, and all are out of warranty. The customer periodically requests service to calibrate the flowmeters. The customer sends the items to your technical department to have the items calibrated. When taking the order, your service personnel create a calibration order.

Figure 11.15 shows a calibration order for finished goods items that have unique serial numbers.

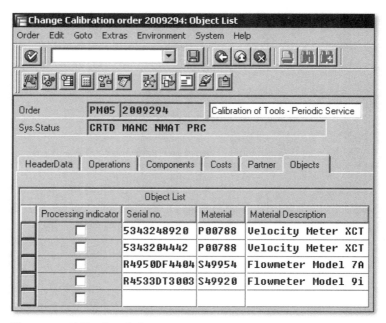

Figure 11.15 Calibration Order

Repair Order

A repair order is created when your customers send in items for repair because it's faulty or damaged. The repair order can be used when items are not covered under warranty or guarantee.

Repair orders

 **Example**

A customer has an electric motor that has been installed at a drill station. The motor is nonfunctional and needs repair. The motor is sent to the manufacturer for repair, which results in a repair order being created on receipt.

Figure 11.16 shows a repair order for a single item that has been sent for repair at the manufacturer's site.

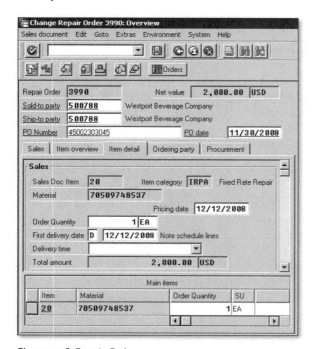

Figure 11.16 Repair Order

A repair order goes through several stages. The technician examines the item to ascertain whether it can be repaired. If not, then it may

Scrapping items

be returned to your customer based on agreements you have that customer. If the customer doesn't want the item, then it may be scrapped.

If the item can be repaired, then the customer is informed, and the repair continues. Depending on your pricing strategy for repairs, the price can be all-inclusive or based on time and materials.

Ex **Example**

> A customer has sent in a pneumatic driver for repair. The item isn't un-der any warranty, and the customer has indicated that the item can be scrapped if it can't be repaired. After an initial inspection, the service technician makes an assessment that the driver can be repaired, but the cost will be based on time and materials. The customer is informed and approves the repair costs. The item is repaired, returned to the customer, and an invoice is sent to the customer for the labor costs and materials used in the repair.

Figure 11.17 shows a repair order that was sent in for repair by a customer. A business decision was needed before the item was repaired at a fixed price. The item was repaired and returned to the customer.

Figure 11.17 Repair Order with Business Decision Matrix

After the work has been performed on the item for the order, the technicians must enter their time and confirm that the operations have been completed. Next, we'll look at how the confirmations are entered.

Confirmations

When the service order or repair order is processed, each operation needs to be confirmed as completed. This is to ensure that the progress of the order can be monitored and that the labor expended on the order can be recorded.

Operations confirmed as completed

The completion can be entered into the system as each operation is finished, or it can be added collectively. Service departments have different methods, either after each operation or at the end of each technician's shift.

Ex   Example

A technician is working on two work centers, each of which has a repair order in progress. The technician can alternate between the two as diagnostic tests are being run. At the end of the technician's shift, the technician collectively enters the time spent on each operation of the two repair orders.

Figure 11.18 shows the collective entry of confirmations for two service orders. The technician has entered time for a number of operations on the two orders.

Order	Op...	Act. Work	Unit	Pers. No.	Plnt	Postg date	Work Ctr
5994092	0010	1	HR	27505	1000	11/14/2008	TECH-01
5994092	0020	3.5	HR	27505	1000	11/14/2008	TECH-02
5994092	0030	2.5	HR	27505	1000	11/14/2008	TECH-02
5994106	0010	1	HR	27505	1000	11/14/2008	TECH-01

Figure 11.18 Collective Confirmations for Service Orders

Tip

> Each service order should contain all of the time and materials that were used. If these are not included at the time of the confirmation, they may be missed at billing and not be included.

After the confirmations have been entered and the order is completed, the next phase is to bill the customer for the work done.

Billing

Based on agreement when placing service order

The customer is billed depending on the order that was completed. If the service order was based on time and materials, then the customer will be billed by your accounts receivable department for all of the labor expended and the materials used. If the service order was a fixed price, then the billing will be for the agreed price, and nothing more. Your company may also offer some service work free of charge. This is often used by companies who want to improve their standing with the customer. Your sales department will be involved in these kinds of decisions.

Ex **Example**

> A customer requested on-site service for an installed motor that was faulty. The motor wasn't under warranty, and the customer didn't have a service agreement. The service technician completed the work on-site and entered his time and the parts he used in the service order on his return to the service department. Because the customer was in negotiation to purchase a service agreement for several of its facilities, the sales department wanted to show some goodwill. The sales director decided to invoice the customer just for the technician's time at the site and not the travel time or the parts required for the repair.

Figure 11.19 shows an invoice for a service similar to the preceding example. Only the technician's time has been charged to the customer; all other charges have been removed.

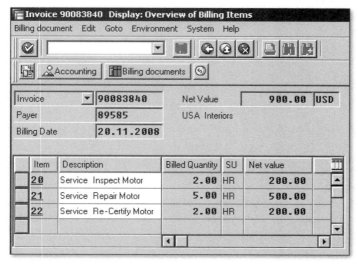

Figure 11.19 Invoice from a Service Order

This section has examined a number of sales processes that are available to your company in the CS component. Service notifications are an excellent method of collecting information so more investigation can take place. Service orders allow your technicians to identify all of the tasks to be performed and to monitor those tasks as they progress. It's important to identify all of the activities performed in the service order so that the correct billing can take place.

Summary

This chapter reviewed the functionality that comprises the CS component. Many of the functions in CS can be seen in other components in SAP. The notification and order process is similar to that found in plant maintenance (PM) and sales and distribution (SD). This is helpful because after you become more familiar with PM and SD, you'll be able to identify those same processes in the CS component. Key points to remember include the following:

299

> The structures you'll find in CS include materials, equipment, and functional location. Items such as equipment and functional location can be found also in PM.

> Service agreements have similarities with the SD component. Service contracts and agreements use the same structure as the documents you'll find in sales.

> However, the warranty is something unique to CS and that may be something that your company is involved in or considering. Understanding the warranty process is important in the CS component.

> Processing service notifications, service orders, and repair orders are similar to the processes found in SD and PM. The key to successful customer service is to ensure that the correct tasks are being performed and that each task is recorded so that the customer is billed correctly.

This chapter has given you an overview of the CS component, and you should spend some time looking at the system now that we've explored some of the major concepts.

In the next chapter, we'll turn our attention to transportation management.

12

Transportation Management

In this chapter, we'll discuss the SAP Transportation Management (SAP TM) component, including both transportation scenarios: inbound and outbound. Without transportation, no finished goods would reach their intended customers, and no raw materials would ever reach the plant. Although it's often overlooked, the transportation management component of your company's implementation is as important as any other.

We'll discuss how transportation is planned and what functions need to be performed before any goods leave the facility. The planning function is able to plan and optimize shipments for whatever method of transportation you decide to use. Secondly, we'll look at how shipment costs are processed. Finally we'll examine how the transportation process is executed, with respect to creating and monitoring shipments.

Figure 12.1 shows the integration points between SAP TM and other SAP components.

The SAP TM component provides the functionality to efficiently ship deliveries from your facility to the customer. The component is fully integrated with the SAP sales and distribution (SD), quality management (QM), and finance (FI) components.

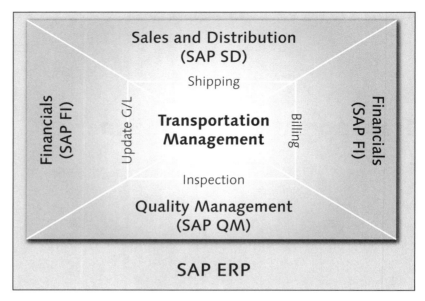

Figure 12.1 Integration Between Transportation Management and Other SAP Components

Transportation is an important part of the logistics function because it allows your staff to plan shipments that provide on-time customer deliveries at the lowest cost possible. The freight charges are a major part of any shipping cost, and your staff should work with forwarding agents and freight companies to minimize this.

So let's start this chapter by looking at the first of those topics, transportation planning.

Transportation Planning

Planning shipments reduces shipping costs

Transportation management is at the core of every movement in and out of your company's facility. Planning shipments by your transportation department can help minimize the costs of delivering your finished products. Reducing these costs means that those savings can be passed on to your customers, and perhaps you can gain an advantage over your competitors.

To begin, we'll look at the SAP transportation structures that are and then review the activities that must occur before a shipment leaves your facility.

Transportation Planning Point

Depending on the structure of your transportation department, there may be one or more locations where transportation activities occur. These locations may be where transport planning occurs or be a physical location where shipping occurs. Each distinct location is defined in the SAP software as a *transportation planning point*.

The department that coordinates shipments

> **Ex** **Example**
>
> A company is based in a single facility that operates production, ware-housing, and transportation activities. The transportation department operates as two teams: one set of employees focuses on domestic shipments, and one set deals exclusively with international shipments. When defining the organizational structure for an SAP implementation, the company creates two separate transportation planning points for the distinct separation of activities between the two transport teams.

Figure 12.2 shows the transportation planning points for one company. The company has decided to create points for each group of employees dealing with different modes of transport and has a separate point for international shipments.

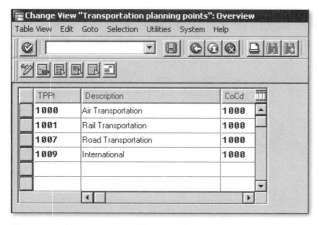

Figure 12.2 Transportation Planning Points

303

After you've addressed the planning points, the next step is to understand the different shipping types in the transportation functionality.

Shipping Type

Method of transportation

The shipping type allows your transportation personnel to enter in the system the relevant transportation methods that your company uses. These shipping types are used when calculating costs and in constructing routes, which we'll look at in the next section.

 Example

> A company has been using its vehicles to transport finished goods from its manufacturing plant to local customers. The company was purchased, and customers are no longer just local but also national and international. The company has to use many more transportation methods than just its own vehicles, so other shipping types such as train, air, and ocean freight were added to the system.

Figure 12.3 shows the shipping types that have been added, including Mail, Air Freight, Surface Freight, and Sea.

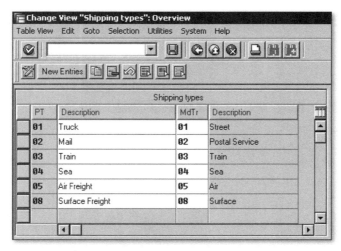

Figure 12.3 Shipping Types

The shipping type is used in defining a route, which we'll look at in the next section.

Routes and Stages

Some companies have a large number of customers who have regular deliveries. Instead of making transportation personnel create a route each time a shipment is needed, your staff can predefine routes and stages. This will significantly reduce the time required to create a shipment. The route can be defined so that it contains the shipping type, the transit time, and the stages that comprise the route.

> **Ex Example**
>
> A customer regularly purchases finished goods. Because the customer is located in a remote area, transportation takes more than one method. A route can be predefined in the SAP software so it doesn't need to be replicated each time a shipment is created.

Figure 12.4 shows the routes that have been defined by transportation staff. The route shows the shipping type (ST) and the number of day's duration (Transit Dur) that the route will take.

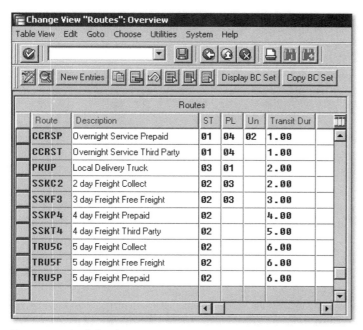

Figure 12.4 Predefined Routes

The other elements that you can define are the stages that make up the route. There can be a number of stages that make up a route, including a stage that is by air transport and then a second stage where the shipment is transferred to a trailer for delivery.

Ex Example

A company has created a route for a customer that requires two stages to complete the shipment. The first stage covers the majority of the distance and is completed by air. The second stage is completed by a local courier service.

Figure 12.5 shows a route that is made from two stages.

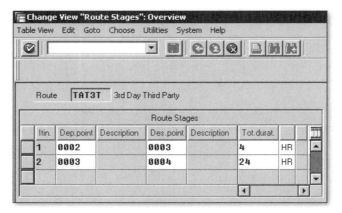

Figure 12.5 Route Containing Two Stages

Your transportation staff can also enter stages manually in a shipment rather than using the predefined routes.

In the next section, we'll discuss the role of the forwarding agent, who can be used to help with your shipping issues for a price.

Forwarding Agent

The *forwarding agent* or *freight forwarder* is a vendor to your company who acts as a facilitator between you and the shipping companies. A forwarding agent generally doesn't have any shipping assets, such as trucks and airplanes, but contracts with the shipping companies that do own the assets. The forwarding agent can collect a commission from the shipping company and a fee from the shipper to make all of the arrangements, pick up the shipment, and monitor the shipment to its destination. Some forwarding agents also may take responsibility for loss and damage to the shipment.

The forwarding agent is especially useful to your company if you don't own any shipping assets, and you don't have any contracts with carriers or are having issues finding a reliable carrier.

Useful if you don't have shipping assets

 Tip

Forwarding agents can provide an invaluable service for companies who have limited resources in their transportation department.

Many companies use forwarding agents exclusively for overseas shipments. A forwarding agent collects and processes all of the relevant documentation for shipping overseas.

 Example

A company has contracts for shipping with several carriers. Some of the finished products are potentially hazardous materials and require specialty packing and storage while being transported. The carriers currently under contract won't take the items that are potentially hazardous. The company could not find a local carrier to take the material, so they asked a forwarding agent to find a suitable carrier and organize the shipments that contain the potentially hazardous items.

 Tip

Forwarding agents are often used by large companies for international shipping. They generally have significant experience shipping products internationally and can perform tasks more efficiently than in-house resources.

If your company decides to use forwarding agents, that information can be added to the shipment when it's created. In the next section, we'll look at the creation of a shipment.

Shipment

Shipments contain one or many deliveries

A shipment is comprised of a delivery or a number of deliveries. When your transportation staff members create a shipment, they can select deliveries and add them to the shipment. The deliveries can be added if they meet certain selection criteria that your staff can decide upon. The shipment is created for a specific transportation planning point. The staff has to select a shipping type, such as air or truck, and can add a forwarding agent if one is needed.

Figure 12.6 shows the creation of a shipment from transportation planning point 0001. The shipment isn't being given to a forwarding agent, and the shipping type is a truck shipment. Deliveries will then be added to this shipment.

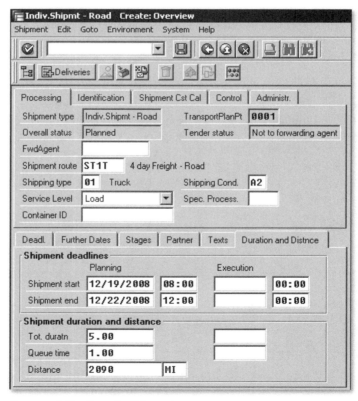

Figure 12.6 Creation of a Shipment

Ex Example

> The transportation department creates a shipment to a customer without using a forwarding agent. They use selection criteria to find other deliveries for that customer and also for customers in the same geographical area. To ensure that the shipment is a full truckload, a number of deliveries are assigned.

Shipment Status

When the deliveries are assigned to the shipment, it's given a status of "planned." At this stage, deliveries can be removed from the shipment. This can be due to capacity issues with the carrier or the customer might want to change the date it needs to accept the delivery. The shipment can be assigned other statuses as well:

Status shows the stage of the shipment

> **Check-in**
> The vehicle arrives at the plant that will contain the shipment.

> **Start Load**
> The vehicle is loaded with the shipment.

> **End Load**
> The loading of the shipment is complete.

> **Shipment Completion**
> The documents are created and printed, posting the goods issue for the deliveries in shipment is performed, and the deliveries in the shipment are billed.

> **Shipment Start**
> The truck containing the shipment leaves the transportation planning point on its way to the customer.

> **Shipment End**
> The shipment is complete and fully delivered to the customer.

Figure 12.7 shows the status of shipment 5051. The shipment is at the Shipment Completion stage. In this shipment, the actual times exceed the planned times for each status. Your transportation staff would see that the shipment is more than seven hours behind at the shipment completion stage.

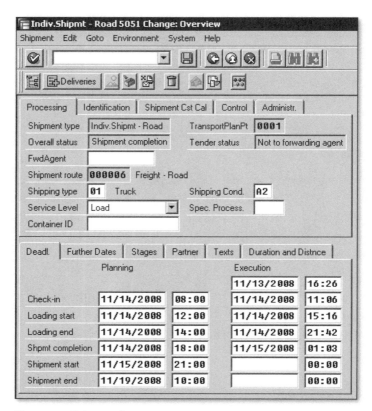

Figure 12.7 Shipment Status

Now that we've looked at the status of a shipment, let's look at the SAP reports that are available to assist your staff in planning activities.

Transportation Planning List

A wide range of selection criteria

The SAP software provides your transportation staff with reports to aid in the creation of shipments. A key report your staff will use is the transportation planning list. It provides a variety of selection criteria from which your staff can choose to locate shipments based on date, route, shipping type, and so on.

The report shows all shipments that are relevant to the selection your staff enters. From the report, shipments can be selected and modified, such as deliveries added.

 Example

> Your company is shipping more deliveries than normal because of a marketing push. For your transportation department to monitor the planning of shipments, the staff members have each been allocated a shipment to monitor based on shipping type and route. To clearly identify the shipments they have been allocated, the transportation staff uses the transportation planning list using the selection criteria they have been assigned to.

Figure 12.8 shows shipments that have been identified using the transportation planning list based on selection criteria 01 for shipment type.

Shipment List: Planning

Shipments   Edit   Goto   Settings   Environment   System   Help

List level: 1   Entries: 5   View: 1

U	Shipment	ShTy	TPPt	ST	L	Route	Container ID
☐	1060	0001	0001	01	4		8579478
☐	1066	0001	0001	01	4		MH CONT 13345
☐	1061	0001	0001	01	4		8579475
☐	1062	0001	0001	01	4		MH CONT 13343
☐	1003	0001	0001	01	4		MH CONT 13387

Figure 12.8 Transportation Planning List

The planning list is a key report for those members of your staff that need shipments with specific criteria. One other report that assists with monitoring planned shipments is the shipment execution monitor, which we'll look at in the next section.

Shipment Status Monitor

Shows shipments
for shifts or up to 7
days

During a shift, the transportation staff has to react to changes in the schedule of shipments due to trucks arriving late, problems with loaded, unloading, or product not being available. To assist your staff with this changing workload, your staff can use a standard SAP report called the shipment status monitor.

 Tip

Shipment status monitor provides real-time information, which should be monitored continually over a shift.

The report is available in two modes: shipments over a shift for one day or shipments for up to a seven-day period. This allows your staff not only to review the workload as it changes during the shift but also as it fluctuates over the coming days. This is a great tool for assessing staffing needs in the short-term.

Ex **Example**

The transportation department has scheduled shipments to be loaded at a rate of two per hour during the shift. However, due to the breakdown of a trailer, the shipments due to be loaded in the first two hours haven't been. The transportation staff works with the shipment status monitor to reschedule the loading times and move some shipments to the next shift.

Figure 12.9 shows the shipment status monitor for a 12-hour shift. Currently there are only 24 planned shipments to be completed in the first six hours. However, transportation staff can change the planned loading times to match the availability of staff and resources over the shift.

Now that we've looked at the shipment planning functionality in your SAP system, we'll look at the important topic of freight costs that concerns so many companies trying to keep expenses down.

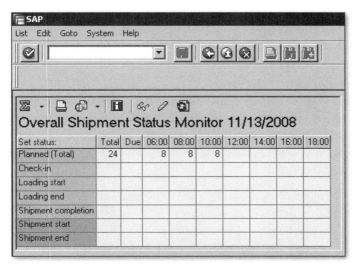

Figure 12.9 Shipment Status Monitor

Freight Costs

When you send a shipment, a number of modes of transport can be used that will affect the cost of shipping. Customers want to pay as little as possible for the cost of their delivery, and every company wants to reduce the amount they charge to increase their competitive advantage.

Moving goods from the plant to the customer

In this first section, we'll look at some of the modes of transportation that are used for shipments.

Modes of Transportation

Your company will most likely use a number of transportation options to get your finished product to your customers. Depending on the product you're shipping, transportation options include air, train, and truck.

Air Transportation

For shipment by air, your company can work with asset-based carriers such as FedEx and UPS, or nonasset-based companies that are air freight forwarding agents.

The asset-based carriers such as FedEx offer a full service. They collect the shipment from your facility; transport by air, and then deliver it to the customer. These companies are sometimes called *integrators* because they are fully integrated and don't rely on any other companies to deliver the shipment.

The air freight forwarders will save your company money on shipping because they purchase large quantities of space on air carriers. Then, they sell small quantities of space to companies. Air freight forwarders are more flexible than integrators because they deal with a large number of carriers and always have the shipping option that companies require.

Air transportation is generally an expensive shipping option, but can help to reduce other logistics costs. By shipping items via air to customers more than 1,500 miles may, your company can forego a regional warehouse, which can be expensive to maintain.

Ex Example

A company based in Boston has a warehouse in Oakland, California that ships by truck to all western states. After a zero growth year, the company assessed the viability of the Oakland warehouse. It concluded that if it closed the warehouse and used FedEx two-day shipping, there would be no degradation of customer service levels. Despite being a very expensive method of shipping, the company would save $100,000 a year in logistics costs.

Rail Transportation

The majority of rail transport is found in industries that are primarily bulk product orientated such as coal, stone, and grain. The ability to load items into a rail car and have them transported directly from the facility is very attractive for some companies. However, the railroad system is limited and with no new investment in infrastructure, it's difficult to take advantage of the lower costs of rail transport is large areas of the United States.

This isn't the case in Europe, where the rail system is far more developed and significantly more used.

Truck Transportation
The majority of all consumer products in the United States are shipped using trucks. The U.S. Department of Transportation identified 4 million miles of road in 2006, which increased more than 500,000 miles from 1960. Conversely, the rail system fell from 207,000 miles to only 97,000 in the same period.

As of 2006, the U.S. has 4 million miles of road

Truck shipments are very flexible for companies and offer excellent price and service for short-haul shipments.

There are a number of options for companies who ship parcels. Companies such as FedEx, UPS, and the U.S. Postal Service offer parcel shipping, but the shipping price per pound is the most expensive for companies.

Convenient parcel carriers are expensive per pound

Transportation by truck can be further divided into less-than-truck-load (LTL) and full truckload (FTL) carriers.

Less-than-Truckload
Most shipments with LTL carriers are less than 1,000 pounds in weight, although LTL carriers will accept much larger shipments even above 10,000 pounds. The LTL carriers collect shipments from companies and consolidate them for transportation in trailers. The LTL carrier will operate a number of set routes between its terminals. Companies have to be aware that transportation by LTL carriers can take longer than other methods.

Compete with parcel carriers for small shipments

The cost advantage of LTL carriers is that it's significantly cheaper than using a FTL carrier. As LTL carriers compete with parcel carriers such as FedEx, their prices seem very reasonable. However, the disadvantages can be found in additional charges that LTL carriers tack on. Extra charges can be made for copies of documents, packing, unpacking, handling costs for heavy shipment, delivery to a private residence, and notifications. Companies should weigh up the additional charges to fairly compare LTL to other carriers.

Full Truckload

Generally the cheapest for heavy shipments

The full truckload (FTL) carrier contracts with a company to provide an entire trailer to a customer. Normally the FTL carrier delivers a trailer to a customer. The trailer is then filled by the customer, and the FTL carrier returns to pick up the trailer and the associated documents.

If your company can use the whole trailer, the more cost benefit you'll get. FTL carriers will charge for whatever amount is in the trailer.

 Example

> Your company has a 12,000-pound shipment to move between two fa-cilities that are 1,000 miles apart. A FTL carrier charges $11.00 per mile, irrespective of weight. Therefore, the cost of the shipment by FTL carrier would be $11,000. The same shipment by LTL carrier would cost $1.45 per pound, with a total cost of $17,400. Therefore, the LTL shipment would be $6,400 more expensive than shipping using a FTL carrier.

Now that we've looked at the modes of transport that you can use, let's look at the shipping rates that can be used by the carriers.

Shipping Rates

Shipping rates vary between carriers

Each carrier that your company deals with will have a variety of rates that your transportation staff has to understand. Rates differ between carriers, and each carrier has a number of rates it offers customers.

 Tip

> Negotiating a low freight cost with freight companies can save your com-pany and customers considerable amounts of money.

Class Rate

The *class rate* is the highest rate that you can pay for a LTL shipment between two points. The class is determined by the product you want to ship.

The definition of a class is catalogued in the National Motor Freight Classification tariff, commonly referred to as the NMFC. Every carrier will have a rate for each of the classes found in the NMFC. Higher shipping rates will apply to higher classes; for example, an item in class 200 will be more expensive to ship than an item in class 55.

National Motor Freight Classification (NMFC) tariff

 Example

> A company wants to ship some building materials to another facility. The transportation department checks the NMFC tariff to find the classes for the items to be shipped. The transportation staff members identify that they have cement bricks, which are class 55; glass bricks, which are class 60; and fiberboard, which is class 70. The selected carrier offers the company rates for each of the classes.

Because class rates are the most expensive rates a carrier can offer, your transportation department should negotiate a discounted rate.

Exception Rate

Sometimes your transportation department can get a reduction in the rate by asking the carrier for an exception in the class. For example, you may be shipping building material that is class 55, but the carrier may give you a rate for class 50, which is used for bulk building materials, especially if the volume to be shipped is large.

Local Rate

If your company is shipping items to points locally, carriers may offer a discounted rate below the class rate for these local deliveries.

Released Value Rate

This discounted rate can be negotiated with the carrier. The discount is applied because your company can agree to have a limit on the amount of any claim you may have for loss or damage. This means an increased risk for your company but a lower shipping rate as a lower class is applied.

Example

> A company wants to move a shipment of automobile carpets to a distribution center. The carpets are class 250 according to the NMFC. The cost is $16.43 per pound. To reduce the cost, the company reduces the value to $12.94 per pound, which is equivalent to class 220. The company takes the lower shipping cost and accepts the added risk because the carpet is sold at approximately $13.25 per pound.

Contract Rates

Contracts with carriers give companies discounts

If your company wants the best shipping rates, a negotiated contract with a carrier or a number of carriers can provide this result. Most carriers offer low rates if your company ships a certain amount of product over a period of time, and the discounts can increase if the amount shipped increases.

 Example

> Your company has negotiated a contract with a local LTL carrier. The discount is 30% on published class rates up to 50,000 pounds of freight per month. If the company ships more than 50,000 pounds in any month, the discount rises to 40% for the shipments after the 50,000 pounds is reached. The contract also states that if the company ships more than 100,000 pounds in any month, the discount will then reach 50%.

Now that we've looked at the various shipping rates that can be found, we'll look at how the shipping costs are calculated in the shipment.

Shipping Costs

Shipping cost calculated in the shipment

Shipping costs are applied to the shipment after all of the relevant deliveries have been added. The shipping costs are calculated by conditions similar to those used in determining pricing for sales orders. The freight charges can be discounted based on the contract your company has with the carrier and any other discount or surcharge conditions that may apply.

With rising fuel prices, carriers have been applying fuel surcharges to shipments, and these need to be included in the shipment costs when they are calculated.

Ex Example

When calculating a freight charge for a shipment, the gross freight charge is discounted by the percentage in the contract, which is 40%. However, there is a surcharge of $0.08 per pound for this shipment because it's below 10,000 pounds, and an additional fuel surcharge of $0.12 per pound. The discounts and surcharges are applied to the gross freight charge to calculate the net freight cost of the shipment.

Figure 12.10 shows the shipping cost for a shipment. The gross freight rate has been calculated, and then the discount offered by the contract with the carrier has been applied. The rate charged to the shipment is the calculated net freight cost.

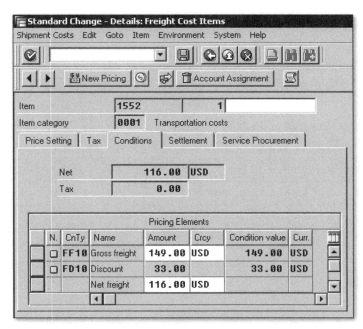

Figure 12.10 Shipping Cost for a Shipment

Now that we've look at shipping rates and the way freight codes are calculated in the shipment, let's look at what is needed to complete the shipment.

Transportation Execution

When shipments are ready for arrival to your site or ready for pick up by your selected carrier, checklists are available in the SAP software for your staff to use.

Checklists collect inbound/outbound information

The system provides a checklist for shipment completion, when your shipments are ready to leave the facility. Conversely, there is a check-in report that your staff can use to collect information on inbound shipments.

The first report we'll look at is the check-in list that can be prepared for incoming shipments.

Check-In List

When shipments are arriving at your facility from vendors and other facilities, the shipments can be checked in by the receiving staff. On arrival, the information can be verified against the check-in list for the shift.

Check-in lists provide real-time status

The shipment can be entered in the transaction as checked in, and the transportation staff can be aware that the shipment needs to be unloaded. The transportation staff can then use resources more efficiently when accurate statuses are maintained.

Figure 12.11 shows the check-in list for a shift. The check-in list shows all of the shipments that are due to arrive at the facility on a particular day. The list in this figure shows that five shipments are due to arrive at the facility.

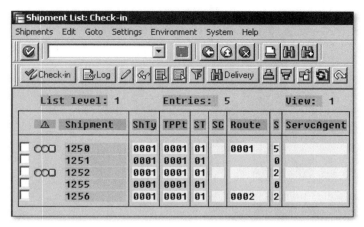

Figure 12.11 Check-In List

In the next section, we'll look at the report that helps your transportation staff with shipments leaving the facility.

Shipment Completion List

This report shows the shipments that are almost ready to leave the facility. All of the planning activities are complete, and only minor tasks need to be completed such as weighing, inspection, and goods issue.

Shows shipments ready to leave your facility

The list is created at the start of a shift so that the transportation manager can use resources efficiently based on the workload.

Changes to the shipments can be made from this list so that the shipment information can be kept accurate during the shift.

Before the shipment leaves the facility it may be required to have one final quality inspection. Depending on the finished product, some companies require the finished product to be tested a final time. For example, for a refrigerated product, the temperature may be checked to make sure it's within the tolerance for shipping. In addition, some companies require that the packaging is checked by quality inspection prior to leaving the facility.

Figure 12.12 shows the eight shipments leaving the facility during a shift.

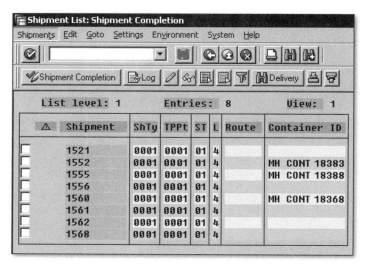

Figure 12.12 Shipment Completion Report

In the next section, we'll examine how the deliveries associated with the shipment are goods issued.

Posting Goods Issue

Posts all accounting and inventory information

When the shipment has been completed, and all activities are performed, it's possible to post a goods issue. This can be for all the deliveries that make up the shipment, which is convenient when a shipment is made up of many individual deliveries.

 **Example**

A shipment is being processed for a FTL, where there are more than 30 deliveries onboard. The shipment has been processed, and all remaining documentation is complete. As the trailer is removed from the facility by the carrier, the transport staff can post goods issue to all of the deliveries contained in the shipment with one transaction, instead of individually processing goods issues for every single delivery.

Figure 12.13 shows the deliveries in the outbound delivery monitor that are relevant for a shipment that has left a facility. Using the selection criteria of the shipment number, the report shows the deliveries that can be goods issued from this single screen.

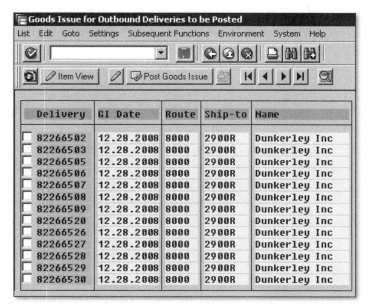

Figure 12.13 Posting Goods Issue for Deliveries in a Shipment

 Tip

Posting the goods issue is important because it then triggers the billing process.

After the deliveries have been goods issued, the inventory changes are posted, and the relevant accounts debited and credited.

Summary

In this chapter, we looked at the SAP Transportation Management (SAP TM) functionality. The transportation of your customer deliveries is a key factor in maintaining and improving customer satisfaction.

SAP TM provides you the ability to manage resources to efficiently load and unload shipments. The functionality also allows you to accurately monitor shipments as they are processed at your facility.

This chapter looked at the information that needs to be created prior to implementation such as deciding on routes used by your company. The use of forwarding agents is a choice that is made by your transport manager based on the shipments you company has. The first section of this chapter also looked at the reports that can assist your staff in successfully planning shipments.

The second part of this chapter examined the modes of transport that can be used to transport shipments and the associated freight costs. Your transportation department will be working to minimize shipping costs without reducing service to your customers. As fuel costs rise and freight costs increase, it will be difficult not to pass these on to your customers. The functionality in SAP TM will help you maximize the efficiencies of your shipping process and reduce the impact of these increased freight costs.

There are a number of key points in this chapter that you should remember:

> Forwarding agents can provide an excellent service for companies that have limited transportation resources.
> The shipment status monitor gives your staff a real-time view of the shipments to be processed over a period of time.
> The use of LTL carriers can reduce shipping costs.
> Contracts with freight companies allow your company to obtain the best rates.
> Goods issue must be processed to ensure that the financial records are updated and billing can be processed.

In the next chapter, we'll look at the timeline and strategy for a successful implementation of SAP ERP. In addition, we'll look at the total cost of ownership (TCO) and consider your potential return on investment (ROI).

PART IV
Implementation and New Technologies

Implementation

Now that we've discussed the logistics function in SAP ERP, we should now look at the implementation strategies that your company can adopt. It's important to implement SAP ERP based on your business requirements. SAP ERP shouldn't be considered just as a technology replacement; it's implemented to allow your company to run its business with increased efficiency and using best practices.

In this chapter, we'll look at how your company can approach the implementation of SAP ERP. We'll discuss the decisions that need to be made with regards to implementation strategy.

In addition, we'll look at the difficult business questions that arise when any implementation of SAP ERP is considered concerning the total cost of ownership (TCO) and the return on investment (ROI).

SAP ERP Implementation

The success of any SAP software implementation depends on the way that system is designed, configured, implemented, and, ultimately,

Business decisions more important than technology decisions

used. Success of the implementation project depends on many of the decisions that your company makes prior to the start of any implementation project.

Companies choose SAP software to transform the way they do business for a variety of reasons. However, it's important to understand that these reasons are based on the various challenges companies face in the marketplace.

Companies have their own issues

Not all companies are the same, and each has its own unique set of problems to overcome. In this first section, we'll look at some of the reasons why companies choose SAP ERP to assist in transforming their business.

Why Implement SAP?

Implementing any enterprise resource planning (ERP) suite is a significant investment. A decision to implement SAP ERP should not be taken without considerable discussion involving all parts of the organization. There can be a variety of business reasons to implement. Some companies do so to increase their presence in the global market. Companies that have been successful in one country or region find themselves unable to break out and compete globally.

SAP functionality is built on best practices

Some businesses implement SAP ERP to adopt business processes that make them more efficient and therefore more competitive in their national market. Increased efficiencies brought about by using best practices embedded in SAP functionality will lead to increased customer satisfaction.

Although world-class companies have been continually transforming their businesses each year, implementing SAP ERP can accelerate business transformation.

SAP SCM and SAP CRM accelerate business transformation

This is particularly true of companies that have implemented SAP in the past and have upgraded their ERP systems and introduced new SAP business suites, such as Supply Chain Management (SAP SCM) and Customer Relationship Management (SAP CRM). These additional business suites enhance the core business functionality and transform businesses further.

SAP is the market leader in the enterprise applications market, and with more than 300,000 customers in 120 countries, the company invests more in research and development (R&D) than any other company in the market. This level of commitment is attractive to businesses of all sizes that see SAP ERP as a long-term investment. SAP ERP has evolved over the past 30 years. The level of R&D shows companies that have significant investments in the product that the evolution of the SAP business suites will continue.

300,000 SAP customers in 120 countries

Companies can evolve their business processes in tandem with the SAP business applications that are developed. Flexibility is a key component to any technology application, and SAP ERP allows businesses to incorporate acquisitions quickly to minimize conflicting business processes and technology.

Company leaders have seen technology implementations fail in the past because the software was too generic for their business processes. The failure of many business transformation projects has been due to the inability of the applications or technology to allow the company to run its business. Applications that were found to be successful in one industry were totally incompatible with other industries. Company leaders have found that with SAP suites, this isn't the case. The business suites have industry-specific capabilities. SAP suites have more than 25 industry-specific solutions, and SAP has developed these industry solutions by listening to the needs of industry leaders and adopting industry-specific solutions based on best practices within the application.

More than 25 industry-specific solutions

Deciding on SAP ERP to transform your company's business may be a difficult decision and should take due diligence and consensus. However, the decisions that you make in the implementation process are directly responsible for the success of the venture. In the next section, we'll look at the implementation process and the important decisions you should address.

Implementation Methodologies

SAP ERP affects employees and business partners

After you've decided to implement SAP ERP, selecting a methodology is the next important process. It's crucial to use a methodology that encompasses all aspects of the implementation, not just the technology and business processes. The implementation won't only affect the company adopting SAP ERP, but every employee, customer, supplier, and business partner.

Some companies have their own strategy or methodology of implementing a software product. This is also true of partners that your company may use to assist in the implementation of SAP ERP. However, the implementation of SAP ERP is significantly different from the implementation of standalone software products, such as the financial package QuickBooks. Many companies have found their SAP software implementations flounder by using methodologies that failed to incorporate all aspects of the project.

 Example

A pharmaceutical company began an implementation of SAP software and decided to use the company's software replacement methodology that they created and had used on all software implementations. After the initial meeting of the project team, a project scope and plan was decided upon. At the next project team meeting, the project plan had been modified over a dozen times to include aspects of the project that had not been addressed in the company's methodology. After consulting with SAP, the company restarted the project using the ASAP roadmap with additional elements specific to the pharmaceutical industry.

In the next section, we'll look at the methodology and roadmaps that SAP developed and continually refines to help their customers achieve a rapid and successful implementation of SAP software.

ASAP Methodology

ASAP is a comprehensive solution for the implementation of SAP business suites. It was first introduced in 1996 and then released worldwide in 1997. The methodology includes the necessary project management; the configuration of business processes, testing, and training aspects; as well as technical implementation activities. The effectiveness of ASAP has been demonstrated as the methodology to use at companies around the world.

The ASAP implementation roadmap provides proven implementation methodology for implementation of all the SAP business suites: SAP ERP, SAP CRM, SAP SCM, SAP PLM, and SAP SRM.

The latest release of the methodology, ASAP Implementation Version 3.8, was released in May 2008 and is fully aligned with the business process structure in the SAP Solution Manager.

ASAP Implementation Version 3.8 released in May 2008

The ASAP roadmap covers the different aspects and phases of an implementation. In the roadmap, a detailed project plan is included for the five phases. The roadmap provides a standard repeatable procedure for implementing SAP ERP, including project management, configuration of business processes, and technical, testing, and training aspects. The ASAP roadmap contains everything you need for your implementation. However, if there are elements to your implementation that your company requires from your own methodology or due to industry requirements, these can be added to the ASAP roadmap.

The five phases of the implementation are listed here:

Five phases of the ASAP roadmap

> Project preparation
> Business blueprint
> Realization
> Final Preparation
> Go-Live and Support

Figure 13.1 shows the ASAP roadmap and the five phases.

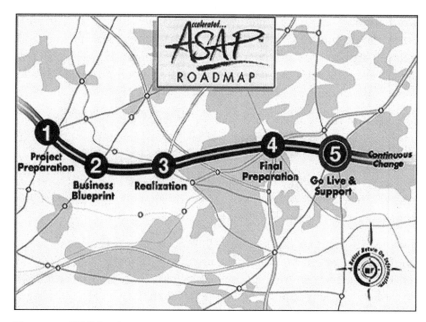

Figure 13.1 ASAP Roadmap

In the next section, we'll look at some of the functional aspects that are part of the first phase of the ASAP implementation roadmap: project preparation.

Project Preparation

Project scope defined in project preparation

In this phase of the implementation, your company's decision makers need to identify the scope of the project and issue a project charter. This is very important because the scope defines the level of resources that will be required, the timeline of the implementation, and the overall budget.

The size and make-up of the project implementation team is directly related to the project scope, which in turn affects the timeline that can be achieved. It's important to the success of your project that the subject matter teams should include knowledgeable resources. Every implementation is different, and, therefore, the project team can be made up exclusively of your employees or can include paid consultants, either from SAP or a consulting firm.

During the project preparation stage, your company needs to begin a change management program. An SAP ERP implementation covers all aspects of your company. This includes employees, vendors, customers, and business partners. Communications are vitally important to ensure everyone is receiving the same information about the implementation: its scope, timeline, and progress. Customers and vendors will be eager to ensure that their interactions with your company aren't disrupted during the implementation.

Successful projects include change management

 Example

A company is implementing SAP software, and the scope includes replacing the current inventory system. As part of the project, the company will replace their current 6-character intelligent item numbers, with 12-character nonintelligent numbers. To ensure that vendors and customers are aware of the changes, the company began sending monthly communications to their business partners with information on progress.

The project preparation stage should include discussion of what business process measurements the company wants to review to help with identifying a return on investment (ROI). Your company justified the implementation based on improvements of certain business areas or processes. The ROI shows whether or not that benefit has been achieved. To do this, certain business process measurements need to be agreed upon prior to go-live so that measurements in the legacy system can be compared to those when SAP ERP is live. Business process measurements can include increases in inventory accuracy, decreases in outstanding accounts receivables, or reductions in manufacturing time. Some ROI measurements may be financial, for example, a reduction in server costs. We'll discuss ROI later in this chapter.

Identify processes to measure ROI

At the end of the project preparation phase, the deliverables need to be approved by the project leadership.

The deliverables at the end of the project preparation stage can include the implementation project plan, budget, communications strategy, scope and timeline, documentation strategy, change management, and data conversion strategy.

Project preparation deliverable include a project plan

Table 13.1 highlights some of the key activities of the project preparation phase.

Key Activities
Develop project scope.
Assemble knowledgeable project teams.
Develop change management strategy.
Develop communications strategy.
Decide on system landscape.
Implement issues database.
Identify objectives for ROI.
Develop data conversion strategy.

Table 13.1 Key Activities for the Project Preparation Phase

The next phase of the ASAP implementation, business blueprint, is examined in the next section.

Business Blueprint

The business blueprint phase is designed to document your company's requirements and the business processes that you want to include in the scope of the implementation.

 Example

In the project preparation stage of an SAP project, the project team decided to include the sales and distribution (SD) component for the first phase of the implementation. In the business blueprint stage, the project team members for the SD component found that their business processes for the customer service (CS) component were undefined. The company decided to leave the CS component out of the first SAP implementation phase because its inclusion would have put the timeline in jeopardy.

During the blueprint phase, the project leaders should start conducting regular meetings. The highest level of meeting is with the project steering committee. The steering committee should include the project leaders and senior company executives. Leadership buy-in is vital to a successful implementation, and it's critical to have honest communication with senior executives regarding the progress of the project. In cases where the project needs additional resources or has a special requirement, the steering committee is the decision-making body.

The introduction of regular team meetings and project lead meetings should begin to ensure information at the lowest level is shared. It's important that there is a complete view of the implementation process. If progress has been impeded, it can impact the project budget, scheduling, resources, and timeline. Project management must coordinate integration aspects between the different project teams.

The project team will work on defining the overall organizational structure. For the logistics team, this includes the plants, purchasing organizations, sales channels, and so on. This level of structure will be defined for all of the components that are included in the implementation.

Organizational structure defined in the blueprint

The business processes should be further defined. The project teams can hold business blueprint workshops with the selected employees in each of the areas that are included in the scope. The project team should receive appropriate SAP software training prior to the business blueprint workshops. The workshop is an effort by the implementation team to understand and document required business processes and for the employees to learn about the functionality within SAP ERP.

 Example

> A business blueprint workshop is held by the plant maintenance team to discuss the notifications process. At the workshop, the plant maintenance staff explain how notifications from the shop floor are passed to the plant maintenance staff and how that becomes a maintenance order. The project team documents the process and identifies any areas that may require further clarification or potential modification.

In the business blueprint workshop, employees are encouraged to share reports that they use to support the business and share whether they have any additional databases or systems they use that have not already been identified.

Interfaces, conversions, and reporting requirements

The blueprint phase should include reporting requirements, interfaces with systems that aren't being replaced, conversion of data, and possible SAP software enhancements.

At the end of the blueprint phase, the project leaders need to present the results of the blueprint to the steering committee. The official sign-off solidifies the organizational structure and the business processes to be implemented.

Table 13.2 highlights some of the key activities of the business blueprint phase.

Key Activities
Introduce project meetings at all levels.
Develop a project team training plan.
Define the organizational structure for SAP.
Conduct business blueprint workshops.
Identify reporting, interfaces, and conversions.
Finalize business processes
Finalize project scope, budget, and timeline.

Table 13.2 Key Activities for the Business Blueprint Phase

Next we'll look at the third stage of the ASAP roadmap: the realization phase.

Realization

In the realization phase, the project team needs to have an integrated and documented solution that fulfills your company's business process requirements.

The configuration of the system is performed by your project team with the help of consultants. This is where the decisions you made in the blueprint phase are technically addressed in the SAP system. The project team works on achieving a baseline configuration, designed to cover around 80% of your daily business transactions with the adopted organizational structure in place.

While the configuration is being carried out, you need to complete other aspects of the realization phase, including defining the business roles.

SAP functionality is covered by a layer of security that restricts a user's access to certain functionality or data. This restriction is based on the role that the user has been assigned.

In the realization phase, the project team should consider the functionality that users will use in their present job capacities.

Ex Example

> A project team member needs to review the functionality that a purchasing clerk needs in the SAP system. In the current system, the clerk reviews all incoming deliveries and has view access of the accounts payable transactions. The project team member sets the purchasing clerk's new role for the SAP implementation as restricted so that the user has access to his own purchasing organization and no access to any accounts payable functionality.

The roles for all of your company's users need to be identified. Some of your employees may need two or more roles to complete their work. This isn't uncommon, and some positions will have many roles. You should remember that you don't want positions to exist that allow employees to perform tasks that cause a violation of company procedures. For example, you don't want an employee to have a role assigned that allows the employee to purchase a material, receive a material, and process the vendor invoice.

Prior to implementation, it's important to test the authorization properties of key roles. Some business processes may not be able to be

Baseline configuration represents 80% of daily transactions

Many positions require multiple user roles

completed if users don't have the correct role assigned to their user ID.

Formal user documentation also needs to be considered in the realization phase. Your company will have many users of the new system. Although many will attend training, user documentation is needed for training purposes and for initial day-to-day operations.

 Example

> Warehouse operators haven't been required to operate a computer system prior to the implementation of the SAP suite. To ensure that all warehouse staff members understand their job requirements and how they will change at implementation, project documentation has been written to give a step-by-step guide.

The realization phase should also produce a set of test plans that will be required to test SAP ERP in the next stage called final preparation.

Table 13.3 highlights some of the key activities of the realization phase.

Key Activities
Configure SAP software based on business processes.
Test unit and integration of configuration.
Develop end user documentation.
Develop roles.
Develop test plans.

Table 13.3 Key Activities for the Realization Phase

The next phase, final preparation, finalizes your company's implementation, resolving any outstanding issues.

Final Preparation

The final preparation phase contains all of the tasks required to get the system ready for go-live. This phase contains testing the configured system, training the end users, and resolving open issues. At the end of the final preparation stage, the project leaders will be in a position to recommend to the steering committee to allow cutover from the existing system to the new SAP business suite.

A key objective of this phase is to follow the test plans and resolve any issues that may arise. It's important that the integration between the different components is tested to ensure that information successfully flows between them.

Test results should be fully documented. The documentation created during implementation can be referred to at a later date when users may ask how functionality was designed. You can use the test results to show what was expected from a transaction and that the process performed as expected.

Test results should show expected performance

As the activities in this phase are completed, your team should implement the cutover plan and complete the final tasks.

The final task prior to cutover is conversion of the transaction data that is moved from the legacy systems to the new SAP system. This includes any open purchase orders, sales orders, and inventory levels. Based on the results of the tasks in the cutover plan, the members of the steering committee will make the final decision to approve the migration to the new SAP system.

Table 13.4 shows the key activities of the final preparation phase.

Key Activities
Test conversion procedures and programs.
Test interface programs.
Conduct volume and stress testing.
Conduct final user acceptance testing.
Implement cutover plan.
Create and follow go-live checklist.
Implement helpdesk procedures.

Table 13.4 Key Activities for the Final Preparation Phase

Next we'll look at the final part of the ASAP roadmap, which is the go-live and support phase.

Go-Live and Support

The final phase of the ASAP roadmap addresses the activities that occur post go-live, when the SAP system is available to end users. All processes previously performed on the legacy systems are then carried out in SAP ERP.

Some initial issues after the go-live   Initially after go-live, there may be issues with security authorizations, missing data, and users' inability to access transactions they need to perform their jobs. The helpdesk or project team can assist with any of these issues.

Business procedural issues may occur, which need to be reported to the project team. Often simple issues occur in processes such as physical inventory, where the process at go-live didn't consider items in the warehouse that are on consignment but not identified as such. The process must be amended to ensure that consignment materials were labeled as such. These procedural issues are assessed by the team to identify if they are business critical. The post go-live issues are prioritized by project leaders and worked on accordingly. The helpdesk keeps records of the incoming calls and informs the project team of SAP components with the greatest volume of calls.

Post go-live is the time for the project team to revisit the business measurements that were identified in the project preparation phase. After go-live, the processes identified in the measurements should be executed to give a baseline result. Subsequent execution of the processes will show improvement over time. You can review the measurements to see if they show the benefits of your company's investment in the SAP business suite.

Ex **Example**

A company has implemented SAP ERP, and the project team is currently supporting end users. The project steering committee is tasked to report to the CEO on the ROI for the project. The project team subsequently identifies 12 processes that can be measured to show increases in productivity.

We'll examine the concept of ROI later in this chapter.

Table 13.5 shows the key activities that are part of the go-live and support phase of the ASAP roadmap.

Key Activities
Support end users.
Correct role issues.
Correct security authorizations.
Correct missing data.
Identify and prioritize post implementation issues.
Identify measurements for ROI.

Table 13.5 Key Activities for the Go-Live and Support Phase

The support phase of the project is determined by the issues that were raised post go-live and the level of calls to the helpdesk. Additional training may be required for end users. Some of the project team may support the first month-end close, which includes closing the financial books for the month and changing the financial period.

In the next section, we'll examine the topic of the total cost of ownership (TCO) of an SAP business suite.

Total Cost of Ownership (TCO)

TCO is a financial estimate designed to inform company executives of the direct and indirect costs that relate to a project implementation. In the case of an SAP implementation, the TCO includes both hardware and software.

TCO includes hardware and software

It's important to your company's executives to understand the TCO associated with the SAP business suite. In the implementation project, the costs were tied to the activities in the ASAP roadmap and limited to a specific timeframe. The TCO give executives a greater understanding of the future costs of maintaining a stable SAP system that continues to bring business benefits for the next 20 to 30 years.

History of Total Cost of Ownership

The idea of TCO was first developed in 1987 by Bill Kirwin of the Gartner Group as a means of clearly addressing the real costs attributed to owning and managing an information technology infrastructure in a business environment.

Direct and Indirect Costs

The two areas that contribute to the TCO are direct and indirect costs.

Direct Costs

Identify and budget direct costs

Direct costs are associated with the purchase of the SAP software and the costs of the implementation, including purchasing servers, building space, power consumption, networking, and infrastructure. The direct costs also include the labor costs, internally from the employees on the project team and externally from the consultant resources, if a fixed price contract is used.

It may be helpful when calculating the TCO to break down the direct costs into the initial costs and the costs that are recurring after the go-live.

Table 13.6 shows the initial project costs of the SAP implementation.

Initial Project Costs
SAP license fees
Server costs
Infrastructure costs
External SAP consulting services
Internal employee SAP consulting
Internal IT support
Project team training
End user training
Data conversion costs

Table 13.6 Initial Direct Costs

The initial costs are budgeted as part of the original project plan. The ongoing costs should have been part of the justification process and identified also. Table 13.7 shows some of the recurring costs.

Recurring costs are part of the justification decision

Recurring Costs
SAP maintenance fees
Future SAP upgrade costs
Internal employee SAP support
Internal employee SAP training
Internal IT support costs
Additional end user training
Infrastructure maintenance costs
Infrastructure upgrade costs

Table 13.7 Recurring Direct Costs

Indirect Costs

Indirect costs are harder to quantify. The indirect costs can only be estimated at the time of the project. Training costs are an example of an indirect cost because they can only be estimated at the time of the project conception. The training of end users can vary from project to project within your own company. Indirect costs can also include wasted end user time due to implementation issues, system downtime due to hardware or software issues, and the cost of any delay to the project because of go-live postponement.

Indirect costs only estimated, not quantified

One indirect cost that should concern companies is the decline in customer satisfaction due to poor response or failure to deliver on time. If inadequate funds were spent on the initial implementation that caused core business processes to falter, such as inability to ship products, this indirect cost will be greater than any other.

The Gartner Group identifies in their ongoing business surveys that "despite the difficulty of measuring them, indirect costs can typically represent a substantial component, as much as 60%, of the total cost of managing and owning an IT infrastructure."

Table 13.8 shows a number of indirect costs found in an SAP implementation project.

Indirect Costs
System downtime
Poor system performance
Retraining of end users
Additional SAP support staff
Low end user productivity
Business process inadequacies

Table 13.8 Indirect Costs

Poor direct cost spending contributes to high indirect costs

Indirect costs such as system downtime can be attributed to the decisions made in direct cost spending. For example, a decision to spend less on SAP consulting reduces the direct cost. However, if reduced spending created a go-live delay or system downtime after implementation, this causes greater indirect cost.

Calculating the Total Cost of Ownership

Companies want to understand what the TCO is for an SAP business suite. The most accurate estimates are achieved by companies that understand the initial budget has to accurately reflect the real direct costs of the implementation.

High indirect costs can inflate TCO

TCO varies greatly if the initial project budget was too small, forcing inadequate direct cost spending. The indirect costs can greatly inflate the TCO beyond initial estimates.

If the initial budget restrained spending on direct cost items such as SAP consultants and system infrastructure, then this can result in very high indirect costs after the SAP business suite goes live.

Example

> Company executives asked for a reduction in the budget for their SAP ERP implementation. The project leaders obliged by reduced training costs so that only 4 shift leaders in production and warehousing were given SAP training, rather than the 40 regular employees. After implementation, the shift leaders were the only resources that could process transactions. Instead of running the production line and the warehouse, they were engaged full-time in data entry and executing transactions. Subsequently, the production process began to slow as decisions were not made, and the warehouse workers were not picking deliveries, forcing delays in customer shipments. The company subsequently had to train all of the end users and suffer the costs of delayed production and missed delivery dates.

The TCO may be far greater for companies that incorrectly estimate the initial project implementation and show the company executives a small budget. The correct way to provide a sound estimate for the TCO is to create an initial budget that shows the real direct costs required for a successful SAP implementation.

The TCO is important because it provides an understanding of the true cost of an SAP implementation. When it's combined with the ROI, it can be used to show the economic value of that investment. In the next section, we'll look at the other economic benchmark that companies examine closely: ROI.

Return on Investment (ROI)

The return on investment (ROI) is a performance measure to calculate the success of an investment. If we consider the investment to be an SAP implementation project, then the ROI can be calculated to be the benefit that the SAP implementation has given the company.

ROI is a performance measure

Although the calculation of return on a financial investment is based on the monetary value, the ROI of an SAP project is based on a combination of subjective and objective measurements. Every SAP implementation is different because every business's definition of success has different measurements.

345

Example

> A company decided to combine their implementation of SAP software
> with the implementation of SAP software at a subsidiary. The two imple-
> mentations were very similar in nature with only small differences at a lo-
> cal level. The success of the implementation was based on an agreed set
> of measurements. However, the company found that the measurements it
> put forward, such as reduction of purchasing processing costs and inven-
> tory reduction, were not relevant for the subsidiary. They had addressed
> those issues and had optimized those functions. The subsidiary's indica-
> tors of success revolved around vendor and material rationalization.

Agree on
measurements
before go-live

To determine the ROI of any SAP implementation, the measurements
need to be agreed upon in the project preparation stage of the ASAP
roadmap.

In the next section, we'll look at some of the objective measurements
that can be used by your company in determining the ROI.

Objective Measurements

Calculating
objective
measurements

A number of measurements can be made to show the benefits of the
new SAP system. They can be financial or functional. For example, a
common measurement is the reduction in IT spending. An implementation of SAP software allows the decommissioning of legacy systems
and the hardware they run on. The savings in software maintenance
costs, hardware costs, and hardware maintenance costs can be quantified and used as a measurement in the overall ROI calculation.

In the project preparation phase, a number of objective measurements are identified. In some projects, these may be referred to as key
performance indicators (KPIs).

The business drivers behind the SAP implementation should determine some, if not all, of the measurements for the ROI.

Accountability
ensures targets are
achieved

The executive of that specific area is responsible for ensuring that the
measurements can be measured and the target can be reached. For
example, if a target is set for a reduction in the headcount in the

purchasing department, then the director of purchasing should be accountable.

 Example

> As part of the SAP implementation, the senior executive in charge of warehousing is accountable for a number of metrics relating to the implementation. One of those measurements is to reduce the cost of warehousing by 20% over a two-year period after implementation.

In addition to objective measurements, there are subjective measurements, which we'll look at next.

Subjective Measurements

In contrast to the objective measurement, the subjective measurement can't be as easily defined. Whereas a monetary savings can be identified on a report based on accounts and transactions, a subjective metric such as customer satisfaction or performance may not be accurately measured.

Subjective measurements aren't as empirical

Allowing subjective metrics to be part of the ROI equation doesn't detract from the overall ROI calculation, but it does allow a less intrinsic value to be considered.

 Example

> A company implementing SAP software defined a number of business benefits that could be measured. The executive vice president for sales was accountable for a performance indicator regarding customer satisfaction. A survey of 100 customers was performed prior to the SAP software implementation, and they gave their opinion on a number of aspects of their relationship with the company. The survey was to be repeated at selected periods to identify if there was an upward trend in customer satisfaction. Although the data is purely subjective, the company believed that the value of the measurement was still important to its ROI.

The ROI calculation differs between companies implementing SAP software. Each company is unique, and there is no one set of metrics that will determine the ROI for all companies. Each company has to

Business benefits differ for every company

identify the business benefits that it expects from an SAP implementation. The business then has to use those expectations to derive measurements that it believes will prove the benefits have been achieved in a certain period of time.

 Case Study

A Mexican manufacturer of electrical components made a business decision to implement SAP ERP at its locations in Mexico and Costa Rica. The implementation was, in part, justified using a ROI requirement of 20% within two years of implementation. The company used the ASAP roadmap for the implementation methodology and brought in a top-tier SAP consulting firm to assist with the project.

During the project preparation stage, the project team created a number of KPIs that reflected the initial business benefits identified in the selection of SAP software originally. The KPIs reflected measurable savings in IT infrastructure, a reduction of warehouse facilities, a reduction in production resources, an increase in inventory accuracy, and an increase in customer satisfaction.

The KPIs were measured one month after go-live and again at three-month intervals during the first two years. The results were unable to quantify an exact ROI percentage for the company executives. There were several reasons why this was the case. Five months after the go-live, the company purchased a medium-sized component manufacturer in Panama and began work on moving the acquisition over to SAP software. Just after the first year anniversary of the SAP implementation, the company sold two of its product lines to a competitor, which included a production facility and two warehouse locations.

The company believed the SAP implementation was a success despite the fact it wasn't able to quantify this with the ROI it required. However, the company was able to acquire another manufacturer and divest itself of mature products that it found to cost more to produce than they were sold for. This was due in part to the SAP software.

Summary

In this chapter, we've looked at some of the business aspects of an SAP implementation; the ASAP roadmap, TCO, and ROI. Following are some key points to remember:

> The ASAP methodology is the key to a successful implementation. It's a full function methodology that has been tested in hundreds of successful implementations. ASAP is used by multinational companies and mid-market companies alike with the same result—a successful implementation.

> The success of the project can be measured by looking at the TCO or the ROI.

> Executives look at the TCO to see if the cost of the implementation exceeded budget, and the success can be seen in financial terms. But this is a narrow view and doesn't look at the benefits a company gets. The TCO in itself is subject to interpretation due to the nature in which the costs are calculated.

> The ROI can take into account the business benefits, both financial and functional, but there is no universal ROI calculation for an SAP implementation. Changing the way in which a company does business may not allow a measurement of the benefits gained, and the ROI won't reflect that.

In the next chapter, we'll look at some of the new SAP technologies, as well as some of the other business suites that you may come into contact with, and review some of the concepts we've examined throughout the book.

14

New Technologies and Conclusion

In this chapter, we'll look at some of the technologies that you'll find when you look at other SAP implementations, such as SAP NetWeaver and service-orientated architecture (SOA). We'll also examine some of the other SAP business suites that complement the logistics functions in SAP ERP. In the final part of this chapter, we'll review the concepts discussed throughout the book.

SAP NetWeaver

SAP NetWeaver is the technical foundation that all current SAP solutions are based on. SAP NetWeaver is also the first Internet-based cross-application platform that can be used to develop not only SAP applications but others as well. SAP NetWeaver allows a developer to integrate information and processes from geographically dispersed locations using diverse technologies, including Microsoft .NET and IBM WebSphere. It can assist companies in integrating their current systems with portals, data management, and development environments.

SAP NetWeaver is a cross-application platform

SAP NetWeaver is comprised of a number of components that can be traced back to components in earlier releases of SAP software. Table 14.1 shows the SAP NetWeaver component and the equivalent in previous releases.

SAP NetWeaver Component	Component in Earlier Release
SAP NetWeaver	SAP BASIS
SAP NetWeaver Application Server	SAP Web Application Server
SAP NetWeaver Mobile	SAP Mobile Infrastructure
SAP NetWeaver Portal	SAP Enterprise Portal
SAP NetWeaver Business Intelligence	SAP Business Information Warehouse
SAP NetWeaver Exchange Infrastructure	SAP Exchange Infrastructure
SAP NetWeaver Composite Application Framework	SAP Composite Application Framework

Table 14.1 SAP NetWeaver Components

Integration

Full integration with .NET and WebSphere

Many companies have invested in the Microsoft, Sun, or IBM solutions, so SAP NetWeaver's ability to fully integrate with these technologies allows your business to be extremely flexible. Because SAP is committed to making sure that SAP NetWeaver is interoperable with IBM and Microsoft solutions, the use of SAP NetWeaver should continue to rise. SAP has also committed to cooperating in development strategies, field engagements, and competency and support centers.

Key Benefits

SAP NetWeaver is the platform for SOA

The goal of SAP NetWeaver is to deliver an integrated, open, and adaptable SOA-enabled platform for enterprise applications. We'll discuss SOA later in this chapter.

SAP NetWeaver can deliver a number of key benefits:

> **Open and adaptable**
  SAP NetWeaver is an open development platform because it provides the capability to integrate SAP and non-SAP applications.
  Due to SAP NetWeaver's integration with .NET and WebSphere,
  it's highly adaptable.

> **Solid platform for SOA**
  SAP NetWeaver provides a seamless integration between different
  components across the enterprise. It's a solid platform for the development of SOA.

> **Sustainability**
  SAP NetWeaver can simplify the deployment of enterprise applications because it can be situated on the same platform. It also
  provides the possibility of extending your current systems because
  they can be integrated with the other systems. SAP NetWeaver can
  save companies money because it allows systems to continue and
  not be replaced. SAP NetWeaver can connect databases and legacy
  systems with Internet-based information.

SAP NetWeaver is the platform that allows companies to adopt SOA,
and we'll examine that technology in the next section.

Service-Orientated Architecture (SOA)

SOA has evolved since the initial development of services offered
over the Internet. Before we look at SOA, we need to look at services
and service-orientated architecture.

Services and SOA

A service-oriented architecture is essentially a collection of services.
A *service* is a task that is performed to achieve a desired result for a
service consumer. In the world of SOA, a service is an application that
may be a modular part of a larger application or a standalone application. These applications can be used by different users both inside
and outside a company. New applications can be built by combining
services from the central repository. SOA applications are built out of

Services are tasks performed

a selection of software services. Instead of the services communicating via programming code, SOA provides protocols to describe how one or more services can talk to each other. SOA then relies on a business process expert to link and sequence services that are required by a company.

SOA saves companies money

One result of SOA is to have functionality strung together to form loosely bound applications that are built entirely from existing software services. This is a great cost saver for companies looking to extend their existing legacy systems. They can combine additional services to their legacy systems to add functionality that they could not have obtained without new ERP software.

Figure 14.1 shows how different components can be used with SOA.

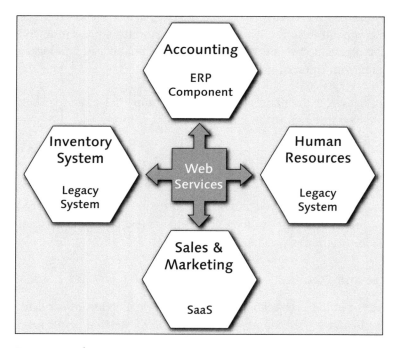

Figure 14.1 Software Services with SOA

SOA is used for small modular services, unlike the large application found in SAP ERP. However, SAP has developed a way of using SOA with the enterprise application. We'll look at this in the next section.

SOA with Enterprises

SOA allows your company to use your ERP system with other Web Services as you would in any SOA environment. The ERP system is transformed into a number of business processes that are Web Services. Each service is based on a business process, which can be selected so that your company can use as part of the SOA solution.

SOA Business functions as individual services

SAP has created these enterprise services so that they can be used as the process would be used in SAP ERP, allowing users to create, update, and delete records in the transaction, such as create, change, or delete a purchase order.

 Example

> In SAP ERP, an inventory clerk uses a menu path to select the transaction to create an inventory count document. If the inventory clerk performed the same task using SOA, the clerk would access the enterprise service operation, "Create Inventory Count."

Figure 14.2 shows a typical SOA environment with SAP and non-SAP services using SAP NetWeaver to achieve a composite application.

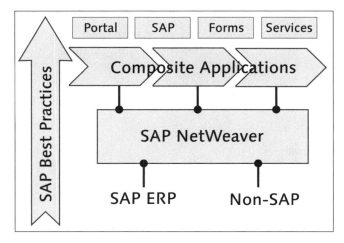

Figure 14.2 SOA Environment

SAP has developed enterprise service bundles that can save your company time and effort. We'll look at these enterprise bundles in the next section.

Enterprise Services Bundles

A collection of related services

SAP has created a number of enterprise service bundles (ES bundles) that allow companies to achieve a rapid return on their SOA adoption. An ES bundle is a collection of enterprise services and related documentation. Each bundle is grouped by main SAP business scenarios and processes. They allow companies to select groups of business processes that have already been identified. This saves your company a significant amount of time in selecting your individual SOA services.

There are many ES bundles, such as Demand Planning, Service Parts Management, and the Available-To-Promise Check.

Let's take a look at one of these ES bundles in more detail.

Example of an Enterprise Service Bundle

The Service Parts Management ES bundle is made up of a number of business process components. Table 14.2 shows the components in the Service Parts Management ES bundle.

Business Process Components in Service Parts Management ES Bundle
External Procurement Trigger and Response
Interchangeability Group Management
Location Data Management
Product Data Maintenance
Purchase Scheduling Agreement Processing
Service Parts Planning
Source of Supply Determination
Supply and Demand Matching

Table 14.2 Business Components

This bundle can be used alone or can be used with external services such as an external service parts inventory planning/optimization application. SOA allows seamless integration rather than cumbersome interfaces.

Each of the ES bundles contains a number of business process components that can be integrated with either legacy or external services to create a composite application for your company.

ES bundles contain business process components

Now that we've looked at the SOA solution in SAP, let's turn our attention to some of the other business suites that SAP offers in addition to SAP ERP, which may be of interest to logistics users.

SAP Supply Chain Management (SAP SCM)

The SAP Supply Chain Management business suite (SAP SCM) gives companies greater visibility of the information in the supply chain. SAP SCM connects the areas of supply, planning, manufacturing, and distribution. This gives companies flexibility in their supply chain and enables them to make timely and informed decisions.

SAP SCM supplies supply chain info

Flexibility in the Supply Chain

The SAP SCM business suite was designed to allow companies to change their linear supply chain into an adaptive one. Supply chains were linear in the fact that everything was very sequential in operation. The aim is to make supply chains adaptive, which means that companies can make decisions quickly to adapt the supply chain processes to market changes. These changes can be identified by the availability of timely information supplied by the components of the SAP SCM business suite.

React to changing market conditions

Phases for an Adaptive Supply Chain

SAP SCM identifies five key phases for an adaptive supply chain: planning, executing, sensing, responding, and learning.

Adaptive supply chain phases

Planning

SAP SCM gives companies the ability to plan using push and pull processes. For example, a *pull* is where you request inventory to be replenished, and a *push* is where inventory is replenished because of an actual demand.

SAP SCM includes demand and supply planning, demand forecasting, safety stock planning, distribution planning, and service parts planning.

Executing

SAP SCM provides your company with the ability to respond to changes by using real-time distribution, transportation, and logistics processes.

RFID and voice recognition in the warehouse

In the warehouse, the SAP SCM business suite can provide your company with the ability to use Radio Frequency Identification (RFID) technology and voice recognition to increase response times.

Sensing

The SAP SCM business suite can alert your staff to events as they occur. The analytics built into SAP SCM provides staff members with the information to make decisions on when changes are required in the supply chain. Having the data available so that it can be responded to immediately allows your staff to sense when change is needed.

Responding

When your staff is aware of changes that need to be made due to demands or deviations in the supply chain, they need to respond quickly. The problem with the linear supply chain was that the decisions weren't made quickly, and the changes required failed to address problems later in the supply chain.

Immediate response to supply chain changes

An adaptive supply chain requires that responses are immediate. Sometimes the response can be made internally, but often the response is outside the control of your staff.

Ex **Example**

> A customer's requirements have changed, and because of this, additional
> finished product is required. Your staff can move the production order up
> and get additional resources to cover the order, but additional raw mate-
> rial is needed. If your collaboration with suppliers is such that you have
> a seamless integration, then the changes will be communicated to them,
> and additional raw material will be sent in time.

If your supply chain isn't integrated with business partners and suppliers, then your company won't be able to adapt to changes.

Learning

The adaptive supply chain allows companies to make changes. However, efficiencies can only be gained when responses to these changes
are learned. When there is an event in the supply chain that requires
an immediate decision, it's difficult to make that decision when it's
the first time that event has occurred. But if that event occurs again,
then your staff needs to have learned what the response should be to
make it quicker than before. The learned response rapidly increases
your company's ability to successfully adapt to changes in the supply
chain.

Learned responses
increase efficiency

The SAP SCM business suite helps with a company's need to react to
changes in the supply chain. In conjunction with the SAP ERP business suite, it creates an environment for efficient relationships with
suppliers and business partners. It increases the visibility and velocity
of response, enhances collaboration with suppliers, helps to create
an environment for an adaptive supply chain, and improves supply
chain planning and execution.

In the next section, we'll look at another business suite of interest to
logistics users: SAP Supplier Relationship Management (SAP SRM).

SAP Supplier Relationship Management (SAP SRM)

The SAP Supplier Relationship Management (SAP SRM) business suite
is key in coordinating your company's business processes with your

SAP SRM manages
supplier spend

trusted suppliers. It provides tools for enabling document exchange and electronic business transactions. It has features that can assist in identifying sourcing opportunities and negotiate with your suppliers.

Core SRM Functionality

The SAP SRM functionality provides a number of tools that can give your company greater efficiency throughout the source-to-pay process. SAP has identified a number of core functions that can assist in providing those efficiencies.

E-Sourcing Application

E-sourcing provides a sourcing-to-contract management process

The E-sourcing application uses SAP NetWeaver to help maximize savings with suppliers. The functionality looks at spend analysis and provides sourcing-to-contract management. It also provides the ability to create forward and reserve auctions to gain favorable pricing from suppliers.

Spend Analytics

The Spend Analytics application is a business user focused application that brings together essential procurement measures across your organization. It allows your purchasing staff to create key performance indicators (KPIs), conduct analyses, and create procurement initiatives.

SAP Contract Lifecycle Management (SAP CLM)

Tighter control over contracts

SAP CLM allows your company to manage all aspect of the contract process. SAP CLM can operate with any type of contract and help with standardized language and reporting to reduce any legal, financial, or regulatory risk. The SAP CLM function is powered by SAP NetWeaver.

SAP Cost and Quotation Management (SAP CQM)

SAP CQM ensures accurate quotes

Providing customers with an accurate quote can mean the difference between a sale or not. The SAP CQM functionality provides your company with a more accurate quotation function to win business that will provide a profit. The SAP CQM functionality is powered by SAP NetWeaver.

Supplier Collaboration

SAP SRM offers functionality that allows collaboration with suppliers. Being able to integrate with your suppliers can streamline purchasing processes. With SAP NetWeaver, you can use web-based supplier portals. This can allow you to exchange documents with suppliers, as well as receive purchase orders (POs), shipment notices, and invoices.

Streamline the procurement process

Supplier Base Management

When your company has relationships with a large number of vendors, it's difficult to understand and manage the information. Supplier base management allows web-based self-registration for vendors. It enables your company to maintain performance management information, which allows periodic review of vendors.

The SAP SRM business suite provides the functionality for your company to organize and streamline relationships with your vendors.

In the final section, we'll review the logistics function in the SAP ERP business suite.

Conclusion

In this book we've examined the logistics functions within the SAP ERP business suite. Let's review the lessons learned.

Lessons Learned

In Chapter 1, we looked at the components of the SAP ERP business suite that make up the logistics function. Most of the logistics function is contained within SAP ERP Operations. We identified three specific areas within SAP ERP Operations: procurement and logistics execution, product development and manufacturing, and sales and service. These three areas are examined in full in the subsequent chapters.

Three areas of SAP ERP logistics

Chapter 2 began the examination of the procurement and logistics execution section of the SAP ERP Operations. This chapter looked at the procurement function specifically. The organizational structure within

Procurement functionality

SAP ERP was described and the relationships examined among company code, plant, and storage location. This organizational structure is basic to the logistics function. We examined the structure within the purchasing function, including the function of the purchasing organization with the plant and the use of the purchasing group.

The chapter goes on to examine the procurement process. The function begins with a purchase requisition that can be lead to a request for quotation (RFQ) sent to a selection of vendors. The replies are entered into the system as quotations, a vendor is selected, and a PO is issued.

The accounts payable function concludes Chapter 2. The traditional three-way match is examined as well as the two-way match, called evaluated receipt settlement.

SAP Inventory Management (SAP IM)

Chapter 3 continued the procurement and logistics execution discussion with an examination of SAP Inventory Management (SAP IM). The various goods movements, goods issue, goods receipt, returns, stock transfers, and transfer postings were discussed. These goods movements are used every day at your company facilities. A goods movement is used to move material from one location to another or from one status to another.

The second part of the chapter examined the physical inventory function. It's important to ensure inventory accuracy to avoid delays in production or customer deliveries.

SAP Warehouse Management (SAP WM)

Chapter 4 looked at the SAP Warehouse Management (SAP WM) function. We examined the structure of the warehouse, including the role of the storage type, storage section, and storage bin. SAP WM integrates with SAP IM at the storage location level. The storage location is linked to a warehouse. Goods movements in SAP IM trigger movements in the SAP WM system. The movements defined in SAP WM are transfer requirements and transfer orders. The transfer requirement plans the movement, and the transfer order creates the actual movement.

Inbound and outbound logistics

Chapter 5 examined the inbound and outbound logistics functions. On the inbound side, we looked at the shipping notice sent from vendors, inbound deliveries, and goods receipts. On the outbound side, we looked at the outbound delivery process, including picking, packing, and the goods issue.

Chapter 6 began the examination of the product development and manufacturing section of the SAP ERP Operations. This chapter reviewed the product planning functions in SAP ERP. It started with SAP Sales and Operations Planning (SAP SOP). The SAP SOP function is a useful tool for planning in the long- and medium term. It brings together sales, marketing, manufacturing, and finance. The second planning function discussed in this chapter is demand management, which is driven from customer's planned sales orders. Information from demand management can be used as inputs for the MRP function. The final product planning function examined in Chapter 6 is materials requirements planning (MRP). This is the most popular planning tool in industry. MRP calculates planned orders based on inventory, production orders, sales orders, and purchase orders. Planned orders can be converted to purchase orders or production orders.

Product planning

Chapter 7 examined the manufacturing operations that you can operate at your company. The chapter described the structures found in manufacturing, such as work centers, routings, and bill of materials (BOM). The elements of the production order were also examined. The production order has a number of operations based on the routing of the material to be manufactured. Each operation is confirmed when it's completed on the shop floor. When the order is completed, you can settle the costs associated with the production order.

Manufacturing operations

The final section of Chapter 7 examined product costing. This functionality calculates finished goods inventory values by combining the cost of the direct materials, labor, and the overhead that are consumed when your company produces a finished product.

Chapter 8 examined the plant maintenance (PM) component. This functionality is critical to companies that maintain their equipment on the shop floor. PM covers three main areas: prevention, inspection, and repair. Preventive maintenance is used to prevent the failure of equipment before it actually occurs. Breakdowns can lead to delays in production and customer deliveries. Maintenance notifications are

Plant maintenance (PM)

raised when there is an issue with a piece of equipment; if required, this can be converted to an order if the repair needs to be planned and perhaps include the purchase of spare parts.

Quality management (QM) In Chapter 9, we looked at the quality management component. This functionality is similar to PM because it operates with notifications and orders. Products are inspected based on a set of characteristics. In the quality planning, you can determine how the inspection is to take place and the item characteristics to be inspected. Notifications are issued when a problem has been identified with an end product or items from a vendor. The inspection lot function allows an inspection of your company's product. Most inspection lots are automatically triggered by either a goods receipt or a goods issue. On completion of an inspection lot, a usage decision can be made as to whether the material can be accepted or rejected.

Sales order management Chapter 10 began the examination of the sales and service section of the SAP ERP Operations. The chapter examined the sales order management functionality. The first section described the sales structure that can be found in SAP ERP. The structure of the sales organization, channel, and division are combined to create a unique sales area. The sales order function can commence with a customer inquiry to your company, which should reply with a quotation. If the quotation is approved by the customer, a sales order will be sent from the customer. Depending on your relationship with the customer, a contract can be created so that you can guarantee sales while offering a preferential price to your customer. Orders are shipped and an invoice is sent to the customer as part of the billing process.

Customer service (CS) Chapter 11 reviewed the functionality used in customer service (CS). Many items that are serviced are materials that have serial numbers because the number uniquely identifies the item. If the item is worked on a number of times, that information can be held against the specific serial number. Service agreements are similar to contracts, except they relate to the service provided by your staff to maintain and repair items. Similar to PM, the CS function has notifications and orders. Customers call with an issue with their equipment, and a notification is created. A notification order can result in a sales order being created for the customer's service need, except the item being sold is a service call. The CS function does contain warranties, which are not found in any other component. Not all companies offer warranties for their items, but if you do, the CS component offers all the necessary functionality.

Chapter 12 discussed the SAP Transportation Management (SAP TM) component. This covered the inbound and outbound transportation. The transportation structure is based on the transportation point where all shipments are issued through. A shipment is made up of a number of deliveries and given a specific route. Companies are interested in keeping down freight costs as discussed in Chapter 12. The final part of this chapter examined the execution of the shipment and the posting of the goods issue.

SAP Transportation Management (SAP TM)

Chapter 13 looked at the SAP ERP implementation. Methodology is an important aspect of any implementation, and the ASAP roadmap methodology has been helping customers with their implementation for more than 10 years. The methodology incorporates five distinct phases: project preparation, business blueprint, realization, final preparation, and go-live and support.

Implementing SAP ERP

The other sections in this chapter are becoming more important to companies as financial pressures are more prevalent. Total cost of ownership (TCO) is a calculation of the costs, both direct and indirect, that have been spent on the SAP ERP implementation, prior to and after the go-live.

Total cost of ownership (TCO)

The return on investment (ROI) is a performance measure to calculate the success of an investment. Measurements can be made objectively, for example, by measuring the decrease in hardware costs, or subjectively, such as customer satisfaction.

Return on investment (ROI)

Future Direction

In this chapter, we've looked at some of the new technologies that SAP is involved in. SAP NetWeaver was the first Internet-based cross-application platform that can be used to develop not only SAP applications but also non-SAP applications. It can integrate your systems

SAP NetWeaver

without expensive interfaces and can integrate legacy systems, SAP ERP, and Internet applications on the same platform.

SOA

SOA takes the SAP NetWeaver application and creates SAP business processes that can be selected and operated alongside other SAP NetWeaver applications.

SAP Supply Chain Management (SAP SCM)

This chapter also looked at two other business suites that should be of interest to those working with logistics. The SAP Supply Chain Management (SAP SCM) business suite gives companies a greater visibility to the information in the supply chain. SAP SCM connects the areas of supply, planning, manufacturing, and distribution. SAP SCM can be used in conjunction with SAP ERP, and we encourage you to learn more about some of the relevant functionality in the SAP SCM business suite.

SAP Supplier Relationship Management (SAP SRM)

The other business suite that is relevant to logistics people is the SAP Supplier Relationship Management (SAP SRM). The E-sourcing function in SAP SRM looks at spends analysis and provides sourcing to contract management. The SAP Contract Lifecycle Management (SAP CLM) function allows your company to manage all aspects of the contract process. The SAP Cost and Quotation Management (SAP CQM) functionality provides a more accurate quotation function to win business that will provide a profit.

This book has given you an understanding of the logistics functionality in SAP ERP that will make your experience with SAP ERP an enjoyable and productive.

A Bibliography

Britta Stengl and Reinhard Ematinger, SAP R/3 Plant Maintenance: Making It Work for Your Business (Reading, MA: Addison-Wesley, May 2001).

D. Iyer, *Effective SAP SD*, (Rockville, MD: SAP PRESS, February 2007).

Douglas M. Lambert, *"Supply Chain Management: What Does It Involve?"* Supply Chain & Logistics Journal. (Fall 2001).

Federation of Tax Administrators, "Evaluated Receipts Settlement (ERS) and Tax Compliance." (September 1998).

Gartner Research, "PC Virtualization TCO: The Best of All Worlds, or the Worst?" (June 2004).

Gartner Research, "When Thin Clients Can Narrow Your TCO." (August 2004).

Gartner Research, "CIO Update: To Control TCO, It Must Be Measured and Managed." (April 2003).

Gartner Research, "Market Share: ERP Software, Worldwide, 2006." (July 2007).

Gartner Research, "Market Share: SCM Software, Worldwide, 2006." (June 2007).

Industry Directions Inc., "Executive Brief: Driving Adaptive Supply Chains: 5 Laws of Adaptive Supply Chain Management." (Spring 2003).

J. Michael Tarn, David Yen, and Marcus Beaumont, "Exploring the Rationales for ERP and SCM Integration." Industrial Management & Data Systems Journal, Volume 102, Issue 1 (January 2002).

M. Holzer and M. Schramm, *Quality Management with SAP* (Rockville, MD: SAP PRESS, January 2006).

Michael K. Evans, *Practical Business Forecasting*, (Boston: Blackwell Publishers, March 2002).

R. Neil Southern, Transportation and Logistics Basics (Memphis, TN: Continental Traffic Publishing Company, October 1996).

Stephen N. Chapman, *The Fundamentals of Production Planning and Control* (Upper Saddle River, NJ: Prentice Hall, March 2005).

B Glossary

Account Assignment When creating a purchase requisition, charge the goods and/or services to a specific cost object and general-ledger account on the Account Assignment screen.

Account Assignment Category Determines which account assignment details are required for the purchase order item (e.g., cost center or account number).

Accounts Payable Liabilities currently owed by a person or business. These debts arise mainly from the purchase of goods or services.

Advanced Shipping Notification (ASN) Document received from vendors indicating the material that is on the way to the warehouse.

Americas' SAP Users' Group (ASUG) User group for more than 45,000 SAP users in North America.

ASAP (ASAP) Standardized methodology for SAP software implementations.

Assembly Products that are combined. An assembly can be used as a component in another assembly.

Authorizations Access to a transaction in the SAP system is based on a set of authorized values for each of the fields in the system. Users are given access to the appropriate fields, screens, and data using the authorization or security programs.

Availability Check Check that is run as part of a goods movement to make sure the material stock balance doesn't go negative.

Backflushing Automatic issue of materials after they have been used in a production order or physically moved.

Barcode Group of lines and spaces that can be recognized by an optical scanner.

Base Unit of Measure The unit of measure for a material from which all other units of measure for the material are converted.

Batch An amount of material that is unique and managed separately from others.

Batch Determination Function that allows a program (e.g., a sales order) to select a batch based on selection criteria.

Bill of Materials (BOM) List of all of the items, including quantity and unit of measure, that make up a finished product or assembly.

Billing Document   A generic term for invoices, credit memos, debit memos, and cancellation documents.

Blanket Order . Standing purchase order (contract) with fixed start and end dates for repetitive purchases from a single vendor. Requisitioners can purchase against the order until the amount of the blanket order is depleted or the blanket order expires.

Catalog   Catalogs in QM contain characteristic attributes, usage decisions, tasks, and defect types.

Change Management   The change involved in implementing an SAP system with new processes and procedures requires a level of change management to assist employees and management with the effects of change.

Characteristic   Description of a material that is defined by the user, such as color, viscosity, and so on.

Characteristic Value   The value that is assigned to a characteristic when it's used to describe a material; for example, for the characteristic Color, the value may be entered as blue.

Chart of Accounts   Consists of a group of general ledger accounts. For each GL account, the chart of accounts contains the account number, name, and any technical information.

Client   A self-contained unit in the SAP system with its own separate master records and set of tables.

Company Code   Used to represent an organizational unit with its own complete, self-contained set of cost objects for reporting purposes.

Condition   Used to calculate prices, discounts, taxes, and so on, according to the selection of vendor, customer, material, and so on.

Configuration   The formal process of establishing the SAP settings to support a company's specific business rules, validations, and default values.

Consumption-Based Planning   A generic term for the procedure in materials resource planning (MRP) for which stock requirements and past consumption values are critical.

Contract   Long-term outline purchase agreement against which materials or services are released according to user requirements over a specified period of time.

Cost Center   Organizational unit within a controlling area that represents a separate location of cost incurred. Cost centers can be set up based on functional requirements, allocation criteria, activities or services provided, location, or area of responsibility.

Cost of Goods Manufactured (COGM)   Sum of the material and production costs incurred in the production of a material.

Cost of Goods Sold (COGS)   Sum of the costs incurred in the value-added process.

Credit Memo   A credit memo is normally created if the goods or services are defective or the price charged is incorrect.

Customer   A business partner with whom a relationship exists that involves the issue of goods or services.

Customer Inquiry   A customer request to your company for a quotation or for sales information.

Customer Quotation   An offer by a sales area to a customer for delivery of goods or services.

Customizing   The process of configuring the SAP system to meet the business needs of the company.

Cycle Counting   The physical inventory that is performed on materials several times during the year, unlike a yearly physical inventory.

Delivery Monitor   Processes and displays open and completed deliveries.

Demand Management   Plans the requirement quantities and requirement dates for finished products.

Distribution Channel   A structure through which saleable materials or services reach customers. Distribution channels can be assigned to one or more sales organizations.

Document   The electronic record of a transaction entered in the SAP software. Examples include a material document or an accounting document.

Electronic Data Interchange (EDI)   Electronic communication of business transactions—such as orders, confirmations, and invoices—between organizations.

Equipment   An individual object that is to be maintained independently.

Equipment Task List   Maintenance task list linked to a piece of equipment.

Evaluated Receipt Settlement (ERS)   Procedure for the automatic settlement of goods receipts, where the vendor doesn't issue an invoice. Also known as a two-way match.

External Services   Functionality that supports bid invitation, award, and acceptance cycle for the procurement of externally performed services.

Factory Calendar   Defined on the basis of a public holiday calendar. Shows the workdays for the client.

FIFO (first in, first out)   Materials and products are withdrawn from stock for sale or use in the order of their acquisition.

Financial Accounting (FI)   The SAP module that monitors real-time values from financially relevant transactions and maintains a consistent, reconciled, and auditable set of books for statutory reporting and management support.

Forecast   Estimation of the future values in a time series.

Forwarding Agent   A person or business that specializes in the shipment and receiving of goods.

Freight Cost   The compensation paid to the contracted carrier for the transportation services performed.

Full Truckload (FTL)   A shipment comprising a full or almost full load on a truck. A full or almost full load is considered to be between 39,000 and 44,000 pounds.

Functional Location   An organizational unit that structures the maintenance objects according to functional, process-oriented, or spatial criteria.

GL Account (general ledger account)   A six-digit code that records value movements in a company code and represents the GL account items in a chart of accounts.

Goods Issue   A reduction in warehouse stock due to a withdrawal for consumption in-house or the delivery of goods to a customer.

Goods Receipt   Denotes a physical inward movement of goods or materials.

Handling Unit (HU)   A physical item consisting of a material and packaging material. An HU has an identification number that can be used to recall the data on the HU.

Implementation Guide (IMG)   Explains the steps in the implementation process. The structure of the IMG is based on the application-component hierarchy and lists all of the documentation that is relevant to implementing the SAP system.

Inspection Characteristic   Characteristic on the basis of which an inspection is performed.

Inspection Lot   Request to a plant to carry out a quality inspection for a specific quantity of material.

Inspection Plan   Description of the quality inspection process for materials in a plant.

Inventory Adjustment   Correction to the material stock level due to physical inventory or goods movements.

Inventory Valuation   Process of calculating the value of the material in the plant.

Invoice   Bill sent to the client from a vendor for goods or services delivered.

Invoice Split   The creation of several billing documents from one sales order or delivery.

Invoice Verification   Vendor invoices are compared with the purchase order and the goods receipt.

Item Category   Indicator that identifies whether certain fields are allowed for a material.

Kanban   A procedure for controlling production and material flow based on a chain of operations in production.

Less Than Truckload (LTL)   Shipments that weigh less than required for the application of a truckload rate.

LIFO (last in, first out)   Materials and products are withdrawn from stock for sale or use in the order of the most recent purchase.

Lot Size   A defined quantity to purchase or produce.

Maintenance Notification   The means by which internal company notifications are entered and managed. Notification types are maintenance requests, malfunction, and activity reports.

Maintenance Order   A detailed planning tool for maintenance tasks to be performed. Order types are investment, calibration, and refurbishment orders.

Maintenance Plan   A list of maintenance and inspection tasks to perform on maintenance objects.

Maintenance Schedule   A part of the maintenance plan that contains the scheduling data and is responsible for scheduling.

Maintenance Task List   A description of a series of maintenance activities that are executed repeatedly in a company.

Master Production Scheduling (MPS)   Manufacturing plan that quantifies significant processes and other resources to optimize production and to anticipate needs and finished products.

Material Group   A group that classifies materials by commodity or service type and is used by the purchasing department for reporting purposes.

Material Type   A grouping of materials with the same basic attributes such as raw materials, semi-finished products, or finished products.

Material Requirements Planning (MRP)   A term for procedures in production planning that take into account and plan future requirement during the creation of order proposals.

Movement Type   Indicates the type of goods movement. It enables the system to use predefined posting rules determining how the accounts are to be posted and how the material master record is to be updated.

MRP Controller   The person responsible for a group of materials in MRP at a plant.

MRP List   A document in SAP that shows an overview of the result of the MRP run.

MRP Type   A key that controls the MRP process for a material.

Negative Inventory A logical situation where the inventory is below zero due to a goods issue being performed before the goods receipt has been entered.

One-Step Stock Transfer Issue of material in one step where the material is issued and received simultaneously.

One-Time Vendor A vendor master record used for processing transactions with vendors that are not normally or have never been used.

Operation A manufacturing activity step in a routing. Used in production planning.

Outline Agreement An arrangement between a purchasing organization and a vendor for the supply of materials or provision of services over a certain period.

Output Device The name of the printer to which your SAP printouts will be sent, for example, LPT1 or US99. Many SAP printers are labeled with the output device name.

Permit A regulation or condition that must be observed when maintenance work is performed on a technical object.

Physical Inventory The recording of actual stock levels of materials by counting, weighing, or measuring at a given location at a specific time.

Picking Process of grouping materials from the warehouse on the basis of sales orders, deliveries, or staging materials for production.

Plant An organizational unit within the company code where material is produced, purchased, and planned.

Product Group Groups together materials for planning purposes.

Production Order Used in discrete manufacturing to create finished goods.

Production Resource and Tools (PRT) A moveable operating resource used in production or plant maintenance.

Proof of Delivery Acknowledgement of when your customer has received the shipment.

Purchase Order (PO) Document generated by the purchasing department. A PO is an official order sent from the client to a vendor requesting goods and services.

Purchase Requisition A request by a user or a process to the purchasing department to purchase certain material at a specific time.

Purchasing Group A person or group of people in the purchasing department responsible for purchasing a type of good or service.

Purchasing Information Record   An information record that defines the specific details for a vendor/material combination.

Purchasing Organization   An organizational unit that procures materials or services and negotiates the conditions of purchase with vendors.

Putaway   Used in warehouse management to describe the physical movement of the material into the bin locations.

Quality Notification   Description of the nonconformity of a business object with a quality requirement. It includes a request to take appropriate action.

Quant   The stock of material stored in a storage bin, which is only created through warehouse movements. Different batches of a material are identified as different quants.

Quantity Contract   An agreement whereby the terms and agreement of the contract are valid for a quantity of material or services over a period of time.

Quota Arrangement   A purchasing concept that allows the source of supply for a material to be determined via quotas decided upon with a number of vendors: Vendor A supplies 40%, vendor B supplies 35%, and Vendor C supplies 25%.

Quotation   A reply to a request for quotation from a vendor specifying its

terms and conditions for the materials or servers required by the purchasing department.

Radio Frequency Identification (RFID)   A data collection technology that uses electronic tags for storing data.

Release   To approve a purchase requisition or a purchasing document.

Repair Order   A sales document used for recording the processes for processing faulty goods that a customer sends in for repair.

Repetitive Manufacturing   Method of manufacturing where the same products are continually and repetitiously manufactured.

Request for Information (RFI)   A standard business process whose purpose is to collect written information about the capabilities of various vendors.

Request for Proposal (RFP)   An invitation for vendors, through a bidding process, to submit a proposal on a specific product or service.

Request for Quotation (RFQ)   A request to a vendor or number of vendors for a quotation to supply materials or services.

Request for Tender (RFT)   A structured invitation to vendors for the supply of products or services.

Reservation   A request to the warehouse to ensure that certain materials are available on a certain date.

Return Delivery   A delivery returning goods to a vendor. It is linked to a purchase order or goods receipt.

Return Material Authorization (RMA)   The recipient of material arranges to return defective goods to the supplier to have the product repaired or replaced or to receive a refund.

Return on investment (ROI)   A performance measurement to calculate the success of an investment.

Returnable Packaging   Material that was used to package the material for delivery but is to be returned to the vendor.

Route   The distance between a beginning point and an end point. It can be made up of several legs.

Routing   Defines one or more sequences of operations for the production of a material

Safety Stock   The level of material in stock below which a material shortage may occur.

Sales Area   A combination of sales organization, distribution channel, and division.

Sales Division   A logistics organizational unit based on responsibility for sales or profits from saleable materials or services.

Sales Office   A logistics unit in a geographical area of a sales organization. A sales office establishes contact between the firm and the regional market.

Sales Order   A customer request to the company for delivery of goods or services. The request is received by a sales area that then fulfills the contract.

Sales Organization   A logistics structure that is responsible for selling material and services.

SAP Environmental, Health & Safety (SAP EH&S)   A key functional area of SAP that provides a comprehensive solution to environmental, health, and product safety issues.

SAP Extended Warehouse Management (SAP EWM)   Component of SAP Supply Chain Management (SAP SCM). Originally developed to manage replacement parts.

SAP NetWeaver   Internet-based cross-application platform that can be used to develop SAP and non-SAP applications.

SAP Sales and Operations Planning (SAP SOP)   Forecasting and planning tool for setting targets for sales, production, and other supply chains based on historical, current, or estimated data.

SAP Service Orientated Architecture (SOA)   Allows companies to use their ERP system with other Web Services as in any SOA environment.

Scheduling Agreement A purchasing agreement with a vendor where the vendor supplies material to the customer at agreed upon days and times.

Serial Number A unique number assigned to a single item. Each item has a unique number. For example, each vacuum cleaner produced at a plant has its own serial number.

Service Contract Agreement covering the content and the scope of services to be performed for a customer. A service contract describes which services are performed.

Service Notification Means by which notifications from a customer are entered and managed in CS.

Service Order Agreement between service provider and service recipient, in which one-off services are specified by the service recipient in the order and then billed by resources when the order is completed.

Service Orientated Architecture (SOA) This technology is a collection of services. The services interoperate with each other without knowledge of the underlying platform implementation.

Shipment A grouping of goods at a transportation planning point, which have been shipped together.

Shipping Point The part of your business responsible for the type of shipping, the necessary shipping materials, and the means of transport.

Shipping Type An indicator that shows which means of transport and mode of transport can be used to carry out a shipment of goods.

Six Sigma Set of practices originally developed by Motorola to systematically improve processes by eliminating defects.

Stock Transfer Refers to the physical movements of materials in a plant.

Storage Bin The smallest addressable unit of space in a warehouse; it can be referred to as a "slot."

Storage Location Organizational unit allowing differentiation between the various stocks of a material in a plant.

Storage Section Logical or physical division of a storage type. Storage bins with the same characteristics are placed into one storage section.

Storage Type Physical or logical division of a warehouse, distinguished by the warehouse procedures used or its organization form or function.

Subcontracting A form of outsourcing, where an external vendor produces material for the customer.

Total Cost of Ownership (TCO) A financial estimate designed to inform company executives of the direct and indirect costs that relate to a project implementation.

Transfer Order   A warehouse management term that describes the request to move material to or from a storage bin.

Transfer Posting   A logical movement of material.

Transfer Requirement   Material is planned to be moved from one warehouse location to another.

Transportation Planning Point Organizes the responsibilities in a company according to, for example, shipment type, mode of transport, or regional departments.

Two-Step Stock Transfer   A procedure whereby the stock is issued from one plant and then received at the receiving plant. This is the same for transfers between storage locations.

Unit of Measure   Defines the amount or size of the material or service such as bottle (BT), each (EA), hour (Hr), and so on.

Universal Product Code (UPC)   Standardized number used in the United States to uniquely identify a material. The EAN number is used in Europe.

Valuation   The process of estimating the value of the company's stock.

Value Contract   An agreement with a vendor whereby the terms and agreement of the deal are valid for given period of time up to a certain monetary value.

Variant Configuration   Description of complex products that are manufactured in many variants, for example, cars or aircraft.

Vendor   A business partner from whom materials and services are purchased.

Vendor Evaluation   The functionality that allows the vendors to be evaluated based on price, quality, service, and delivery reliability. The evaluation can determine how a material is sourced.

Warehouse   An organizational structure that resides within the warehouse management functionality. It can be linked to materials management via the storage location.

Warranty   A warranty for a material usually covers specific conditions, usually within a limited time period.

Warranty Counter   Represents the wear and tear of an object, or the use or consumption of a supply within the validity of a warranty.

Wave Picking   Picking method where there are simultaneous picks of multiple customer orders.

Work Center   A location used in production planning where a manufacturing operation is performed.

Index

Gain a holistic understanding of SAP

Make SAP-related decisions with ease

Learn about the SAP landscape, products, solutions, strategies, and more

Nancy Muir, Ian Kimbell

Discover SAP

If you're new to SAP and want to learn more about it, or a decision-maker pressed for time, who needs to gain a holistic understanding of SAP, then this book is for you. A practical, reader-friendly guide for busy professionals, this comprehensive book helps you make quick sense of SAP solutions such as CRM, as well as application integration, SAP NetWeaver and enterprise SOA, embedded analytics, and many other core topics. Plus, learn about SAP as a company, its history, vision, strategies, and much more.

426 pp., 2008, 34,95 Euro / US$ 34.95
ISBN 978-1-59229-117-5

>> www.sap-press.de/1376

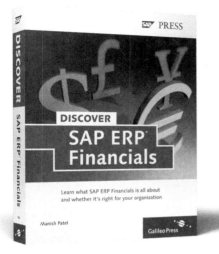

Discover what SAP Financials (FI) is all about and whether it's right for your organization

Lean how this powerful, time-tested tool can improve your financial processes and save you money

Explore the major modules, including receivable and payables, tax accounting, cost accounting, payroll accounting, travel management, and more

Manish Patel

Discover SAP ERP Financials

Business financials are an essential part of every business, large or small. Whether you just need basic accounting or you perform complex financial audits and reporting, your business needs a software tool that meets your needs.   Discover SAP Financials explains how SAP can provide this solution. Using an easy-to-follow style filled with real-world examples, case studies, and practical tips and pointers, the book teaches the fundamental capabilities and uses of the core modules of SAP Financials. As part of the Discover SAP series, the book is written to help new users, decision makers considering SAP, and power users moving to the latest version learn everything they need to determine if SAP Financials is the right solution for your organization.

This is the one comprehensive resource you need to get started with SAP Financials.

544 pp., 2008, 39,95 Euro / US$ 39.95
ISBN 978-1-59229-184-7

>> www.sap-press.de/1672

Provides managers and consultants with a complete guide to what SAP CRM is

Teaches about the benefits of using CRM to build profitable customer relationships

Includes practical insights from customers using SAP CRM successfully

Srini Katta

Discover SAP CRM

The book provides manager, consultants, power users, and aspiring users with a detailed guide to all things CRM, including what it is, why SAP CRM is important, and what the many application interfaces are (Call Center, E-Commerce, Mobile, and Channel). The book teaches about the core areas of CRM, including marketing, sales, and service, and explains the different ways SAP CRM can be used and integrated into a business. It also explains the technology and tools behind CRM (Netweaver, Web Services, Business Server Pages, Java, ABAP, etc.), and covers the various user access modes used to utilize the applications (desktop, laptop, tablet PC, PDA, & smartphone).

406 pp., 2008, 39,95 Euro / US$ 39.95
ISBN 978-1-59229-173-1

>> www.sap-press.de/1641

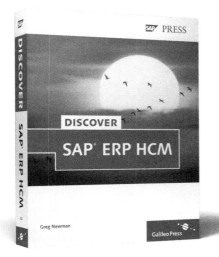

Teaches readers what SAP ERP HCM is
and how it can benefit their company

Provides a detailed overview of all core
functionality

Includes practical insights and real-world
case studies to show HCM at work

Greg Newman

Discover SAP ERP HCM

This book is an insightful, detailed guide to what SAP ERP HCM is all about and how it can
make companies more effective in managing their own HR processes. The book details all
of the major components of SAP HCM, explaining the purpose of the components, how
they work, their features and benefits and their integration with other components. It uses
real-world examples throughout to demonstrate the uses, benefits, and issues encountered
by existing SAP HCM users to ground the book in reality rather than just marketing hype.
After reading this book, readers will have a broad understanding of SAP's HCM offering and
insight into existing customer experiences with the product.

approx. 400 pp., 39,95 Euro / US$ 39.95
ISBN 978-1-59229-222-6

>> **www.sap-press.de/1846**

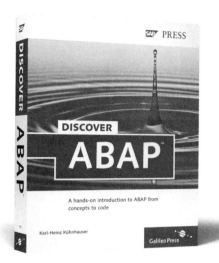

A hands-on introduction to ABAP from concepts to code

Task-focused education with coverage of all the most important commands

Short exercise units featuring a wealth of code examples and screenshots

Karl-Heinz Kühnhauser

Discover ABAP

This book, specifically designed for beginners, introduces you to all relevant ABAP language elements in a series of clearly structured lessons. Adhering to the motto, "As much theory as necessary and as little as possible," you'll methodically familiarize yourself with one ABAP programming aspect at a time – each directly relevant to solving the tasks described in the corresponding lesson. Based on an extended, real-life example that's referred to throughout the book, you'll quickly develop your own programming solutions, starting right from the first page. Then, take your new skills to the next level as you successfully use your custom source code in practice. By reading this book, you can develop the knowledge and skills needed to leverage ABAP tools and methods in your everyday work.

503 pp., 2008, 39,95 Euro / US$ 39.95
ISBN 978-1-59229-152-6

>> www.sap-press.de/1531

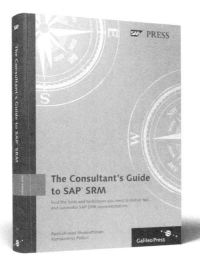

Find the tools and techniques you need
to deliver fast and successful SAP SRM
implementations

PadmaPrasad Munirathinam, Ramakrishna Potluri

Consultant's Guide to SAP SRM

**Find the tools and techniques you need to deliver fast and successful SAP SRM
implementations**

Consultants hold many roles during an SAP implementation, from business consultant
during the blueprint phase, and product specialist (techno-functional expert) during the
realization phase, to trainer after go-live. This book provides all of the information a
consultant needs to hold these roles effectively and to ensure that they are delivering the
most value to their customers.

Based on SAP SRM 6.0, the book targets the specific needs of consultants and provides a
comprehensive guide to implementing SAP SRM and purchasing best practices. Each
chapter covers a specific process of supplier relationship management, ensuring that
implementation teams can utilize their time efficiently. Going beyond standard SRM
scenarios, the book arms consultants with practical tips for enabling complex customer
requirements, and provides insightful troubleshooting tips and techniques.

512 pp., 2008, 79,95 Euro / US$ 79.95
ISBN 978-1-59229-154-0

>> www.sap-press.de/1558

Provides a comprehensive overview of the entire delivery process

Teaches functions, processes, and customization

Covers dangerous goods management, availability checks, user exits, and much more

Othmar Gau

Transportation Management with SAP LES

This in-depth reference provides readers with practical and detailed knowledge on all aspects of shipping and transportation with SAP Logistics Execution System (LES). Using this book, employees in the warehouse and shipping departments, as well as consultants, can benefit from proven best practices for working successfully with the Transportation Management module. The author describes the entire shipping and delivery process, from the creation of a delivery in the SAP system, to mapping the internal supply chain, and from transportation planning to invoicing and settlement with forwarding agencies – and everything in between. Plus, readers also learn how to master system configuration, and much more.

574 pp., 2008, 79,95 Euro / US$ 79.95
ISBN 978-1-59229-169-4

>> www.sap-press.de/1594